Bankers *with a* Mission

Bankers *with a* Mission

The Presidents of the World Bank, 1946–91

Jochen Kraske

with

William H. Becker
William Diamond
Louis Galambos

Published for the World Bank

OXFORD UNIVERSITY PRESS

Oxford University Press

OXFORD NEW YORK TORONTO
DELHI BOMBAY CALCUTTA MADRAS KARACHI
KUALA LUMPUR SINGAPORE HONG KONG TOKYO
NAIROBI DAR ES SALAAM CAPE TOWN
MELBOURNE AUCKLAND

and associated companies in

BERLIN IBADAN

© 1996 The International Bank for Reconstruction
and Development / THE WORLD BANK
1818 H Street, N.W.,
Washington, D.C. 20433, U.S.A.

Published by Oxford University Press.
200 Madison Avenue, New York, N.Y. 10016

Oxford is a registered trademark of Oxford University Press.

Manufactured in the United States of America
First printing September 1996

The findings, interpretations, and conclusions expressed in this study are entirely those of the
authors and should not be attributed in any manner to the World Bank, to its affiliated organizations,
or to members of its Board of Executive Directors or the countries they represent.

Photos: All the photographs are from the World Bank photo archives. Page 114, by Fabian Bachrach;
first page of photo insert, by Edwin Huffman; last page of photo insert, by Michele Iannicci

Design: Joyce Petruzzelli

Library of Congress Cataloging-in-Publication Data

Bankers with a mission : the presidents of the World Bank, 1946–91 /
 Jochen Kraske . . . [et al.];
        p. cm.
  Includes bibliographical references and index.
  ISBN 0-19-521112-X
  1. World Bank—Presidents—Biography. 2. Bankers—Biography.
3. World Bank—History. I. Kraske, Jochen, 1932– .
HG3881.5.W57B367   1996
332.1'532'0922—dc20
 [B]   96-34639
                                         CIP

Contents

Preface

When I accepted the assignment as the World Bank Group's historian, my friends and colleagues in the Bank presented me with a set of photographs of the Bank's presidents to decorate my new office. The presidents of the Bank have always been a fascinating subject for the staff of the Bank. Not only were they the source of power in the institution; they were also the ones the staff looked to for signals that would indicate the Bank's primary mission and its operational priorities in a changing world. Thus surrounded by the images of the Bank's past presidents, I felt I should make them the focus of an in-depth inquiry.

The general preoccupation with the presidents of the Bank has given rise to a rich store of anecdotes and myths. The growth of the institution increasingly limited the opportunity for direct contacts and exchanges of views between the president and the main body of staff members. Remoteness tends to stimulate the imagination. At the same time, it distorts perceptions, just as the passage of time often presents events and personalities in a nostalgically tinted light. These perceptions tend to shape the discussions about what the institution has done, what it is, and what it can be. They affect, in particular, the interpretation of the part former presidents played during their administrations. These perceptions also surface in any discussion about the role of the president and the contribution that is expected of him. To confront these perceptions with the record should not only serve to modify and correct them but also assist the ongoing discussion about the future of the Bank.

As far as possible, I have tried to rely on the written record to present the actions of the presidents and the course of their thinking. Their speeches, especially those to the annual gathering of the Bank's shareholders, present an overview of the challenges faced by the institution and the agenda they adopted to address them. I have been able to supplement the evidence offered by the written record with interviews and informal discussions with former colleagues, as well as with the oral histories they recorded.

I would not have been able to complete this study without the active support and assistance of many individuals. I am deeply indebted to the contribution of my associates in the Office of the Bank Group Historian, William Becker, William Diamond, and Louis Galambos. William Becker, professor of history at George Washington University, prepared initial drafts of the chapters dealing with Eugene Meyer, A. W. Clausen, and Barber Conable and compiled most of the material used in these chapters. William Diamond, a former staff member and trained historian, assembled the material for the McCloy chapter and prepared an initial draft of it. Louis Galambos, professor of history at Johns Hopkins University, contributed to the conceptual design and focus of the book. All three followed the production of the various drafts in the course of regular monthly meetings. They pointed out inconsistencies, elaborated the historical context, and provided invaluable editorial assistance.

Many others aided generously and graciously in the preparation of the text by drawing my attention to particular sources and through their comments. Among them I should mention in particular Warren Baum, Aaron Broches, Shirley Boskey, Sven Burmester, Richard Demuth, Johannes Linn, Franz Oppenheimer, Davidson Sommers, Ernest Stern, Wilfried Thalwitz, and Willi Wapenhans, each of whom reviewed some of the chapters of the book.

The members of the team currently working on a comprehensive history of the World Bank under the auspices of the Brookings

Institution took a close interest in my work. I am indebted to John Lewis, Richard Webb, and Devesh Kapur for their suggestions and for sharing with me the insight they had gained on the basis of their much more extensive research into the history of the Bank.

I owe a debt of gratitude to those who helped me find and organize the documentary sources. The staff in the Bank's Archives, in particular Charles Ziegler, have given me invaluable assistance by guiding me in my search and responding to my requests with unfailing promptness. Marie Gallup worked with great diligence on the organization of the material and in the process was inspired to prepare a *Guide to the World Bank Archives,* which was published recently. Paola Brezny copyedited the final draft, and Barbara Malczak and Abigail Tardiff proofread the book.

I am grateful to all of them and to the World Bank for its support and the freedom it allowed me to pursue the task I had set for myself. Although the Bank supported me, I am responsible for the conception of the book, the views it reflects, and its conclusions. The book is dedicated to Huda—faithful companion and supportive colleague through three decades of World Bank history.

Introduction

June 1996 marked the fiftieth anniversary of the opening for business of the International Bank for Reconstruction and Development (IBRD). The anniversary provides an appropriate occasion to look back and reflect on how the Bank started and how it came to be where it is today. From small beginnings it has grown into a global institution. It has become the World Bank—a nickname that originally reflected aspirations more than accomplishments. It has become a critical source of finance and advice for developing countries; more generally, it has become a principal intermediary between industrial and developing, rich and poor nations.

The past half century has seen major changes in the world economy and in the Bank. Although the era was not free of violent disruptions, there was nothing comparable to the two world wars of the first half of the century. Despite social revolution and a cold war between communist and noncommunist states, on balance the past fifty years were characterized by relatively peaceful evolution. It was a period of spectacular technological and significant economic progress. In particular, it was an era of unprecedented global economic and financial integration—stimulated by technological and economic developments, but also fostered by new international financial and economic organizations, including the

1

Bank. These organizations were created to help control and ease tension between nations and to promote trade and economic activity. They came to epitomize a new spirit of international cooperation.

When the conference at Bretton Woods drew up the charter of the Bank—its Articles of Agreement—in 1944, World War II was still in progress.[1] Although the war's outcome could be predicted with some assurance at that time, the shape of the postwar world and its economic problems were matters of conjecture. Indeed, the officials who assembled at Bretton Woods were trying to apply the lessons of the past. They had experienced the collapse of the international economic order in the 1930s and the outbreak of World War II, and they were determined to create institutional safeguards that would prevent another breakdown of trade and financial relations. The Articles of Agreement, drawn up in the course of the three-week conference, proved to be not only a workable prescription for the immediate postwar period but also an adequate framework for governance during the next fifty years. With rare and minor amendments, the Articles of Agreement provided a structure that allowed the Bank to adjust to changing demands smoothly and effectively. Change has indeed been the central theme in the evolution of the Bank.

These changes did not involve revision of the institution's basic mission, as set forth in the Articles of Agreement. Rather, they called for adjustment, first, in the focus of the Bank's activities, and then in the interpretation of its mission and in its specific operational objectives. Weighing heavily on the minds of the people who met at Bretton Woods, and on the Bank's principal members when the Bank opened its doors two years later, was the need for reconstruction of postwar Europe. That task became the institution's initial focus. The phase of reconstruction lending was short-lived, however, because the task proved far beyond the financial capacity of the Bank. Instead, it was the Marshall Plan that provided the funds needed for Europe's reconstruction, leaving the Bank free to devote itself to the financing of development. This task became synonymous with the institution.

Economic development was a subject little understood in the early days of the Bank, and the views of what would prove effective in supporting development changed with experience. The Bank's operational objectives expanded over time, from supporting infra-structure investment to encouraging the growth of industrial and agricultural production; to developing human resources through improved education, health care, and family planning; to dealing with the special needs of women; to caring for the environment. As the agenda expanded, the Bank's concerns moved beyond the con-ditions directly affecting the performance of the projects it sup-ported; it began to deal with the economic policies that determined the direction and performance of investment in its member coun-tries. The Bank's contribution increasingly included technical as-sistance and advice—packaged together with the transfer of essen-tial resources.

The Bank's goals underwent change as well. The Articles of Agree-ment had linked the institution's activities rather generally with "raising productivity, the standard of living and conditions of la-bor" in its member countries.[2] Once support of economic develop-ment moved into the foreground, the Bank sought to narrow the gap between rich and poor countries. The cold war was an essen-tial part of the context for the Bank's assistance to its developing members. But the quintessence of economic backwardness was al-ways the pervasive poverty it represented. The relief of economic misery was the main test of the Bank's success, even though it was not until the 1970s that poverty alleviation was explicitly adopted as a primary goal.

The views about appropriate remedies for economic backward-ness evolved, along with the analyses of its causes. Inadequate sav-ings, excessive external debt service, unfair trade practices, acceler-ating population growth, the adoption of inappropriate priorities, corruption and waste—all were identified as key problems at vari-ous times and in various countries. The Bank's activities reflected the changing perceptions of the intricate development challenge and the problems it generated. If the transfer of needed capital resources represented the unchanging core of the Bank's business, the effective use of those resources remained its principal challenge. From sound project selection and design, the emphasis shifted to institution building. The key role attributed to the adoption of effective sector and macroeconomic policies was amplified by the concern about institutional factors—about governance in general and political participation in particular. As the complexities of the development process became apparent, the Bank changed to deal with them and, in the process, became a more complex organization.

The nature of the institution changed over the years. The report of Commission II, entrusted by the Bretton Woods conferees with working out the charter of the IBRD, concluded that "it was accidentally born with the name Bank . . . mainly because no satisfactory name could be found in the dictionary for this unprecedented institution."[3] Nevertheless, this designation seemed to define adequately the institution's behavior for the first fifteen years of its life. The Bank took pains to present itself as a sound financial undertaking and adopted standards common to commercial financial institutions. Economic backwardness was regarded as a problem that could be dealt with by relying on the normal process of financial intermediation, that is, by raising capital in the richer countries and transferring it to the needy ones. Once the depth and complexity of the problems faced by the developing countries were recognized, the conventional terms of investment lending became an unwieldy, even dysfunctional constraint. The concept of the Bank as a financial institution modeled on traditional investment banks gave way to a new vision of a development finance institution. Ten years of experience were enough to bring about this transformation in the concept of the Bank.

These changes in orientation were neither accidental nor automatic; they reflected decisions by the Bank's leaders. The Bank's presidents, each in his fashion, recognized the needs of the member countries and sought to satisfy those needs. They moved the institution to identify appropriate ways of intervening and to respond to the needs of its members. They tried to anticipate changes in the economic and political setting and to address the economic and financial problems of the Bank's membership in a timely fashion. They were able to persuade the Bank's shareholders to provide the mandate for the Bank's expanding activities and support new roles for the organization. To find out who the presidents of the Bank were and to examine their actions and the reasons for their decisions are therefore useful and illuminating ways of understanding the history of the institution.

Our story of the seven men who presided over the Bank from 1946 to 1991 throws light on the importance of leadership for the building and performance of an institution, especially a global institution. Each president made a distinct contribution to building the organization and to defining its mission. While their contributions necessarily reflected their times and the problems they confronted, their personalities and their personal experiences also shaped the style and content of their presidencies.

All the Bank's presidents have been U.S. citizens. According to an unwritten convention, it is the prerogative of the United States to nominate the president. The custom was based less on the position of the United States as the Bank's largest shareholder than on the critical importance of the Bank's access to the U.S. capital market. Reportedly, Harry White (with the strong endorsement of Lord Keynes) wanted to become the first managing director of the International Monetary Fund (IMF) but had to back down when U.S. Treasury Secretary Fred M. Vinson decided that "the Bank would have to be headed by a U.S. citizen in order to win the confidence of the banking community, and that it would be impracticable to appoint U.S. citizens to head both the Bank and the Fund."[4] Ever since, the managing directors of the IMF have come from Europe, and the presidents of the World Bank have come from the United States.

The chapters that follow describe who those presidents were, how they came to the Bank, and what experiences they brought with them. The essays also analyze the problems these men encountered during their tenure and how they dealt with them, discuss the impact each president had on the evolution of the Bank— on its policies and operations and on its organizational character—and, finally, describe the legacies of these presidents. To the extent that a history of the Bank's presidents can provide a window on the evolution of the institution, this book also provides a brief overview of the history of this important international institution.

CHAPTER ONE

Eugene Meyer

The Bank's First Steps

ugene Meyer was not President Harry Truman's first choice to head the new IBRD. In the early spring of 1946 the president was having a difficult time finding a candidate for the position. There was some urgency in Truman's search because the Bank was scheduled to begin operations in May 1946. In April, Truman endorsed the head of a major U.S. insurance company for the job, only to be rebuffed publicly a few days later. The White House considered other potential candidates, all of whom ultimately refused to take the job of president of the World Bank. The one senior-level candidate reportedly interested in the position, U.S. Secretary of the Treasury Fred M. Vinson, was taken out of the running when President Truman nominated him to the Supreme Court on June 6, 1946.[1]

Truman's difficulty in finding a president for the new institution was not a good omen. It bespoke the uncertainty surrounding the mission of the Bank and the responsibilities of its president. To be sure, Truman had other pressing matters to attend to in the first half of 1946. There was the Paris Peace Conference between April and October, which considered the peace treaties with former allies of Germany, and sharp disagreements with the U.S.S.R., which prompted serious rethinking about U.S. postwar foreign policy. From the beginning of the year the president confronted the contentious partisan issue of ending wartime price controls. During these same months, Truman also turned his attention to proposals for the international control of atomic energy. In the press of coping with these other issues, the administration did not consider the Bank a matter of high priority, nor was the Bank's imminent opening something that attracted much public attention.

This is not to say that the Bank lacked supporters. Indeed, the officials who in 1944 had designed the IBRD and the International Monetary Fund (IMF) were intensely interested in the success of the new institutions created in June and July 1944 at meetings in Atlantic City, New Jersey, and Bretton Woods, New Hampshire. U.S. officials from the State and Treasury departments had been prominent among the designers of the two new institutions. From the ranks of these individuals—and men of similar position and experience from France, Greece, the Netherlands, and the United Kingdom—were drawn some of the Bank's first executive directors and professional staff.

The governors of the IBRD assembled in March 1946 in Savannah, Georgia, for the organization's inaugural meeting. The sessions, which included many of the people who almost two years earlier had designed the Bank and the Fund, addressed the issues of the Bank's location, the responsibilities of its executive directors, and the compensation that they should receive. Over the strong objections of the U.K. delegation and its leader, John Maynard Keynes, the United States insisted that the Bank be located in Washington, D.C., close to officials of the Treasury and State departments, away from the investment bankers of Wall Street, under the purview of a Congress somewhat skeptical of the IMF and the IBRD, and near the foreign diplomats assigned to the United States. The Bank's placement in Washington made clear that U.S. officials at the Savannah gathering expected to exercise decisive influence over the activities of the new institution.

The U.S. insistence that the Bank be in Washington and that its executive directors should serve full time and receive competitive salaries highlights the tension that existed in the views of the Bank. It was to be an institution that served the interests of U.S. foreign policy and, at the same time, operated according to commercial standards acceptable to the private sector. Emphasis on one or the other of these approaches to the IBRD was one source of the conflict that marked the first presidency of the Bank.

Although the questions of location and salary, as well as other issues, proved contentious, the United States prevailed in most respects. It was, after all, the country that had provided one-third of the capital to establish the Bank, and it had one-third of the votes. The Bank would get under way at the first meeting of the executive directors scheduled for May 1946. The major topic of business would be the appointment of a president, whom everyone expected to be an American in view of the magnitude of the U.S. contribution to the new Bank.[2]

The scheduled launching of the Bank in May put pressure on Truman to find someone to head it. The administration missed the deadline, although not for want of trying. But in early June 1946, Truman and Secretary of State James F. Byrnes persuaded Eugene Meyer to accept the position of president of the IBRD; he took office on June 25.

Meyer appeared to be a good choice. In 1945–46 he had gained wide public attention by leading a well-publicized U.S. effort (the famine emergency committee) to aid the starving in postwar Europe. He had practical organizational experience as the publisher of the *Washington Post,* a newspaper he had refashioned to reflect his own pragmatic, open-minded approach to domestic and international issues. Perhaps of more importance, Meyer, a Republican, had broad government experience. He had served as a member of the committee that directed the War Finance Corporation (1918–20), as commissioner of the Federal Farm Loan Board (1927–29), as a governor of the Federal Reserve Board (1930–33), and as the first chairman of the Reconstruction Finance Corporation (1932). Truman's choice was a familiar figure to leaders on Capitol Hill, officials in the Department of the Treasury, and members of the securities and banking industries.

Meyer brought other valuable attributes to the job. Before turning to government service, he had established a successful brokerage house on Wall Street. He had an enviable reputation for innovative practices and careful dealing. His firm had pioneered in detailed economic analyses of the institutions in which Meyer's and his clients' funds were invested. By the time he dissolved the brokerage to work with the War Industries Board in 1917, Meyer had built a sizable fortune.[3]

Nevertheless, despite Meyer's appropriate experience, his assignment at the IBRD proved to be a difficult time for him and the Bank. He took charge of an institution still in need of definition without having strong ideas about the direction it should take and without receiving clear guidance from President Truman as to what he hoped the Bank's first president would accomplish. Moreover, he encountered men already on the scene—in the Bank and in the U.S. government agencies charged with oversight of the new institution—who had distinct ideas about what the Bank should become. Their hopes for the IBRD had taken shape in the course of the planning for the postwar economic order, in the detailed elaboration of the agreements that finally established the IBRD and the IMF, and in the debate in the U.S. Congress between January and July 1945 that led to U.S. approval of the IMF and the Bank.

These men, in short, had thought seriously about international monetary stability, postwar reconstruction, and economic development. Most of them believed that the exchange and financial markets in general, and private international bankers in particular, had failed miserably in the late 1920s and 1930s—a failure for which the United States and the rest of the industrial world had paid a high price indeed. Those in the United States and abroad who created the Fund and the Bank formed a community of officials with a vision of a multilateral, interdependent world economy guided by international institutions that had to answer to the governments which created and sustained them. Certainly these men had clearer ideas about how to stabilize the international economy than did Eugene Meyer or Harry Truman.

Between June and December 1946, confronting the issues of global monetary stabilization and economic reconstruction for the first time, Meyer found himself involved in sharp clashes with the IBRD's executive directors. Personalities played a part in this conflict, and Meyer and several of the executive directors developed strong antipathies to each other. But underlying problems in the division of responsibility among Bank officials were the immediate source of the conflict. Fundamentally, the debate revolved around the authority of the president with respect to that of the executive directors in setting Bank policy and around the role of the United States and the United Kingdom in the IBRD.

In Meyer's six-month presidency he faced up to issues that would define the institution in the next decades. Although he failed to resolve the question of the authority of the president in relation to that of the executive directors, his unhappy experience as president pointed up that his successor needed to resolve the issue of the president's authority before taking the job. Even so, Meyer began the task of organization building. He recruited senior staff, many of whom were to have long and distinguished careers in the Bank. He began the work of defining policy toward loans and of hiring the professional personnel capable of analyzing loan proposals. He also began the important task of building confidence in the Bank on Wall Street, a process that helped the Bank to define the terms on which it would raise funds in the securities markets. Meyer took care to distance the IBRD from the United Nations, which he thought seemed anxious to make the Bank an instrument of U.N. policies.

Founding the IBRD

World War II leaders in the United States believed that the failures of the post–World War I generation of statesmen had helped cause the global conflict of the 1940s. U.S. officials, from President Franklin D. Roosevelt down, were quite self-conscious about avoiding the diplomatic, military, and economic mistakes of those who ended World War I at the Versailles Peace Conference. In the economic sphere, they were determined that the United States, as the world's leading economic power, would not again shirk its responsibilities to promote order and stability in international exchange, finance, and trade.[4]

Among the many consequences of the resolve to avoid the errors of the past were the Bretton Woods meetings in July 1944. The plans for the IMF and the IBRD were tangible results of the U.S. effort to bring about a new postwar international economic order.

Even before it entered World War II, the United States was re-thinking the postwar world economy. In the 1930s, key officials had already been reexamining foreign economic policy. Taking the lead was Roosevelt's secretary of state, Cordell Hull. The former Tennessee congressman advocated a Wilsonian vision of international cooperation and supported the Democratic Party's traditional commitment to lower tariffs. During the 1930s Hull promoted a series of reciprocal trade agreements that lowered tariffs on a bilateral basis.

As the United States drew closer to involvement in World War II, forward-looking politicians, journalists, academics, and business leaders discussed what the aims of the war should be. Among the ideas that caught Roosevelt's attention were concepts of international economic cooperation that in practical terms would promote stable currencies and lead to increased flows of trade and capital. Such ideas, general as they were, nevertheless enlarged the cramped vision of free trade propounded by Hull. The Atlantic Charter, announced by the United States and the United Kingdom in August 1941, extolled these ideas in what was a general statement of the war aims of the two English-speaking powers. Only in April 1942, in the Lend-Lease agreement, were the implications of these ideas perceived in operational terms. Each side assigned technical advisers to work out the details of the arrangement. This requirement of ongoing negotiations, as Hull said, laid the foundation "for all our later postwar planning in the economic field."[5]

Roosevelt's secretary of the treasury proved no less influential than Hull in promoting ideas for changing the international economic order after the war. Henry Morgenthau Jr., like Hull, believed that the United States had a responsibility to improve international commercial and financial institutions. By the end of the 1930s, Morgenthau's rhetoric trumpeted such changes as contributing to the security of the United States.[6] Although Morgenthau's ideas about the link between economic and national security were unexceptional, the secretary himself remained a controversial figure. He had a penchant for offending members of Congress, and his willing loyalty in carrying out Roosevelt's schemes of monetary gamesmanship in the early years of the New Deal had won him intractable enemies on Wall Street. He also made no secret of his belief that the mismanagement, shortsightedness, and greed of investment bankers had brought on and then prolonged the consequences of the collapse of 1929. Indeed, he believed that the government should impose order on international finance in much the same way that the New Deal had increased government regulation of the domestic banking, finance, and securities industries (117).

Morgenthau owed his important post to a close friendship with Roosevelt, who was his neighbor in Duchess County, New York. Even though his family had been in the investment banking business, Morgenthau was a gentleman farmer who happened to be the confidant of a man who became governor of New York and then president of the United States (24–26).

Morgenthau made no pretense of expertise in financial matters, a fact quickly observed by academics, bankers, and studious members of Congress. As a result, the secretary relied heavily on a group of talented expert advisers. One in particular, Harry Dexter White, provided Morgenthau with plans for cooperative institutions to strengthen the international financial system.

White was a key figure among the men planning postwar economic policies. Before becoming a close adviser to Morgenthau, he had headed the Treasury's division of monetary research. White, with a Ph.D. in economics from Harvard, was smart, imaginative, and pragmatic. These qualities—along with a penchant for hard work, an ability to be genial when it suited him, and a commanding personality—brought him a following among the experts and officials preparing financial policies for the United States to pursue after the war. Unfortunately, as the quintessential staff man, White was also undiplomatic, often failing to show proper deference to those having lesser intellects but holding positions of greater power and influence than he had. As a result, he made enemies easily not only for himself but also for his ideas and the proposed institutions that grew out of his clever mind (43–56).[7]

Together, Morgenthau and White were a powerful twosome in their ability to frighten Wall Street and conservative members of Congress. Even so, Morgenthau was determined to give life to the ideas linking future peace and U.S. security to an open but integrated multilateral system of commerce and finance. Influential U.S. investment bankers agreed that greater cooperation was essential to the smooth international flow of trade and capital. Nor did they downplay the important role the United States had in the world economy. Their disagreement with Morgenthau, White, and many of the other experts assembled by the Roosevelt administration was over the appropriate role of the U.S. government in maintaining a system of greater international economic cooperation. Simply, Wall Street opposed the high degree of direction from Washington that was included in the plans White devised during the war.[8]

Serious planning for what was to become the IMF and the IBRD began at the Department of the Treasury in early December 1941, when Morgenthau instructed Harry White to design institutions that would enhance international economic cooperation. White produced a memorandum ("Suggested Program for Inter-Allied Monetary and Bank Action") that sketched his thinking about a fund to stabilize the exchange of currency and an international bank to promote postwar reconstruction. White was not alone in thinking about such a bank. A month after he delivered his report to Morgenthau, experts working for the Department of State, in consultation with the British, proposed an international development corporation. As early as February 1940, a group of specialists drawn from the State and Treasury departments, the Federal Reserve System, and the Federal Loan Agency had proposed an inter-American development bank.[9] White had been among the Treasury officials Morgenthau assigned to work on the 1940 proposal for such an institution. Although the proposal was never taken up, it clearly influenced White's thinking, and parts of it ended up in the IBRD's Articles of Agreement. Thus White's basic thinking, as presented to Morgenthau late in December 1941, was not entirely original.

Nevertheless, the document that influenced the later official conversations about a development organization was a revised and expanded version of White's December 1941 memorandum. Released by the U.S. Treasury in April 1942, the revision was entitled "Proposal for a United Nations Stabilization Fund and a Bank for

Reconstruction and Development of the United and Associated Nations." Morgenthau circulated the document to other agencies of the U.S. government; favorable responses prompted Roosevelt to appoint a cabinet-level committee to pursue the proposal's ideas. The treasury secretary appointed White chairman of the technical committee assigned to prepare the staff work for the cabinet committee (17).

In November 1943 White's committee produced a proposal as the basis of discussion with other governments. Many of the technical experts from the U.S. side to appear at Bretton Woods had served on White's committee or were drawn from other parts of the U.S. government interested in what White was working on. These included staff from the Department of State, which in September 1943, under the direction of Emilio G. "Pete" Collado, chief of the State Department's division of financial and monetary affairs, had developed its own proposal for an agency devoted to international development. Others contributing to White's effort came from the Federal Reserve Board, the Securities and Exchange Commission, the Export-Import Bank, and the Department of Commerce (17).

In early 1944 the Treasury used the November 1943 document, a "Preliminary Draft Outline of a Proposal for United Nations Bank for Reconstruction and Development," to initiate conversations with U.S. allies about a development bank. These discussions led to revisions and clarifications, but substantially the document described what was to become the IBRD. By the time experts from the United States and other countries gathered in Atlantic City in late June 1944 to prepare the agenda for the Bretton Woods meetings, the British in particular had responded positively to the idea of special arrangements for postwar reconstruction (12, 18f.).

What was to become the IMF was the focus of attention for most of the officials planning for substantial changes in the postwar management of the international economy. Even so, a development bank was gaining support. Indeed, at the Atlantic City meetings none other than John Maynard Keynes produced a draft proposal for a bank built on the initiative of U.S. officials and reflecting the views of his delegation and that of European representatives.

At Bretton Woods, a draft amalgamating the ideas presented by White and Keynes served as the basis for discussion of what became the Articles of Agreement of the Bank. Although most of the official discussions at Bretton Woods were devoted to the Fund, there was keen interest in the Bank. Representatives from developing countries wanted a development bank, and the U.K., European, and Soviet representatives saw the proposed institution as an instrument for helping their postwar reconstruction (21f.).[10]

At Bretton Woods, Keynes chaired the commission responsible for creating the Bank. In part, he took this assignment to reduce his visibility in the discussions about the Fund, although he cared most about the problems of currencies, as did White. Neither man, however, wanted to jeopardize the establishment of the Fund—the primary goal of Bretton Woods—by drawing the ire of conservative U.S. bankers, members of Congress, and businessmen, all of whom thought Keynes unsound and perhaps reckless, if not an out-and-out radical. The committees and subcommittees of Commission II, the one entrusted with planning the Bank, collected suggestions and comments. A small drafting committee had the responsibility of writing the Bank's Articles of Agreement. Dean Acheson, assistant secretary of state, was the chairman of the committee, and Edward E. Brown, chairman of the First National Bank of Chicago—and one of the few professional bankers present— was among the members, along with Collado of the State Department and James W. Angell from Columbia University. The drafting committee worked quite informally, and high-level delegates would drift in and out of its meetings. Keynes was joined at these gatherings by Pierre Mendès-France, the leader of the French delegation, or by his counterparts from the Netherlands and Greece, J. W. Beyen and Kyriakos Varvaressos, respectively. These three heads of delegation were, along with Collado, among the first executive directors of the IBRD.[11]

Interpreting the Articles of Agreement became an important, ongoing task in the history of the Bank. They were a complex set of rules designed to meet the varying needs of those participating in the Bank. They also reflected the times in which they were written. As circumstances changed, the drafters' intentions became an important test in determining how to modify Bank procedures. In the first six months of the Bank's history, under Meyer's presidency, four aspects of the articles came up for interpretation: development versus reconstruction, the role of guarantees versus loans, the primacy of project loans as opposed to program loans, and the Bank's relationship with the United Nations.

The IBRD was not really a bank in the ordinary sense of the word. It was owned by governments, it did not accept deposits, and its operations were limited to loans and guarantees. Loans could be made to the governments that were the Bank's shareholders or, with their guarantee of repayment, to public and private institutions within the countries' territories. Guarantees could be provided for borrowings by these governments (and institutions guaranteed by them) in the financial markets.

The Bank had an unusual capital structure. Its authorized capital in 1946 was $10 billion, of which $7.5 billion was subscribed.[12] Members were to pay 2 percent of their subscription in gold or dollars and 18 percent in their own currency. If necessary, 80 percent of the subscription was payable to meet the Bank's own obligations arising from guarantees issued by it or as a result of its own borrowings. In a sense, the callable 80 percent portion could be described as a guarantee fund. The 2 percent portion was freely available for lending, but the 18 percent local currency portion of each member could be used only to the extent permitted by that member. Because the United States was the only country that initially released its 18 percent, that amount, plus the 2 percent payable by the membership in gold or dollars, constituted the funds available to the Bank. The Bank's creators envisioned an institution whose primary operations would be guarantees rather than loans. The acceptability of the Bank's guarantees and of its debt was measured not by the Bank's paid-in capital but by members' obligations to meet calls on the 80 percent portion of their subscriptions. In 1946, and for many years thereafter, the market treated the callable portion of the U.S. subscription as the limit of the Bank's creditworthiness.[13]

The Bank's founding countries had two objectives: reconstruction and development. Which was to receive priority was a matter for Bank officials to determine later. At Bretton Woods, however, the greatest interest was in assistance for reconstruction. The nature of the loans the Bank guaranteed or made was a source of much discussion before, during, and after Bretton Woods. Essentially, the issue was the specificity of purpose in loans: should loans be made to support specific projects or more generally, broader programs? Article III, section 4(vii) reflects the compromise worked out by the Bank's founders: "Loans made or guaranteed by the Bank shall, except in special circumstances, be for the purpose of specific projects of reconstruction or development." The interpretation of the key phrase, "except in special circumstances," became an issue during the Meyer presidency, when countries first approached the Bank about loans.[14]

Finally, the Bank and the Fund were part of an effort at the end of World War II to create an international system that provided incentives for the great powers to cooperate with each other. None of the organizations created was more important than the United Nations, at least in the thinking of Western, especially U.S., leaders at the time. To ensure the integration of the world community, the U.N. charter mandated that specialized agencies, such as the Bank and the Fund, develop a formal relationship with the United Nations. The interpretative issue that arose during Meyer's tenure revolved around the degree of subordination such an arrangement would impose on the Bank (54–59).

An even more important issue was the relationship between the Bank and the U.S. government. The U.S. Congress determined that relationship in the course of the debate over ratification of the Bank and Fund. In considering the two institutions between January and June 1945, Congress ensured that the U.S. executive directors at the Bank and Fund would follow the directives of U.S. policy. Before ratifying the Bretton Woods Agreement Act—where debates revealed considerable nervousness, especially about the Fund— Congress established the National Advisory Council (NAC) on International Monetary and Financial Problems to coordinate the work of the U.S. executive directors at the Bank and Fund. Council members included representatives from the Department of State, the Federal Reserve Board, and the Export-Import Bank, all of whom served under the chairmanship of the secretary of the treasury (33f.).[15]

Eugene Meyer, Financier and Professional Public Servant

Even those skeptical of the IBRD saw Eugene Meyer's appointment as a positive development. The *New York Times* said in an editorial that he had a "rare combination of hard-headedness and a broad humanitarian viewpoint."[16] Meyer was a well-known figure on Wall Street and in Washington, with a long history of public service. Although closely associated with the Republican administrations of the 1920s, he had begun his public career during World War I under Woodrow Wilson. After purchasing the *Washington Post* in 1933, he redirected the staunchly Republican editorial policy of the newspaper to reflect his own pragmatic view of domestic politics and his internationalist perspective on the United States' role in the world. [17]

Eugene Meyer was born in 1875 in Los Angeles, where his father was a prosperous merchant. In the 1880s the family moved to San Francisco, where the elder Meyer joined the French merchant banking firm Lazard Frères. Meyer spent his youth there and began his higher education at the University of California, Berkeley. At the end of his first year in college, however, the elder Meyer became a partner at Lazard Frères in New York City, and the family moved east. Young Eugene interrupted his education to work in the bank in New York for a year.

After that apprenticeship, he enrolled at Yale University. Meyer— experienced in business and educated in Greek, Latin, and French— was more mature than most undergraduates. He applied himself to a broad curriculum, which included English literature, Spanish, German, ethics, economics, and social science (taught by William Graham Sumner, the celebrated exponent of laissez-faire). He completed three years of course work in two and received his degree in 1895, graduating near the top of his class (19–23).

He returned to Lazard Frères in New York but eventually struck out on his own. In 1901, at age 26, he had earned enough money ($50,000) in the stock market to buy a seat on the New York Stock Exchange, and soon after, he established his own brokerage house. By 1917 he had made a personal fortune (estimated at between $40 million and $60 million) by focusing on investments in the copper, gold, automobile, and chemicals industries (126f.).

As the years passed, Meyer developed a reputation on Wall Street as a solid manager of investment funds and as an innovator. Eugene Meyer and Company pioneered the use of a research department—scientific investing—to perform detailed economic analyses of the businesses in which the firm invested. Nevertheless, the stock market was a rough way to make a living, and Meyer was known for toughness and a sharp, cutting tongue. Indeed, some of his associates thought that his superior intellect and rapid success made him a bit arrogant (36, 52, 68, 101f.).

Yet there were other dimensions to Meyer that went beyond his success in the brokerage business. His privileged background and elite education had stimulated an interest in literature, painting, and the theater. Despite his extraordinary success as a broker, Meyer more than once came close to financial ruin—experiences that served to chasten him. The death of people close to him also softened his outlook. He felt keenly the death of a 26-year-old younger brother—his closest confidant and business partner—in the *Titanic* disaster of 1912. More generally, as a Jew, he faced antisemitism throughout his life, a circumstance that made him determined to succeed. Although antisemitism kept him out of clubs in high school and fraternities at Yale, he worked hard at making friendships with a wide range of people. According to his biographer, antisemitism also contributed to Meyer's profound realism, to a sense of having to see the world as it was, rather than as he would have liked it to be (11, 111f., 139).

His realistic view of the world contributed to a life-long interest in people less fortunate than himself. As a teenager in New York, he explored the slums to learn how the burgeoning immigrant population lived. In London he walked through the poorest parts of the city to see firsthand the underside of British society. Once he had amassed a fortune, he became a contributor to charities and an active philanthropist (65).

His wealth also allowed him to turn to public service. In this regard he was like Bernard Baruch and Joseph P. Kennedy, who made fortunes in the stock market and then pursued other spheres of activity. Indeed, Meyer received his first public position on the recommendation of his friend, and at times business associate, Bernard Baruch. Meyer's public service during World War I culminated in his appointment to the board of the War Finance Corporation. His Wall Street expertise proved indispensable to that body's work of stabilizing the bond market and financing enterprises that were expanding facilities for the war effort. A stint at the Versailles Peace Conference introduced Meyer to the problems of postwar economic readjustment. In the 1920s, as commissioner of the Federal Farm Loan Board, he learned much about the adjustments necessary in the troubled U.S. agricultural sector. In 1932 President Hoover turned to Meyer to head the Reconstruction Finance Corporation, an agency designed to help railroads and industries cope with the depression (217–26).

In the years Meyer held these public positions, he and his wife became important figures in the social life of the capital. In Washington and at an estate outside of New York City, they maintained a busy schedule of entertaining. Wealth, public prominence, and adroit attention to finding interesting guests put the Meyers in the company of artists, intellectuals, religious leaders, and philanthropists, as well as business and political leaders.

When the Hoover administration ended in 1933 and Meyer left his post at the Reconstruction Finance Corporation, he purchased the *Washington Post*. This venture provided a new venue for his interest in public affairs and a good reason for remaining in Washington. Even though Meyer's independent-minded editorial policy was at times critical of the Roosevelt administration, the president called on him during World War II for service on the National Defense Mediation Board. At the end of the war, at age 70, Meyer returned to private life and planned to devote himself to his newspaper.

But not for long. It was, in fact, Meyer's continuing interest in public service and his concern for the troubled and less fortunate that brought him to the attention of the public. These qualities also brought him into contact with President Truman in the spring of 1946, when the vacant presidency of the IBRD was becoming something of a problem for the U.S. government.

In the fall of 1945, Congress cut $550 million from the funds destined for the United Nations Relief and Rehabilitation Administration (UNRRA). Officials at the Department of Agriculture also feared that the United States would fail to send overseas the million tons of wheat per month promised earlier. Meyer used the *Washington Post*'s editorial page to criticize Congress and alert the public to the serious problems of hunger in Europe during the winter of 1945–46 (343–46).

Meyer drew from his wide circle of influential acquaintances to put together a high-level famine emergency committee. The committee's campaign asked U.S. citizens to conserve food so that more would be available for shipment abroad. President Truman provided official sanction to the committee at a White House ceremony in March 1946.

Although the record is not entirely clear on how Truman settled on Meyer to head the Bank, it is not unreasonable to assume that Meyer's highly visible campaign to help the hungry in Europe had something to do with the president's turning to the experienced financier and public servant to take on the job at the IBRD. In any event, two months after the emergency food campaign began, Secretary of State James F. Byrnes offered Meyer the presidency of the IBRD, already known as the World Bank. The offer followed a luncheon at Meyer's home. Meyer, surprised by the offer, protested that at 71 he was too old and too busy with his newspaper. Byrnes assured him, according to Meyer's biographer, that the president only wanted him to get the organization going. In a telephone conversation with the president the next day, Meyer reluctantly agreed to take on the position (343–47).

Launching the Bank

Officially, the Bank opened for business on June 25, 1946, the day Meyer arrived at the offices of the IBRD. He was ready to go to work. On June 11, within a week of his appointment, he had closeted himself with the U.S. executive director, Emilio Collado. As the representative of the United States, which had the largest stake in the IBRD, Collado had served as the de facto head of the IBRD during the six weeks between the inauguration of the Bank and the appointment of its president.[18]

During that time nothing of consequence occurred; the board occupied itself only with general discussions. But these conversations were conducted in a friendly, informal atmosphere among a number of people who had worked together earlier on creating the

IBRD and the IMF.[19] Collado and the British executive director, Sir James Grigg, were leading figures in these conversations. Collado's influence was not simply a result of his representing the largest stakeholder in the new enterprise; his long-standing role in the detailed planning for the Bank gave him added weight with his fellow executive directors.

Meyer set as his first task the recruitment of a staff. As one of his initial acts he appointed as vice president Harold Smith, who, at 47, had distinguished himself as director of the U.S. Bureau of the Budget. Success in that governmental post suggested an ability to manage complex operations, and almost immediately after his appointment to the vice presidency, he turned to organizational issues in the Bank. One of the earliest documents in the Bank archives is a detailed analysis of the IBRD's organizational needs prepared for Smith by a former colleague at the Bureau of the Budget. Smith did not become close to Meyer, and his role seems to have been that of providing administrative support rather than developing policy. Overall, the vice president had responsibility for much of the Bank's day-to-day office work and clerical staff.[20]

In not consulting the executive directors before making the important appointment of vice president, Meyer unwittingly got off on the wrong foot with them. In any event, Smith failed to develop a rapport with the executive directors. His problems with them might have been the result of his building an administrative structure for the Bank; the executive directors were much interested in the Bank's organization being responsive to them, and they might have seen his work as a threat to their prerogatives.[21]

Meyer's next major appointment, that of Chester A. McLain as general counsel, worked out better for the president. Meyer had tried to recruit John J. McCloy for the post, but McCloy had only recently returned to law practice in New York from wartime assignments and was not interested in leaving his private business so soon. McLain, who took up his duties in July, was a Harvard Law School graduate, had served on the *Law Review,* and was for a time a professor of law at his alma mater. As a member of one of the most prestigious Wall Street law firms, he had lived in Italy and France while representing U.S. banks in Europe. In addition, his clients' business took him to Germany and Romania.[22]

The general counsel quickly became a key figure in the Bank's first months of operation. Meyer relied on McLain's advice, judgment, and toughness—the latter quality a characteristic of a corporate lawyer with extensive trial experience.[23] During Meyer's tenure the two worked closely on hiring senior staff, a process made more time-consuming by the need to pay some attention to the nationality of candidates and because joining a new organization might strike potential candidates as a risky career move. It was also slow going because Meyer believed, as reported in the *New York Times,* that "care is more important than speed in filling . . . positions."[24] The appointment of top-level staff was completed only at the end of October, when Meyer hired Charles C. Pineo to take charge of what became the loan department. By that time, in addition to the president, vice president, and general counsel, the Bank also had a personnel office, a legal department, a secretary, and a treasurer. Many of the staff members Meyer and McLain chose were to make long careers at the Bank—men such as Leonard B. Rist, Richard H. Demuth, Morton M. Mendels, Aaron Broches, and Martin M. Rosen. By the time Meyer resigned in December 1946, the Bank's staff had grown to 150.[25]

The need for a senior staff was a clear-cut responsibility that Meyer tackled immediately. Less obvious was the shape of the organizational structure that the new Bank should have. The executive directors had begun discussions of organizational issues before Meyer's arrival. Once Meyer was on the scene, and a rudimentary staff was in place, he appointed representatives on the committees the executive directors had set up.

Ultimately, final decisions about the structure of the organization had to await a clearer definition of the Bank's mission and of the division of responsibility between the president and the executive directors. When that was accomplished—something that had not yet happened in 1946—the Bank could then clarify its relationship to other organizations such as the IMF, as well as important constituencies in Wall Street, the U.S. Congress, and the Treasury and State departments.

In 1946 the Bank's mission remained what the Articles of Agreement stated. That is, the Bank was to promote both reconstruction and development primarily through the guarantee of private loans.

The interest of U.S. officials in European problems, and the prominence of the United Kingdom, France, and the Netherlands in the work of the Bank, tilted the institution toward reconstruction. The first genuine request for assistance, however, came from Chile, a developing country. And the request was for a loan, not to a private institution but to the government, for a variety of projects. The U.S. executive director championed making Chile the Bank's first customer.

Even so, if reconstruction was the preference of most in the Bank, how it was to be accomplished—to say nothing of the magnitude of the task—was unclear when Meyer took his post. When the Bretton Woods meetings set up the IBRD, the United States and Allied governments had contemplated the use of Lend-Lease, UNRRA, and commodity-stabilization programs to assist in the postwar rebuilding of Europe. These programs either did not survive into the postwar period or were substantially cut back by the U.S. Congress. Equally unclear, when Meyer took over, were the role that the U.S.S.R. would play in the Bank and the dimensions of its postwar needs in rebuilding. The U.S.S.R. had been interested in the Bank during its planning, and the assurance that a country's political system would not be a consideration in making loans had specifically addressed Soviet concerns. Although relations between the United States and the U.S.S.R. were strained during 1946, the worst of what was to become the cold war was still in the future.[26]

In short, the Meyer presidency operated in a period of great flux. The United States and its allies had created the Bank and the Fund to avoid the mistakes of the 1920s and the 1930s. It remained to be seen how they would cope with the unprecedented problems of the post–World War II period. The nature and magnitude of those problems had already changed between Bretton Woods and the Bank's opening. The future direction of international politics and the world economy was only dimly perceived in the six months of Meyer's presidency.[27]

Even though a sharp definition of the Bank's mission was in the future, certain organizational issues could be dealt with immediately. One of the earliest successful organizational initiatives was the establishment of a research department. Whatever final form the Bank would take, it was going to require staff work to provide senior officials with the data needed to make decisions about loans and guarantees, judgments about the conditions in the countries seeking assistance, and assessments of the availability of capital.

The record is unfortunately silent on whether Meyer or someone else initiated the planning for a research department. In any event, he supported the idea. In July 1946 Leonard B. Rist, who had been among the first group Meyer had hired, provided the president with a report outlining the capabilities a research department should have and the kinds of personnel that would be needed. Within three months, a research operation was under way.[28]

The resolution of other organizational issues proved more tentative. The executive directors' ad hoc committee on organization produced a number of reports, culminating in a broad statement in early December 1946. The committee recommended that Bank policy be determined by, and in important respects be administered through, several high-level committees of the executive directors. An administrative committee, the report suggested, would make recommendations about personnel, salaries, benefits, housing, and the like. An information committee would have responsibility for both the Bank's research operations and public affairs. Other committees would monitor the Bank's relations with organizations such as the United Nations, and a special joint standing committee would take responsibility for devising procedures for working with the IMF. Major policy committees would draw up procedures for loans, and the financial policy committee would monitor the Bank's activities in financial markets.[29]

Meyer resigned within days of receiving the ad hoc committee's report. Creating a well-articulated organizational structure with clear lines of responsibility became the task of the next president. Even so, during Meyer's short tenure, important initiatives had been taken and long-term policies were in the process of formulation. It is clear that the December report of the committee was not simply a document about how things should be done in the future; it was also a prescriptive document on how to codify and organize what in fact the executive directors were trying to do.[30]

On balance, Meyer's influence on the future of the Bank was probably felt more directly in his work outside the institution than inside. Meyer's reputation on Wall Street was one of the strongest assets he brought to the Bank. In August 1946, less than two months after his arrival, he arranged a meeting at the Federal Reserve Bank in New York. Attending the session were representatives of insurance companies and of investment, commercial, and savings banks. A report of the meeting indicated that the security industry representatives welcomed Meyer's remarks, especially his promise that "he intended to operate the Bank on sound banking principles in the same manner as he had previously operated the War Finance Corporation, the Farm Loan Board, and the Reconstruction Finance Corporation."[31]

Although the meeting was a way for Meyer to introduce the Bank to the market, the security industry representatives took the occasion to convey some suggestions. They made the point that the Bank's own debentures would be more easily marketed than guaranteed issues. The question of making loans instead of issuing guarantees would become prominent in the following year, as European countries made requests for loan assistance. Industry representatives also made clear the investment community's interest in the Bank by emphasizing that "one of the primary interests of the market representatives present was the relaxation of state laws restricting investments by insurance companies, savings banks, and trustees" in the Bank's securities.[32]

In regard to the last piece of advice, representatives at the August meeting did not tell Meyer anything he did not already know. Indeed, proponents of the Bank had started a campaign to change state laws soon after the United States and twenty-eight other signatories activated the agreements on December 27, 1945. As early as February 1946 the Investment Bankers Association of America began examining the Bank's prospects, and in March officials of the Federal Reserve System reminded member commercial banks that the Fed's rules would allow them to purchase IBRD bonds. Under the regulations of the time, there were also few restrictions on trust companies' purchasing Bank securities.[33]

Important markets for Bank securities, however, would be the savings bank and insurance industries. Both were highly regulated by the states, and restrictions would have to be removed before the Bank would be able to tap into the industries' rich sources of capital. Even before the Bank opened, the Securities and Exchange

Commission and the NAC had begun a campaign to convince the states to change their laws. Most state regulators preferred to await the formal beginnings of IBRD business—a position that reflected skepticism not so much of the Bank itself as of foreign lending in general (127f.).

By the time Meyer joined the Bank, progress had been made with the states. Indeed, Collado, the U.S. executive director, had taken part in the successful initiative to get New York State to change its laws. The positive action of the state legislature in March was an important achievement because many states would follow New York's lead. Meyer joined in the effort to persuade other states to modify their regulations, freely trading on his reputation for prudence to convince officials that there was nothing to fear in authorizing banks and insurance companies to invest in the IBRD's bonds. The *New York Times* reported in November that the New York savings bank industry had "been developing an increasingly high regard" for Meyer, who they thought would not be in favor of "charity loans."[34]

Although the opinion of Wall Street was critical to the future of the Bank, the nature of relations with the new United Nations was also an important issue in the earliest months of the Bank's history. If mishandled, the fledgling relationship could have enmeshed the Bank with the United Nations. Both Meyer and the executive directors feared that the United Nations would politicize the Bank, a circumstance that would undermine Wall Street's confidence in the IBRD.[35]

Both the Bank's Articles of Agreement and the U.N. Charter anticipated some relationship between the two institutions. The Bank's founders were much less specific about the arrangement, mandating only that the IBRD cooperate with other international organizations. The U.N. Charter provided for close relations with the specialized agencies established by intergovernmental agreement and with wide international responsibilities. The charter called for the United Nations to coordinate these agencies' activities. In the view of the U.N. secretariat, these agencies included the Bank (54–59).

Meyer and his staff delayed when approached by U.N. officials. In truth, the Bank was far from being fully organized, and Meyer had no interest in complicating the IBRD's business by obligating it to the United Nations. A final agreement between the two institutions had to await McCloy's presidency (54–57).[36]

Important as Wall Street and the United Nations were to the future of the IBRD, the division of authority between the president and the executive directors was the critical issue for the institution's future. Although Meyer's staff took part in the numerous meetings of the executive directors' committees over organizational and policy issues, it was clear that the executive directors conceived of themselves as the initiators of policy. They met twice a week and conferred often with each other and with members of Meyer's staff. At times, various executive directors attended the president's staff meetings. Meyer routinely provided all of them with reports on these meetings.[37]

In their first annual report, issued in September 1946, the executive directors stated their position unequivocally: "Matters of policy determination are the responsibility of the executive directors, while operational, administrative, and organizational questions are the responsibility of the president, subject to the general direction and control of the executive directors. The president is the presiding officer of the executive directors and is entitled to a deciding vote in the case of an equal division."[38] This position reflected an interpretation of the provisions in the Articles of Agreement that spelled conflict. The executive directors' views were also reflected in several of the draft reports of the directors' committee on organization. It was only a matter of time before there would be a serious clash over how the Bank was to be organized and who had the authority to propose policies and initiate lending proposals.

In October 1946 the Netherlands' J. W. Beyen demonstrated the strong-willed independence of the executive directors. In a speech to the New York State Savings Banks Association meeting in Quebec, he indicated that the Bank would borrow almost $2 billion in 1947. Meyer's quick disavowal of the remarks did not mitigate the impression on Wall Street that the Bank was off to a troubling start and that the president was not in charge.[39]

As embarrassing as the incident with Beyen proved to be, at least it was over quickly. Loan policy, however, was the source of a drawn-out and contentious confrontation between the president and the executive directors, especially U.S. Director Collado. In

September 1946 the Chilean government submitted a $40 million package of projects for funding. Collado was determined to make a loan by the end of 1946 to demonstrate that the Bank was in business, and he pressed Meyer hard to accept the Chilean request.[40]

Meyer and his staff responded cautiously. For one thing, Wall Street still did not know enough about the Bank and its operations. For another, a prudent investment banker would not simply approve the Chilean request without knowing much more about the projects they wanted funded.[41] Meyer had made his career on Wall Street by careful research into potential investments. He was quite capable of moving quickly when necessary, but it was not his style to act without a thorough investigation and clear purpose.[42]

Collado's disappointment over what he saw as Meyer's foot-dragging fueled his effort to ensure the primacy of the executive directors in the Bank's policymaking. At the time, observers tended to view the disagreement over the Chilean loan as a clash of personalities. To be sure, personality differences played a part. Collado was smart, ambitious, and a skilled bureaucratic tactician. He held a Ph.D. in economics from Harvard and had worked for the Department of the Treasury, beginning in 1934, and then for the Department of State. In the years following, he became deeply involved in the planning for the postwar international economic order. He worked closely with key figures from both the United States and Allied governments in drafting the Bretton Woods agreements. Early in 1946 some officials in the Department of State had even considered him as a potential first president of the Bank.[43]

Be that as it may, Collado was half Meyer's age, and his entire experience had been as a staff man. He was no match for Meyer in experience or stature. Nor was Collado a match for McLain, who approached bureaucratic battles by "slugging it out" rather than engaging in negotiation. The general counsel was tart in his criticisms of the executive directors' attempts to develop policy. Still, Collado had won the respect and support of his colleagues among the executive directors. Among them were proud and determined men—some, like Mendès-France, destined for high office in their own countries—who supported Collado's determination to begin making loans.[44]

Even so, larger issues were at stake in the dispute over the loan to Chile. Collado's authority derived from the NAC, on which Congress had insisted when it approved U.S. participation in the Bank. So long as Collado could count on at least the tacit support of officials in the Treasury and State departments represented on the NAC, he could continue to assert the prerogatives of the executive directors.[45]

Ironically, Meyer's sudden resignation on December 4, 1946, ultimately undercut the efforts of Collado and the executive directors to maintain control over the direction of the Bank. During the negotiations between John J. McCloy and the Truman administration about the presidency of the Bank, Meyer and McLain persuaded McCloy to insist that the primacy of his authority be clearly established before he took the post. McLain, who stayed on as general counsel, ensured that McCloy understood the problems that Meyer had faced. Under the new circumstances, Collado's resignation became inevitable.[46]

As for Meyer's sudden resignation, he steadfastly maintained that President Truman had only asked him to launch the Bank and that he had always seen his assignment as short term. Observers at the time thought that Meyer seemed to lack the vitality necessary to cope with building a new institution in an occasionally contentious environment. Meyer's private comment about the situation, related to his secretary, was, "I could stay and fight these bastards, and probably win in the end, but I'm too old for that."[47] Moreover, Meyer had never seen himself as a man committed to a particular institution for any length of time. His style was to move in and out of organizations as he was needed and as it suited him. After all, he had the wealth to support a patrician way of life and a large number of interests to occupy him. Although his talented son-in-law Philip Graham had taken over the *Washington Post* before Meyer went to the Bank, he still retained a great personal interest in the paper.

By resigning as he did, Meyer created a situation that allowed those who remained, especially McLain, to ensure that the power of the next president was sufficient to build an effective organization. But the next president also had to begin his tenure by attend-

ing to apprehensions on Wall Street. The *New York Times* described
Meyer's departure as "a serious blow."[48] Meyer's abrupt leaving
unnerved potential investors who were already concerned about
the Bank's future after the Wisconsin Banking Commission had
refused to allow banks in that state to purchase World Bank securities.

Short as Meyer's tenure was, the groundwork was set for policies that continued for a long time. Meyer learned from Wall Street
that issuing guarantees was not going to be the Bank's major operation—that it would have to issue its own securities to find out
whether it could play a role as an effective intermediary. The board
and staff in those months also determined that all borrowers would
be charged the same interest rate and that security for loans would
not be required of public authorities.[49]

Certainly, Meyer's few months as head of the Bank cannot com-
pare with the long years of service of some of the men who followed. But important appointments were made during his tenure,
and he and his advisers began to confront issues that would be on
the Bank's agenda for years to come. His excellent reputation on
Wall Street and his conservative approach to public service served
to allay the fears of the Bank's erstwhile opponents while hearten-
ing those who looked to the IBRD as a major force in the effort to
build a cooperative international economic order after World War
II. Although Meyer did not take big steps, he did take the Bank's
first steps.

CHAPTER TWO

John J. McCloy

Starting Up the Business

John J. McCloy assumed the presidency of the World Bank on March 17, 1947. When he was elected two weeks earlier, March 15 was suggested for the event; but the U.K. executive director of the Bank suggested that Saint Patrick's Day would be a more auspicious date than the Ides of March.[1] Whether the 17th was better than the 15th remains unknown.

When the World Bank was designed at Bretton Woods in 1944, optimism was rife. "One World," a slogan of the time, was the expectation of many. It was understood that there would be an urgent task of reconstruction in Europe and a longer-run task of development in poorer parts of the world, still largely colonial. Indeed, reconstruction and development provided the rationale for the World Bank's given name, International Bank for Reconstruction and Development. It was not widely foreseen that two worlds would emerge; that each would be dominated by one of the victorious powers; that the task of reconstruction, and even the membership of the World Bank, would be affected by a sharp line drawn north and south through Central Europe; that the colonial and developing world would be the object of aggressive competition between the West and the Soviet bloc; that the job of reconstruction would be far more costly than the World Bank, as constituted, could finance; and that development would be inhibited by more serious obstacles than finance. Edward Mason and Robert Asher no doubt had these scenarios in mind when they wrote in 1973, "One is struck by both the magnificence of the achievement and the lack of prescience of the founding fathers."[2]

When Eugene Meyer became president of the World Bank, the outlines of the cold war had begun to take shape. When John McCloy became president nine months later, the relation between the two worlds had frozen into confrontation, with important implications for the World Bank's evolution.

McCloy's Agenda

The years of the McCloy presidency, 1947 through 1949, proved to be a challenging time for the Bank. The period was marked by a series of international developments that shaped the next forty years. On one side, Eastern Europe was integrated under Soviet leadership. On the other side, the Truman doctrine for the defense of Greece and Turkey, the Marshall Plan and the Point Four Program of technical assistance, and, above all, the creation of the North Atlantic Treaty Organization (NATO) firmly aligned Western Europe with the United States. The partition of Korea, unrest in Indochina, and the revolution in China brought much of Asia into the confrontation between East and West. At the same time the struggle for independence in the colonial world, which would lead to a steady expansion of the Bank's membership, picked up momentum and became a fertile field for cold war competition. This was the world in which the Bank was defined and came of age. Of course, almost every era, seen close up, seems a volatile one, full of uncertainties, in flux. McCloy's era, however, was probably the most uncertain in the World Bank's history, and these uncertainties affected the Bank's membership, its policies, the scope and direction of its operations, and indeed the rationale for its existence.

In a full scan of McCloy's career, his twenty-seven-month stint as president of the World Bank is not much more than a blip. Of the 663 pages of his comprehensive biography, only 24 deal with his time at the Bank. Of two major reviews of that book, one does not mention the Bank at all, and the other does so only incidentally, in a listing of the principal posts he held.[3]

Those twenty-seven months were a crucial period in the history of the Bank. The Bank started to borrow in the capital market; defined its basic policies and operational procedures; made its first loans, both for reconstruction and for development; filled out the management team; and doubled its staff to almost 400. Most important, it settled the crucial question of how the Bank would be run. Would it be guided primarily by an autonomous "management," a new word in the Bank's lexicon? Or by a board of executive directors elected by its growing number of member states, virtually all of which would be potential borrowers as well? Management "won" what was in fact a political power struggle over the extent of control of the largest shareholder, the United States. That, in essence, would be the way it would remain.

To characterize McCloy's presidency as the period in which the World Bank started up its business does not imply that nothing had happened in the previous nine months. Much important spade-work had been done, including the recruitment of the core staff, the discussion of basic policies, the initiation of a dialogue with potential borrowers, and the first contacts with the New York bond market. But perhaps most important, Meyer's six-month administration and the three-month interregnum that followed had focused attention on the fundamental issue in the governance of the Bank: the ambiguity in the relative roles of the executive directors and of the president. Who would exercise leadership in the institution? Who would manage it? That ambiguity and the tension it caused were at the core of the institution in 1946. The confusion about leadership would have to be resolved if the Bank were to realize the expectations of its founders and its members.

Obtaining resources, starting up lending operations, strengthening the staff, and clarifying the governance of the Bank—not only the respective roles of the board and the president, but also the Bank's relations with the United Nations and with its dominant shareholder, the United States—were the major elements of McCloy's agenda when he assumed the presidency of the Bank. They were closely interrelated and had implications for policies, staffing, and organization. Lending, which was to be the Bank's visible output, depended on its operational policies and on the resources it could muster. If the Bank was to be an ongoing business, it would have to borrow rather than limit its lending to its small amount of usable capital. If it was to borrow, lenders would need to know who ran the Bank, how it would use its resources, and the conditions on which these resources would be made available. In dealing with these issues, McCloy had the advantage of the knowledge Meyer had gained the hard way—the realization that the corporate world was not the world of the Bank.

Preparations: Protecting Big Business and the Nation

John Jay McCloy was born on March 31, 1895, on the wrong side of the "Chinese wall," a stone viaduct that once, physically and symbolically, separated Philadelphia's upper classes from its poor.[4] Not quite "on the wrong side of the railroad tracks," as McCloy liked to say, but in a modest, undistinguished neighborhood on the right side. The McCloy family was not rich, hardly even well-to-do, but not poor either. His father was a clerk with the Penn Mutual Life Insurance Company. Young Jack had a long way to go before he could be identified—as he was much later—as "the most influential private citizen in America" and as "Chairman of the American Establishment."[5]

Jack was 6 years old when his father died at age 39. His mother Anna was left with the burden of making a living and educating her son. She worked as a hairdresser and never married again. She "did heads," McCloy used to say, while one milliner maiden aunt "did hats" and another kept house for the four of them. His mother's main clients were the wives of Philadelphia's wealthy lawyers and businessmen. Anna often took Jack with her in the summer when she went to the homes of her clients in the Adirondacks and New England. She also managed to send Jack, with contributions from his own work and scholarships, to prestigious schools—the Peddie Institute in New Jersey, then Amherst College, and finally Harvard Law School.

His stint at Harvard was interrupted by two years in the army, mostly in Europe. It was followed by twenty years in the practice of law in New York and in Europe, a practice that involved McCloy with some of the country's largest corporations. He worked with the cream of New York's legal establishment and after only five years, at age 34, became a partner at Cravath, de Gersdorff, Swaine & Wood. McCloy's friends, colleagues, and clients were largely conservative and Republican, reflecting his own values and political views. He affiliated, however, with the internationalist wing of the party, which was more interested in foreign affairs than in the domestic economy and focused primarily on the U.S. place in the international order. With the internationalist Republicans he shared a hostility toward President Roosevelt's programs. His firm was principally involved in the famous *Chicken* case, which challenged the linchpin of the early Roosevelt program, the National Industrial Recovery Act—and won it before the Supreme Court. McCloy's brother-in-law, Lew Douglas, was one of the few in his group to join the administration, but he resigned after a few years. McCloy, his biographer notes, shared the biases of his intimates; he was "a man of his times and class"[6]—not of the class he was born into, but of the class to which he had aspired and into which he had been welcomed.

McCloy's political landscape quickly changed with the onset of World War II. President Roosevelt's appeals for national unity actually brought some of McCloy's group, who were ardently pro-Ally, into the administration—most notably Henry L. Stimson, his mentor, as secretary of war. (Stimson had already been secretary of war under President Taft and secretary of state under President Hoover.) Just before the United States entered the war, McCloy went to Washington to be Stimson's consultant and assistant and, before long, his assistant secretary of war.

After the war, in the autumn of 1945, McCloy returned to law practice, this time as a name-partner of Milbank, Tweed, Hope, Hadley and McCloy, whose major clients were the Rockefeller family and its businesses. His first contact with the Rockefeller family had taken place more than three decades earlier, on a trip with his mother to Mount Desert Island, Maine. At his mother's urging, he had rapped one day on the Rockefeller door, looking for a job tutoring the young sons. Although the door was closed on him at that time, it was opened years later to a mature attorney who had proved himself in both private practice and public service. In time, his connection with the family's law firm would lead to the chairmanship of the Chase Manhattan Bank and to further ties with major U.S. firms and foundations.

The various phases of McCloy's career seem to flow seamlessly, each into the next: from his early youth, through college and war, to the business and service careers that preceded the presidency of the World Bank. Throughout, Anna McCloy was a major influence on his life. Jack was the focus of her life; he absorbed her dreams and responded to her determination. Guided by her hopes, he mastered education and the law, making his way into the life of the better-born, beginning with the Philadelphia elite with which she had brought him into contact.

At the Peddie Institute, the school's physical education director reinforced his mother's efforts. His advice, McCloy later recalled, was "'always run with the swift. You might some day come in second.' It was good advice. I took it to heart in all things" (33). At Peddie, Amherst, and Harvard, many of his friends were from elite families, and they would remain his friends and associates. He had the gift of making and retaining friends in high places. Relationships he established in the army and in law practice included the leading figures of the legal and corporate worlds of Europe and of the East Coast of the United States. They constituted a network of VIPs through whom he was to have ready access to the power he came to wield in both private practice and public service.

McCloy used his influence to achieve social as well as individual goals. The national security of the United States was, in particular, a vital and enduring concern for him. With the outbreak of World War I in Europe, while he was still at Amherst, he had become actively involved in the preparedness and interventionist movements. Spurred by the sinking of the *Lusitania* in 1915, he had spent two summers at the military training camps for students and businessmen in Plattsburg, New York. Those encampments were later characterized as a place where "amid simple material surroundings, the upper-class elite underwent a conversion experience of patriotism" (43). Many of those he socialized and trained with—none more so than Stimson—would remain McCloy's friends until his death. The Plattsburg encampment, McCloy's biographer has written, was "the formative political experience of his life" (40). He enlisted in the army in May 1917.

In France McCloy caught the attention of his commanding officer, who tried to convince him to become a regular army officer. But McCloy clearly had more lofty goals in mind. He preferred to return to the law, but not before he had become acquainted not only with General John J. Pershing but also with George Marshall, Douglas MacArthur, and "Wild Bill" Donovan, all of whom would play important roles in his later career.

McCloy's interest and involvement in national security were sharpened by his stellar performance in what was to be his major legal experience, the *Black Tom* case, when he was a partner at Cravath, de Gersdoff, Swaine & Wood. The bulk of the munitions exported to Europe in World War I left from the Black Tom terminus on the New Jersey side of New York harbor. In 1916 the terminus was destroyed by a gigantic explosion felt throughout New York City and as far south as Philadelphia. German sabotage was immediately suspected. Claims were filed and debated for more than a decade by companies that sustained damages, among which were some important clients of Cravath's. The claims were rejected, appealed, reheard, and rejected again. In 1930, McCloy's firm put him in charge of the *Black Tom* case. A decade of largely personal sleuthing on McCloy's part followed. Despite discouragement, rejection by the commission hearing the case, and appeal of one aspect of it to the U.S. Supreme Court, McCloy persisted. Finally, he won the case. *Black Tom* brought him not only notoriety but also the appreciation of his peers and the admiration of Stimson, who had sought to discourage him from pursuing the case. *Black Tom* also took McCloy on extended visits to Europe, where he had the opportunity to enhance his knowledge of Germany and to witness some key events in the Nazi chronology, including the 1936 Olympics, where he sat next to Göring, in Hitler's box (ch. 5, passim).

The knowledge and repute gained in the *Black Tom* affair, added to his general legal experience, led Stimson, now secretary of war again, to bring McCloy into the War Department as assistant secretary. McCloy played a key role in mobilizing the U.S. economy for war, especially in the gigantic task of the planning and production required for D-Day. He was involved and participated in most of the key decisions of the war, including the development and use of the atomic bomb and the occupation policy in Europe and Japan. He was greatly valued as a troubleshooter, a problem solver, and a consensus builder.

Two decisions in which McCloy participated still cast a shadow on his record as assistant secretary. The first was the decision to intern the entire community of Japanese and Americans of Japanese descent—a decision reached over the strenuous objections of the attorney general of the United States. Considered an expert on sabotage since the *Black Tom* case, McCloy said in 1942, "If it is a question of the safety of the country [or] the Constitution of the United States, why the Constitution is just a scrap of paper to me" (146). The second was the decision not to bomb Germany's gas chambers and the rail lines leading to them. In shaping these decisions, McCloy was guided by the absolute priority he felt had to be given to the pursuit of the war. For him, that objective overrode any other considerations—constitutional, legal, or humanitarian. Characteristically, he appeared to have never had second thoughts about these or his other major decisions.

Before McCloy left the War Department in November 1945, he was offered the post of high commissioner for Germany by President Roosevelt, the ambassadorship to the U.S.S.R. by the secretary of state, the presidency of the Standard Oil Company of California by the Rockefellers, and the presidency of Amherst. He turned them all down, preferring to return to the law and "a base from which he could engage in disinterested public service while ensconced within the protective womb of an elite private law practice" (273).

In private practice and in public service McCloy had three principal role models and patrons. Although different, they had important characteristics in common. They were Republicans, but of the internationalist type characteristic of the East Coast business elite, and they were linked to big business. More important, they shared the conviction that the law called for and nurtured a special kind of person, who combined the defense of private interests with public service. The top-notch lawyer, as they saw it, was uniquely capable of identifying the public good and acting as the public's trustee. They found no inconsistency or conflict in this dual role.

During McCloy's youth his mentor had been George Warton Pepper, the exemplar of the Philadelphia lawyer and gentleman, who believed in doing his charitable and civic duty behind the scenes. It was Pepper who advised McCloy not to practice law, as he had planned, in Philadelphia, where his career would be hampered by his modest origins, but to go instead to New York City, where merit ensured upward mobility for the aggressive *nouveau arrivé.* "I knew the pace would be thrilling there," McCloy later recalled. "I knew that was where I would have a chance to run with the swift."[7] Pepper's vision melded into that of Paul Cravath, the founder and senior partner of New York's premier law firm. Cravath was considered one of the sharks of Wall Street's legal establishment, but he also had a profound belief in a lawyer's duty to contribute to the community. Under Cravath's coaching, McCloy honed his ability to deconstruct any problem a client offered, develop a solution, and express it effectively. Cravath once told an audience at the Harvard Law School that "brilliant intellectual powers are not essential [to a lawyer]. Too much imagination, too much wit, too great cleverness, too facile fluency, if not leavened by a sound sense of proportion are quite as likely to impede success as to promote it."[8] McCloy took that to heart.

Looming over Pepper and Cravath, however, was Henry Stimson, whom McCloy had first met at the Plattsburg military training camp. Stimson preeminently mixed private advocacy with service in the cabinets of four presidents, from 1908 to 1946. He was the internationalist hero of two generations of young lawyers and public servants and was McCloy's model, friend, and mentor. It was Stimson who first drew McCloy into public service, which McCloy never fully left. On the wall behind Stimson's desk was the portrait of Stimson's mentor Elihu Root—lawyer, four-time cabinet secretary to two presidents, ambassador, U.S. senator, Nobel Prize winner, founder of the Council on Foreign Relations. "I felt a distinct current running from Root through Stimson to me," McCloy once wrote in his diary. "They were the giants."[9]

Like his role models, McCloy was never, nor was he ever considered to be, an intellectual or an innovative thinker or policymaker. Hard work and persistence were the sources of his effectiveness. He was a problem solver, negotiator, dealmaker, and troubleshooter. Pragmatism rather than ideology dominated his thinking, although ideology no doubt became an instinctive and effective companion of pragmatism. McCloy was always modest and unpretentious, generally jovial, a boon companion: "no one disliked this man except at a distance."[10] He kept a low profile. He was never known for ideology or a political agenda; his influence "grew out of his ability to make the people he dealt with think each idea was their own. . . . Because he was a good listener, one who could guide decisions without noisy infighting, Jack McCloy was considered the consummate wise man."[11]

By the time McCloy became president of the Bank, he had already acquired, not among the public but among insiders in business and government, an immense reputation as a lawyer, wartime manager, and adviser, with close ties to many of the most powerful men in the country. He was considered one of the architects of the American Century heralded in 1941 by Henry Luce, publisher of *Time* magazine. "He and his peers in the U.S. foreign policy establishment provided the rationale for continuing the [wartime] mobilization, this time to build a peacetime national security state. America would turn outward and assume global responsibilities."[12] He and his associates saw the United States taking on the global responsibility for establishing and defining a new world order. This called for continuing to strengthen the country. In 1946, a year before he assumed the presidency of the Bank, McCloy wrote, "We need, if you will, a Pax Americana, and in the course of it the world will become more receptive to the Bill of Rights viewpoint than if we do no more than devoutly wish for peace and freedom" (661).

Given his reputation and his outlook, McCloy could rightly consider himself endowed with *gravitas*. In the 1960s he was to tell Haverford students that the possessor of *gravitas* in ancient Rome "had the respect and regard of his countrymen, whether he was in the forum or on the farm. 'Gravitas' did not imply age nor brilliance, and, least of all, a style or school of thought. It means a core, a weight of judgment and honest appraisal" (575). That was what Pepper, Cravath, and Stimson had in common, and that was what distinguished the McCloy who took over at the World Bank in 1947.

Institutional Governance: Clearing the Decks

The choice of John McCloy to succeed Eugene Meyer seems, in hindsight, to have been eminently sensible. Yet agreeing on his candidacy and persuading him to accept the job was in fact a delicate, difficult, and time-consuming task. By this time, McCloy had an impeccable reputation in both government and business, in the law, banking, and industry. He was politically conservative; however, he was not partisan at home, but rather an advocate of the United States' destiny abroad. He was personally known to the political and business elites in Europe, as well as to those of the northeastern United States. He belonged to the small group of friends, often classmates, who formulated and established the foreign policy that would dominate the United States for a decade after World War II. He was known as a driving and efficient manager and problem solver. He was a natural for the job.

The Truman administration had difficulty finding a suitable successor to Eugene Meyer. The Bank at that time was viewed with skepticism, if not outright hostility, by the conservative banking and insurance communities, which regarded it as a product of liberal, financially unsound, welfare thinking. As if to confirm these suspicions, the Bank was drifting, leaderless, and in a state of "dispirited confusion."[13] The *New York Times,* in February 1947, thought the Bank was "split by dissension, sadly lacking in prestige, and had not lent one dime."[14] No wonder that it was difficult to find a reputable, experienced person willing to accept the challenge of leading this unconventional institution. McCloy later described the situation in a speech to the Investment Bankers Association of America: "Perhaps some of you here have heard me say on other occasions that I made a rough calculation the other day, and I found out that if you took the total of the people who were applying for subordinate jobs in the Bank and added them to the number of people who were trying to get my New York apartment, they approximately equal the number of people who turned down the presidency of the International Bank before I had the nerve to take it."[15]

In fact, several persons were approached before McCloy. Following Meyer's resignation, the executive directors began almost immediately to consider potential successors. Several people were sounded out—chiefly U.S. citizens but also a Canadian—but they showed little interest because the Bank was a dubious proposition. Three board members are reported to have had aspirations to the presidency. The principal shareholders seem to have taken little active interest—until McCloy turned down the first offer.

It is not clear by whom or when McCloy was first approached. Eugene Meyer might have done it informally. They had long known each other: McCloy's prewar law firm handled some of Meyer's personal business, and they had met fairly regularly since 1940 to discuss the progress of the war and related matters. Whether or not Meyer put out feelers, he must certainly have made McCloy aware of his frustrations with the executive directors and with the U.S. director in particular. A more likely source of knowledge of the Bank's plight, and perhaps of feelers about the presidency, was Chester McLain, once McCloy's law partner and now, on McCloy's own strong recommendation, the Bank's general counsel.[16] By all accounts McLain had an influential, perhaps dominant voice in the Bank. Even without McLain's and Meyer's intervention, however, McCloy would have been aware of the situation in the Bank because it was no secret. Nor was Meyer's frequent affirmation that he had resigned because he had completed President Truman's mandate to organize the Bank widely accepted. Insiders attributed the decision to Meyer's age and energy level, but above all to the frustrations of continuing tension with the executive directors.

The first approach from the U.S. government was through Collado, the U.S. executive director. After consultation with the National Advisory Council, Collado flew to New York on December 23, 1946, to offer the post to McCloy. Collado later recalled that McCloy said, "Pete, you've made such a hell of a mess of it, you don't think I'm going to move into the damn thing." All Collado received was McCloy's "half-hearted promise to think about it."[17] McCloy sought the advice of his friends in the business community. Although many of them advised him to take the post, he turned it down. His rejection led both Collado and Treasury Secretary John Snyder to visit him, separately, in New York, where the discussions continued.

McCloy's original rejection may well have been tactical, and so perhaps were his reactions to the discussions that followed. The advice of Meyer and McLain that he insist on appropriate executive authority was reinforced by the advice of friends who, on the same conditions, urged him to accept. Not the least of them was Eugene Black, then a vice president of the Chase National Bank. Black was in Europe when the rumors about McCloy's possible nomination surfaced. On his return, Black later recalled, they met at a Chase Bank committee meeting and he told McCloy about Europe's needs and about the potential importance of the Bank. Black thought he was the first to urge McCloy to accept the post, although that is not likely. He too urged McCloy to insist on having clearly established management authority.[18]

As time passed, the concern of the executive directors mounted. Sir James Grigg of the United Kingdom was in almost daily contact with London, and his communiqués took on a desperate tone. Thomas Basyn, the Belgium alternate director, was much calmer, but he too wrote several long letters a week (sometimes two a day) to the governor of the Bank of Belgium or to its executive directors. His comments on the succession were always labeled *la crise présidentielle*.[19] On January 9, Grigg sent this cable to the Treasury: "I propose to take the line that one fatal thing to do now is to go on hawking the job around. We must therefore patch up some domestic arrangement and carry on vigorously. What this arrangement should be is another matter—probably Collado as temporary chairman with the powers of President."[20] Thereafter, the board consulted the U.S. secretary of the treasury and the undersecretary of state and, in the absence of a negative reaction from them, decided informally to take the action proposed by Grigg, to be executed at a formal meeting on January 15.

But the board had not counted on the steadfast refusal of Chester McLain to accept this decision or on his determination to resign if it were carried out. He felt strongly that the representative of a shareholder and a national official could not credibly hold an international office and that the inherent conflict would be contrary to the fundamental character of the Bank. In response to a phone call from the undersecretary of state, McLain declared that his decision to resign was unalterable. Several members of the staff, despite his efforts to dissuade them, appeared determined to follow

McLain out of the Bank. At this point, the U.S. government became officially concerned.

When the executive directors met informally on January 15, Grigg brought the news from the undersecretary of state that McCloy's decision was not yet final and that the board ought to delay action. The board took that suggestion. The minutes of the meeting reflect dismay and confusion, perhaps even disgust, as the executive directors seemed to suspect that a key issue for McCloy was to have some assurance "that the National Advisory Council would give no formal instructions to the U.S. director without prior consultation with the president of the Bank."[21]

The U.K. Treasury informed Grigg that it was "very much concerned with the present absurd and scandalous position" but firmly instructed him to back off the idea of making Collado temporary president: "We have heard from other sources that McCloy has not finally refused and might accept provided that he is independent of outside pressure. [Under the Articles] the president owes his loyalty to the Bank and to no outside authority, and we assume that the Americans would not wish to make the president, whoever he is, either de facto and still less de jure, a member of the NAC. To sum up if there is still a chance of McCloy we think he would be the best choice, especially as New York might be induced to play with him."[22]

Nonetheless, Grigg visited Snyder and William L. Clayton of the State Department, again expressing concern that the United States would drive a bargain with McCloy, which the executive directors found objectionable. "Snyder said that there could be no misunderstanding between the United States Government and McCloy which diminished the rights etc. of directors under the articles." Snyder had already suggested to McCloy that he talk to the board. "He had also told McCloy in New York that he must give an answer very soon."[23]

Grigg was advised that the chancellor had already written to the secretary of the treasury that the British looked to him "to end the present lamentable [revised from "scandalous" to "lamentable"] situation, which is that the U.S. Government has failed to produce a President, and the Bank is reduced to stalemate."[24] The chancellor's letter was more polite and less blunt but very clear; it reminded

Snyder of his responsibility to deal with the problem: "I should be grateful if, among all your other preoccupations, you could find time to give the difficult but vitally important question your personal attention."[25]

Eugene Meyer was told that the U.S. government had turned down McCloy because he reportedly wanted the right to approve in advance any U.S. decision affecting the Bank. Meyer called McCloy to get his story, and McCloy told him all he wanted was the opportunity to present his views before a final decision was taken on Bank matters. Meyer conveyed this to Snyder and Clayton. Although "Snyder seemed disgruntled about the whole business," both withdrew their objections to McCloy, who now agreed to come to Washington to talk to the board.[26] While he continued to negotiate with the U.S. government and with the executive directors, he was already choosing the principal members of the team he wanted when, and if, he was elected president. Robert L. Garner, whom he had never met, had been strongly recommended to him as vice president; for this position McCloy wanted a strong manager with banking experience, and Garner fitted that role. Eugene Black, whom he had met only recently, was his choice as U.S. executive director and as driver of the Bank's bond-selling strategy.

McCloy met with the executive directors on February 17, 1947. The meeting (McCloy's second with the board) was held in an atmosphere of crisis and must have been very tense indeed. Grigg reported to London that "McCloy. . . was at times unnecessarily truculent." His main concern, and that of other executive directors, seems to have been McCloy's insistence on the dual role of Black as both executive director and staff director of marketing. This posture would raise questions about both conformity with the Articles of Agreement and potential conflicts of interest. At the end, the board agreed that it would accept Black's dual role "if the United States government decides to accept such [an] arrangement. . . . We were in fact presented with an ultimatum. . . . What happens now I don't know but I must say that dirt is a disagreeable diet."[27]

Although the board was ready to give in, McCloy was not yet ready to accept. He returned to New York City to consult with friends and associates about the likelihood of success in a campaign to make Bank bonds legally and economically acceptable to the market. A week later, he informed the U.S. government that he would accept the presidency. He and Garner came to Washington on February 28. Their first stop was at Secretary Snyder's office. Garner's diary entry that day tersely tells the story.

> We explained our position, which was briefly that we were coming down at the request of the Secretary of the Treasury speaking for the NAC, and of the Executive Directors, as we had been informed that they were ready to formally ask McCloy whether he would become president and, if so, elect him; but that if there was not unanimity of support we would clear the air by withdrawing from the situation. The Secretary assured us that he had no question of such unanimity of support.
>
> It was decided, that Mr. Collado's resignation as the Executive Director representing the United States, which the Secretary held, together with the President's acceptance, would be announced, and that the President would forthwith send to the Senate the nomination of Eugene R. Black to succeed.[28]

McCloy then met alone with the board for two hours. Garner joined them briefly to say that "if McCloy took the presidency I would be happy to serve under him and do my best to help in the success of the Bank." After a short discussion among themselves, the directors adjourned "and Collado informed us that the directors were prepared to vote unanimously at the afternoon meeting."[29] They met again at 3 p.m. and elected McCloy president. *La crise presidentielle* was over. Business could at last begin.

Although there is no formal written record of the conditions that McCloy laid down or, more important, those that were ultimately accepted, they can be inferred from the events. Some, such as the president's executive authority, concerned primarily the executive directors. Others, such as the president's relationship with the NAC and with the U.S. director, concerned primarily the U.S. government. All, of course, concerned all member states. Clearly McCloy would be the Bank's chief executive officer. The U.S. government would consult him and seek his approval before appointing its executive director, but his relationship with the NAC was not touched on and would obviously depend on personal chemistry. Finally, the principle was established that the Bank would be independent in its decisions and that the Bank's president would not be subject to the dictates of the U.S. executive director.

It is not clear whose decision it was in the U.S. government to accept McCloy's conditions—Secretary Snyder's or President Truman's—but the decision was made. How long it would last was another matter. Fourteen years later, while Black was president of the Bank, he was asked if the president still had a voice in the choice of the U.S. director. "Well," Black replied, "there's no agreement that he will pick the man, but I think there's an understanding that the U.S. Director should be acceptable to the President . . . . The President of the Bank hasn't got the *right* to select the American Director. That's done by the President of the United States. But if you look back on the history of it, if the American Director has a large share of the votes, it would be an impossible situation if he and the president of the Bank didn't get along. One of them would have to quit."[30] McCloy accepted the view that it would be impractical "for Black to be member of staff as well as American Executive Director."[31] In all but name, however, Black was a member of the triumvirate that ran the Bank while McCloy was president.

The changes in the relationship between the president and the Board were set forth in a report of the Board's Committee on Organization, which the full Board approved in June 1947. The report bluntly stated that while the Executive Directors were responsible for policy decisions, recommendations for such decisions must come from the "management." Although the Board was to be kept generally informed of the progress of the Bank's operational work, the management would decide whether a loan application was to be pursued and would determine the framework for negotiations. It was only after the completion of negotiations that the president would submit a loan proposal to the Board for approval.[32] This was a far cry from the Board's decision of July 1946, which placed control of every stage of the operational process in the hands of the Executive Directors.[33] It is worth noting that the word "management" had now, in 1947, found its way into the Bank's lexicon.

A public sign of the new arrangement for power-sharing appears in the Bank's annual reports. In Meyer's letter of presentation of the first annual report, in September 1946, he wrote that he had "the honor to present to the Board of Governors the Annual Report of the Executive Directors." The report stated that "matters of policy determination are the responsibility of the Executive Directors while operational, administrative and organization questions are the responsibility of the President, subject to the general direction and control of the Executive Directors. The President is the presiding officer of the Executive Directors and is entitled to a deciding vote in the case of an equal division."[34] In the second annual report, McCloy submitted the "Report of the Bank, as approved by the Executive Directors." That report stated, "The President is the Chief Executive Officer of the Bank. Under him, the Vice President acts as the General Manager with responsibility for assuring the effective operation of other offices and departments. It is the Vice President, too, who directs the formulation of policy recommendations for the President."[35]

In the decades that followed—as the Bank grew in membership, size, and impact, as its profile heightened, and as the interpretation of what constituted its fundamental mandate evolved—there would be pressures to modify the relative roles of the executive directors and the president. Tensions, when they occurred, consisted largely of efforts to broaden shareholder influence and to increase borrower influence. But the principles of executive initiative and authority and of nonpolitical lending have by and large held.

McCloy and the team he brought to the Bank had spent their professional lives on Wall Street, in one capacity or another. McCloy saw the Bank not as a distributor of its own, limited usable capital, as some did, but as a sustainable ongoing business. Such a view called for prudence in investment decisions and sound finance. The establishment of the executive autonomy of the president, the emphasis on the mandate of the Articles of Agreement that investment decisions must be made on economic rather than political grounds, the close link between the president and the U.S. executive director were all critical, in their view, to the confidence that the U.S. securities market needed in order to justify financing the Bank. This strategy would enable them to establish the Bank's reputation as an independent development agency, as well as an investment bank.

With the appointment of McCloy and his team, a fundamental decision about the nature of the institution had been made: the Bank was to be not a political or charitable agency but a financially sound lending institution, and the criteria that were to determine the conduct of its business were to be acceptable to Wall Street. McCloy and Black were well known and respected in financial circles in the United States; their presence inspired confidence in the way the institution would be run. In turn, they recognized that earning the trust of the financial community took precedence over meeting the wishes of the shareholders—the member governments—which had appointed them to their positions. To demonstrate that the Bank was in fact autonomous, free from political interference, and run according to sound financial and organizational principles—although its essential role was to provide loans that the private market would not make—thus became a central theme of McCloy's tenure, and later Black's, in the Bank.

McCloy's critical contribution to the Bank was the establishment of those principles. This was largely accomplished in the three months *before* he became president, and it made possible the borrowing and lending that started during his twenty-seven-month presidency and the organization he built up to carry out this strategy. The establishment of these principles might not have been possible had he waited until after his election, when the atmosphere of crisis would have abated, if not dissipated.

McCloy paid a price for his victory. The board's relations with him were never warm, as they were to be with his successor. Executive directors had with good cause felt pressured at the time of his election. McCloy's rigorous and impatient exercise of his prerogatives (his "strong leadership," according to supporters) caused resentment. His vice president's tough, often rough, behavior toward the board did not help. Later McCloy aggravated the resentment when he sought to revive the questions of the tenure and residence of the executive directors, which had been hotly debated at the Savannah meeting and had been settled in favor of a full-time resident board.

The U.K. Treasury, like the other shareholders, had been nevertheless pleased about McCloy's arrival at the Bank. The British were concerned about the growing resource gap created by the closing down of UNRRA, the pruning of U.S. relief, the inability of the British government to make loans, and the inactivity of the World Bank. Hugh Dalton, the chancellor of the exchequer, wrote to Secretary Snyder, "I hope that the way is now clear for the Bank to go full steam ahead without further hesitation or delay—it is essential that it should now act quickly and positively, and should give concrete proof of its powers by beginning operations at once. I have said as much to McCloy, and have promised him that I will give him all the help I can. I know that you will do no less at your end, and I am confident that, with our joint support, he should be able to make the Bank the really live and practical thing which it should be."[36]

Getting into Business

The hiatus in the Bank's leadership and the doubts about the viability of the institution had attracted attention not only in government and financial circles but also among the public at large. The perceived inaction of the Bank attracted a fair amount of criticism. Drew Pearson, in particular, in one of his newspaper columns, attacked the Bank for sitting idly on its capital of $8 billion. McCloy responded to these attacks in a letter to President Truman dated March 25, 1947—within a week of his start at the World Bank—apparently in the hope that publication of his letter would put the matter in perspective. McCloy painstakingly explained that the money usable by the Bank was in fact much less than the subscribed capital. Truman's reply suggested that McCloy take the matter up with the U.S. governor, alternate governor, and executive director. Truman wrote, "I am a little doubtful about the advisability of the publication of the letter at this time."[37]

Meanwhile, the Bank had received a number of loan applications from European and developing countries. That reconstruction would come first in the Bank's lending had been foreshadowed at Bretton Woods, as well as in the congressional debate over the Articles of Agreement. Six of the nine loan applications received by the end of April 1947 were for reconstruction purposes in Czechoslovakia, Denmark, France, Luxembourg, the Netherlands, and Poland. Staff work on these applications was under way when McCloy arrived at the Bank, and discussions with the French representatives had started. McCloy's arrival gave the necessary momentum to the negotiations, and on May 7, 1947, the Bank was able to sign its first loan agreement with the Crédit National, a semipublic French corporation. The loan was for $250 million, an amount that would not be matched until the late 1960s and that in real terms—$2.4 billion in 1994 prices—would make it the largest loan ever extended by the Bank.

Actually the amount was only half of what the French had asked for, but whether $250 million or $500 million, any amount the Bank could provide would be far from enough to cover France's large balance of payments deficit. The loan was in support of the government's reconstruction program, the Monnet Plan, "covering almost every sphere of activity in industrial life—transport, communications, the rebuilding of destroyed factories, and supplies of raw materials for factories."[38] It deviated from what was expected to be the standard pattern for loans. It was not "for the purpose of specific projects of reconstruction or development," as stipulated in the Bank's charter. It was a general purpose loan covered by the "special circumstances" provision, but according to Garner, who led the negotiations, the "feeling at the time was that it was not to form a precedent for the normal operations" (6).

Even though this first loan may not have been representative of what became the Bank's approach to lending, it provided the opportunity to define some of the Bank's most important policies. It is striking how much was accomplished in this area in the first six weeks of McCloy's presidency. When McCloy, Garner, and Black came to Washington in mid-March, they established residence at the Washington home of Nelson Rockefeller on Foxhall Road. In the months they lived together, except while they were on the road lobbying state legislatures, foreign bond holders, and potential buyers of Bank bonds, life was a continuing colloquy. "We spent most of our time working," Black later recalled, "during the day at the Bank and, at night at home, getting the Bank organized and, even more important than that, establishing policies."[39] Senior staff were also working intensively, designing the organization's procedures. Davidson Sommers remembers how he spent long weekends at home with Richard Demuth and Simon Aldewereld drawing up the regulations that would govern the disbursement and use of the funds provided by the Bank.[40]

The Articles of Agreement provided little guidance to the designers of the Bank's lending policies. The discussions at Bretton Woods had dwelt on the problems that the Bank needed to avoid in its lending work but gave little practical advice on how to do so effectively. These discussions were inspired by the experience with international lending in the 1920s and 1930s, which also guided McCloy and his associates in their work. McCloy had been a participant in the experience with foreign lending in the 1920s and 1930s and had seen its impact on investor confidence in foreign portfolio investment. Black later described their position: "[O]ne of the things we had to decide was how we could make foreign loans with safety. The history of foreign loans had been very bad. There had been numerous defaults on foreign loans all over the world. We had to study the causes of those defaults and try to see to it that we wouldn't be guilty of making the same mistakes again. In a way the defaults helped us because we saw what the record was. We could tell the reasons why those defaults took place; and we could set up policies to safeguard the Bank so as not to repeat those mistakes."[41]

The key problems that had to be resolved related to the interest rate to be charged, the security the Bank might require, and the Bank's control over the use of the funds it provided. It was easy to conclude that the interest on the Bank's loans had to be related to the Bank's own actual or prospective borrowing costs. However, whether to vary the interest rate in line with the risks associated with different borrowers became an intensely debated issue. Should the Bank follow the practices of commercial banks? That would obviously enhance its financial position. Yet to classify its members according to the likelihood of their defaulting on a Bank loan would put the Bank in an invidious position and offer little incentive to countries to better their reputation. Eventually, it was decided that the same interest rate would apply to all loans granted at any given time, because "it would be difficult to have different basic conditions for different countries and even very difficult to have different interest rates for different countries."[42] This decision implied a subsidy to less creditworthy, presumably poorer countries but recognized the essential nature of the Bank as a membership-based service institution whose members had equal status and deserved equal treatment.

The designers of the Bank's lending policies realized that it would not be practical to attempt to secure the Bank's loans by requiring collateral. Most prospective client countries did not have the kind of assets, such as gold or convertible currency reserves, that would be acceptable to secure international financial transactions, or, if they did, they needed to have use of those assets. Instead the focus shifted to safeguarding the relative position of the Bank among creditors. The security sought by the Bank thus became the pledge of a member country's full faith and credit and the promise that no future creditor would be able to obtain specific security unless the Bank was secured pari passu. This was the so-called negative pledge.

Persuading member governments to provide this pledge proved difficult at first. The French resisted any reference to the negative pledge in the loan agreement and eventually agreed to deal with the matter in a side-letter to the agreement that would not be subject to parliamentary review. Nevertheless, the negative pledge subsequently became a standard covenant in the Bank's loan agreements. In 1954 the question arose again in negotiations with the French government in the context of a French West African railway loan. At that time Eugene Black overcame French reluctance to accept the clause by explaining that "it would be impossible for the Bank to get the least creditworthy member countries to accept an adequate Negative Pledge Clause if the Bank did not insist on having the substance of the same clause in its contracts with the most creditworthy member countries."[43]

The founding fathers at Bretton Woods and McCloy and his team viewed the real security of the Bank's loans as residing in the loans' purpose. In contrast to foreign lending in the 1920s and 1930s, which had usually been for general, unspecified purposes, the Bank was expected to ensure that the proceeds of its loans would be used "for productive purposes."[44] The Bank's loans would thus contribute to reconstruction and development while at the same time generating the returns that would safeguard the servicing of the debt incurred. Thorough investigation and appraisal of the proposed loan, careful control over the disbursement of the funds, and verification of their actual use for the agreed purposes became the tools the Bank employed to comply with its mandate. Rigorous Bank supervision of the use of its resources was a crucial innovation. The Bank established offices in Paris, and later in Copenhagen, which investigated thousands of vouchers and invoices and prepared specific end-use reports. As in the case of the negative pledge, it proved difficult at first to persuade borrowing member countries to accept such intrusive Bank scrutiny. The French, in particular, considered the Bank's insistence on looking over their shoulders an infringement of their sovereignty. Garner recalled that the French negotiator in 1947 was exasperated: "Mr. Garner, you expect me to identify every lump of coal as to which boiler it's going into?" To which Garner replied: "No, I just want to be sure it is not going to be diverted to Paris night clubs."[45]

The agreement with France helped set the tone for the Bank's principal lending conditions. Although negotiations were difficult, the agreement with a major European member also provided a credible precedent. Other borrowers could not easily reject conditions that France had accepted. This loan thus had important strategic significance in starting the business of the Bank. It was also significant as a signal to the capital market. The Bank needed to establish its credibility as a prudent lender before launching its own first bond issue in the New York market. The loan to France had to be regarded as an acceptable credit risk.

"It should always have been evident that the main problem of the Bank would be to find not borrowers, but lenders prepared to accept reasonable terms."[46] This is how the *Economist* saw the Bank's challenge in 1947. McCloy went to great lengths to explain that despite the subscribed capital of $8 billion, the resources at the Bank's disposal were limited to the 2 percent gold portion of members' subscriptions—that portion which had to be paid in—and the 18 percent portion of the U.S. subscription that the U.S. government had released for Bank use. In other words, the funds actually available to the Bank amounted to less than $1 billion. It was clear, therefore, that the Bank needed to borrow if it was going to become an important lender. Convincing investors that the Bank's loans would be repaid so that, in turn, the Bank would be able to repay its creditors became the principal consideration that shaped the Bank's attitude and policies for the next two decades.

One of the initial obstacles was that the statutes of the various U.S. states did not permit banks and insurance companies to extend loans to foreign borrowers. It would require patient work to persuade federal and state legislators that loans to the Bank should be exempted from these provisions. Although appeals to legislatures and to creditors were important in the short run, over the long run what would count was the effectiveness of the Bank's policies—evidenced not by public declarations but by actual performance: its actual selection of borrowers, the actual purposes for which loans were made, the actual conditions on which they were made, and the actual success in assuring conformity with those purposes and conditions. The bottom line of all this would be the service experience of the Bank's borrowers. Therefore, the determination of the creditworthiness of the Bank's borrowers became a key concern in the lending process.

The assessment of a country's creditworthiness was more a matter of judgment than the result of sophisticated analysis. Quite apart from methodological limitations, the data required to develop a reliable picture of a country's indebtedness were not available. In fact the centerpiece of creditworthiness assessments tended to be an assessment of the country's attitude toward its credit obligations. During the interwar period, failure to meet debt service obligations had become fairly common, with 34 percent of all loans to foreign governments in default in the 1930s. Any credible international lender, therefore, needed to establish that its borrowers would take their debt service obligations seriously, and analysis of behavioral characteristics became a key ingredient of creditworthiness assessments.[47] McCloy's report to the executive directors recommending the first loan to the Netherlands referred to the Dutch people as "skilled and hardworking" and to the government as resting on "solid democratic principles" with proven "stability and wise administration." The report concluded: "The Netherlands have never defaulted on their internal or external debt and have in fact redeemed some of their debts before maturity. . . . The excellence of their debt record, together with their long tradition as a trading and commercial nation, make the Netherlands a good credit risk."[48]

Where there was reason to doubt a prospective borrower's willingness to meet debt service obligations, it became imperative to demonstrate a substantive effort to settle outstanding claims. The Bank was to insist that, as a sine qua non for its support, borrowers had to acknowledge international financial obligations and engage in serious negotiations to settle defaults. McCloy, Garner, and Black were convinced that the Bank would never be able to establish its credit in the U.S. capital markets unless it could demonstrate that it would not entertain loan applications from countries with a record of not honoring their financial obligations. Chile became the first country to be pressured to address the claims of foreign bondholders. It did not receive the Bank's first development loan until agreement had been reached with the representatives of the bondholders.

Many Latin Americans grumbled that the Bank had become a bill collector for Wall Street. The U.S. ambassador in Chile, Claude G. Bowers, was annoyed by the Bank's hard-headed attitude. He complained in a letter to President Truman that the treatment of Chile was unfair and was playing into the hands of the communists. "Our enemies are making the most of this, especially the communists, and charging that the International Bank is under the domination of 'Wall Street' and that we are back to Dollar Diplomacy with the Good Neighbor Policy scrapped. It is very significant that the communists are the only people in Chile who want the International Bank to refuse credit."[49] Truman passed the letter on to his secretary of the treasury. In his covering memorandum Truman said, "I hope you will make it perfectly plain to our friend, McCloy, that the Wall Street crowd are not to control the operations of the International Bank."[50] But McCloy did not budge. The principle that the Bank would not lend to any country which had defaulted on its debts without at least a bona fide effort to settle became firmly established.

Once lending had started, McCloy and Black worked on little else but the first bond offering. This was eventually scheduled for mid-July 1947. They decided to offer two issues simultaneously, one of $100 million ten-year bonds paying 2.25 percent and one of $150 million twenty-five year bonds paying 3 percent. To save the cost of marketing the issues through an underwriting arrangement—which would have been high because the Bank was as yet unknown—McCloy and Black decided to "enlist the selling power of the largest possible number of securities dealers by inviting them to take a direct part in the offering and thereby to spread the sale of Bank bonds as widely as possible."[51] More than 1,700 dealers agreed to participate in the sale, and "on the appointed day McCloy, Black, and Garner stationed themselves on the floor of the New York Stock Exchange and waited anxiously for the first bids."[52] They could soon sigh with relief. Both issues were heavily oversubscribed. The long-term bonds were quoted at 103, and the ten-year issue at 101.5. McCloy was beaming, and the financial press commented in admiring terms on the shrewd judgment reflected in this efficient operation.[53]

To be sure, the issues had the backing of the U.S. government's subscription to the Bank's capital and therefore involved little risk. They also paid higher-than-average interest rates and were thus very attractive. But because of the market's aversion to the unknown, McCloy had felt it was important to make the Bank's first offering attractive in order to ensure its success. The Bank's bonds experienced various ups and downs in a generally volatile market, but in May 1948 a leading financial writer concluded that the Bank's bonds had successfully passed two major tests, "that of comparative market performance and that of acceptability for legal investment in the Nation's major institutional investment centers."[54]

From Reconstruction to Development

Under McCloy's leadership the Bank moved vigorously into the field of reconstruction lending. By the time he left, the Bank had lent about $650 million. This included about $125 million lent to Brazil, Chile, and Mexico, but the bulk of the Bank's assistance had been extended to Western European borrowers for purposes of reconstruction. McCloy had no difficulty understanding the desperate needs of the European continent for investment in reconstruction. He had witnessed not only the devastation of the war but also the hopeful signs that suggested a quick economic response to any sensible program of relief. He understood the concern of those in the U.S. Congress who had ratified the Bank's Articles of Agreement in the belief that the creation of the Bank would absolve the U.S. government of the need to support European postwar reconstruction. At the very least, they had hoped the Bank would moderate the demands for U.S. assistance. There was also the sense among the Bank's supporters that loans to European countries with an unblemished record of debt service would help convince the skeptics on Wall Street of the Bank's creditworthiness.

McCloy was aware, however, that the Articles of Agreement required the Bank to distribute its assistance equitably between reconstruction and development, and he became somewhat defensive about the imbalance in the Bank's lending activities.[55] At the annual meeting in 1947 he said, "The loans which have been granted during the past year have all been to European Nations. I hope that, by the time of the next annual meeting we can report that loans have been made to a number of non-European countries as well."[56] He assured his Latin American critics "that we considered, and our international board of directors was in unanimous agreement, that what we did in the way of assistance to Europe during our first year of operations was a matter of prime importance to all our members and not the least to our Latin American members."[57] A short while later, in a presentation to a U.S. audience, McCloy admitted that the Bank could not possibly finance all worthy projects in the world and had to be selective; "but the Bank does not intend to withdraw from Western Europe during the course of the European program. The more it can do, the greater will be the relief to the U.S. taxpayer."[58]

More telling even than the question of the distribution of the Bank's loans was the disappointment over the limited volume of lending. Some executive directors, including the first U.S. executive director, Pete Collado, had encouraged expectations that the Bank would quickly become a major source of investment funding. "Many felt that the Bank should be borrowing and lending a billion dollars a year."[59] But McCloy understood the concerns of the potential buyers of the Bank's bonds and recognized the constraints the Bank was facing in raising its funds. He felt strongly that "the Bank must attach importance to the views of the U.S.

investor and must conduct its activities in such a fashion that its bonds will be considered a sound business risk by the United States financial community."[60]

The British were especially apprehensive about McCloy's conservative attitude. Even before McCloy became president, the *Financial Times* had written, "on Mr. McCloy's insistence, the U.S. Government is accepting a greatly restricted concept of the Bank's role, thus foreshadowing much smaller World Bank lending in the next two years than was previously anticipated."[61] The British had been relieved when McCloy agreed to run the Bank and expected the Bank "to go full steam ahead."[62] However, McCloy cringed whenever he saw references to the Bank's $8 billion and did everything to lower expectations regarding the magnitude of the Bank's lending. McCloy was concerned about the willingness of the New York market to absorb Bank borrowings much beyond the collateral represented by the usable resources of the Bank. In any event, it was clear that the Bank's ability to borrow was realistically limited to the amount of the U.S. capital subscription. But the British were frustrated by the Bank's cautious approach, which they saw in stark contrast to the great hopes raised by Bretton Woods; the French also felt let down when the Bank cut their loan request in half when the country was facing serious political difficulties. "Despite the political confrontation with the communists in France, or perhaps even because of it," McCloy would not approve the full $500 million. Such a loan, he thought, "could not be justified to the Bank's Wall Street investors" (293).

Because he was not a banker and did not consider himself a Wall Street man, McCloy may have been more cautious than necessary. Davidson Sommers recalls that Black, as a real insider, tended to be much more confident about his ability to tell what Wall Street would or would not tolerate.[63] Nonetheless, McCloy was correct in his belief that it would be a long time before the Bank would be in a position to lend billions of dollars. He recognized the importance and the extent of the financial assistance needed in support of the resuscitation of the European economies. But he concluded that the task exceeded what the Bank could be expected to handle and that if European recovery required massive new loans, these would have to be provided bilaterally by the United States.

McCloy played an important role in persuading George Marshall to adopt the idea of a generous bilateral assistance program and subsequently "lobbied vigorously for the congressional appropriations that would make the Marshall Plan a reality."[64] He recognized that the proposal would affect the role of the Bank and "make it somewhat different from what was envisaged at Bretton Woods." But he did not hesitate to "welcome the proposed program, both because we regard it as necessary for European recovery and because it will enable the Bank to concentrate on the financing of specific productive projects and will relieve it from the pressure of making loans which in effect are intended primarily to meet balance of payments deficits."[65] In due course, the Marshall Plan would make the Bank redundant as a quantitatively significant supporter of European reconstruction, thus facilitating the decisive shift in the Bank's focus toward economic development.

McCloy's vigorous support for the expansion of U.S. bilateral aid did not mean that he was prepared to relinquish the Bank's claims to play a role in that process. In an eighteen-page memorandum addressed to President Truman in January 1949, he presented his views on the relationship between the Bank's and U.S. foreign lending.[66] This intervention was in part inspired by the proposal of the chairman of the Export-Import Bank to expand the operations of his bank substantially. McCloy argued vigorously that the World Bank should be regarded by the United States as the principal public source of long-term international investment capital and that competition of U.S. institutions with the Bank should be avoided. McCloy thought that "nothing would be more productive of ill-will toward the United States than to have the other nations of the world over a long period of time regard the U.S. government as their principal source of foreign capital. Under such circumstances, those receiving aid would not regard it as a favor but as a matter of right, while those who received nothing, or less than they thought they were entitled to, would consider the United States guilty of unfriendly discrimination" (5). For this reason McCloy thought that "any expanded program of financial assistance for development should, to the fullest extent practicable, be under international rather than national auspices."[67]

McCloy saw the Bank principally as a source of finance for long-term investment projects. In contrast, the European recovery program—the Marshall Plan—was meant in his view to address the short-term needs of the European economies, which resulted primarily from the disruptions of production caused by the war and epitomized by the dollar shortage. Once established capacities became productive again and Marshall Plan aid ran out as scheduled in 1952, McCloy expected a renewed role for the Bank in financing the "considerable expansion of productive facilities" (553). In the meantime the Bank could devote most of its time and attention to the problems of its developing member countries. McCloy was confident that it was "well within the capacity of the International Bank to finance all development projects of its member countries which will be ready for financing in the next few years and which can be properly financed with foreign loans."[68]

McCloy's visits to developing countries made him skeptical, however, about the rate of progress that could be achieved. The principal constraint for the Bank in the development field was not the shortage of money but "the lack of well-prepared and well-planned projects ready for immediate execution."[69] Although the Bank's financial and technical resources could be of help, they could not be a substitute for the actions of the developing countries themselves because "low productivity and living standards [were] as much the product of poor government, unsound finance, bad health and lack of education as of inadequate resources or the absence of productive facilities" (555).

Harsh as this conclusion may seem, it actually represented a considerable alteration in McCloy's perspective. His appreciation of the importance of raising the income level of the poorer countries in the world was one of the lessons that his work in the Bank had taught him. The threat to political stability associated with the economic state of the developing countries impressed him because he recognized that "as a result of modern means of communication, the peoples of those countries are becoming increasingly aware of the great contrast between their status and that of the peoples of the more economically advanced nations" (557).

Economic and Political Considerations in the Bank's Decisions

From the outset, there was much concern about the role of political considerations in the Bank's lending decisions. The discussions at Bretton Woods had dwelt on the importance of insulating the lending decisions of the Bank from politics and ideology. The Articles of Agreement made clear that economy and efficiency were to be the criteria that would determine the selection of projects. These criteria were regarded as vital to ensure the viability of the Bank, and they were essential if the Bank was to have continued access to capital markets.

The Bank's autonomy became an issue even before the institution opened for business. A letter from the United Nations, received at the Savannah conference, proposed a cooperative agreement between the United Nations and the Bank. The United Nations charter called for the coordination of the policies and activities of the specialized agencies through the Economic and Social Council. This was reflected in the Articles of Agreement, which required the Bank to "cooperate with any general international organization and with public international organizations having specialized responsibilities in related fields." The Bank was mandated to "give consideration to the views and recommendations" of such organizations in its lending decisions.[70] The United Nations had entered into agreements with some of the other specialized agencies—agreements that gave it much authority and influence over the activities of those agencies—and it was anxious to enter into similar arrangements with the Bank and the Fund.

The president and the executive directors of the Bank agreed that the confidence of investors in the Bank's financial soundness depended on the Bank's arm's-length relationship with governments and with political bodies in general. Anything that suggested that the Bank's management and its decisions might be subject to the influence of outside interests was in conflict with this objective. Initially the Bank tried to defer the overtures from the United Nations as premature because of the early stage of the Bank's organization. President Meyer had thus avoided the issue during his presidency. As the United Nations persisted in raising the issue, both the Bank and the Fund indicated that they could not enter into the kind of agreement that the United Nations had concluded with other specialized agencies.

McCloy was not prepared to compromise the Bank's autonomy. As an internationalist he was a supporter of the idea of the United Nations, but as a pragmatist he found it hard to accept any U.N. interference. His vice president, Robert Garner, was regarded as firmly anti–United Nations. However, McCloy recognized that the problem had to be resolved. When there was some indication that the United Nations would be prepared to take account of the Bank's special characteristics, he instructed Richard Demuth to draft an agreement that would be acceptable to the Bank. Demuth called his draft "in effect a declaration of independence,"[71] but it nevertheless became the basis of agreement between the Bank and the United Nations. In the course of a day of vigorous negotiations, McCloy agreed to take out "a few of our declarations of independence but not very many," as Demuth later recalled (20). A number of members of the United Nations strongly resented the agreement, which was, however, approved by the General Assembly on November 15, 1947. According to the agreement, the Bank became a specialized agency of the United Nations that "is, and is required to function as, an independent international organization."[72]

The protracted negotiations between the Bank and the United Nations did nothing to enhance the respect of their senior officials for each other. Operational relations between the Bank, the United Nations, and the other specialized agencies were strained. U.N. officials thought the Bank arrogant, and the Bank's management and staff were impatient with the United Nations' concerns. In practice, the Bank and the rest of the U.N. family each went its own way, limiting interaction to the formal meetings of the Economic and Social Council. Relations remained distant and tense until George Woods began to look for a more constructive approach during his presidency in the mid-1960s.

Although it was essential for the Bank's leaders to protect its institutional autonomy, the Bank did not operate in a political vacuum, and its decisions would inevitably evoke the political sensitivities of its shareholders in various ways. McCloy recognized that the Bank's need to raise its funds from private capital sources had to be an important element guiding the institution's decisions and the conditions it imposed on its borrowers. He appreciated that it "shields the Bank from political pressures, for if loans were made for noneconomic purposes, the knowledge of this would soon be widespread and an automatic damper on the amount of money available for lending would soon occur."[73] But McCloy was realistic: "The line between political and economic is not always sharply drawn." In practice this meant to him, "We can't and won't grant loans in order to accomplish political objectives; we can and will refuse loans, where the political uncertainties are so great as to make a loan economically unsound."[74] The Bank's lending decisions have continued to reflect this mixture of political and economic considerations. In McCloy's days, the influence of the United States remained strong and was not substantively affected by the realignment of responsibilities between the management and the board. Thus, the urgency and the form of the French loan were in part inspired by Washington's desire to "shore up the French Government" against the threat of communism at the beginning of the cold war.[75]

The intervention of political considerations in the Bank's lending decisions was demonstrated most clearly by the Bank's handling of Poland's loan application. The Polish government had approached the Bank in the fall of 1946 with a request for a $600 million loan. The amount was eventually brought down to more reasonable proportions, and an appraisal team visited Poland in the summer of 1947, looking specifically at a project to improve the coal mining industry. McCloy agonized over the question of whether the Bank should get involved with countries behind the iron curtain. He had raised this issue with his gurus on Wall Street and with Russell Leffingwell, a partner of J. P. Morgan & Co., and one of the pillars of the Wall Street community. Leffingwell thought that it was important to consider how loans to Poland or Czechoslovakia would affect the credit of the Bank, but he also felt that it would be a disaster if McCloy were to accept that the iron curtain was an impenetrable barrier. His advice was that McCloy "should not decide that [he wouldn't] lend money to Poland and Czechoslovakia, but that it [would] take a good deal of convincing to show [him] that the loans to them can be safely made."[76] McCloy himself visited Poland in the fall of 1947 and was favorably impressed with the potential of the Polish coal industry to meet some of the pressing energy requirements of Western Europe.

The Bank entered into negotiations with Poland, but it soon became clear that the United States would not support the loan proposal. Consequently, McCloy and Garner started to back off by raising conditions that the Poles would find difficult to accept. Meanwhile they further reduced the amount of the loan.[77] The Polish executive director, Leon Baranski, pleaded with McCloy that dropping the proposal "would be playing into the hands of those we wished least to help . . . ."[78] Warsaw's representative in the United Nations Economic and Social Council "declared that the World Bank had favored Western Europe in making its loans in the past, and that for some 'sinister reason' it had refused to advance money to Poland for a much-needed coal loan . . . ." The Bank, he said, was "a partner in economic warfare against Eastern Europe."[79] The British, who had favored the loan because it would help Poland achieve a measure of economic independence from the U.S.S.R., were likewise annoyed and thought that McCloy's concern about adverse reactions on Wall Street was a pretext "for avoiding difficult decisions."[80] The Bank's third annual report in 1948 acknowledged the concentration of lending on the Marshall Plan countries: "The Bank is fully cognizant of the injunction in its Articles of Agreement that its decisions shall be based only on economic considerations. Political tensions and uncertainties in or among its member countries, however, have a direct effect on economic and financial conditions in those countries and upon their credit position."[81] To that degree, the Bank's lending decisions reflected the polarization of the international order and the political prejudices of the Bank's creditors.

On to the Next Assignment

Only twenty-seven months after McCloy assumed the presidency of the Bank, he left it. The statement issued to the press on May 18, 1949, was reminiscent of Eugene Meyer's in December 1946. Meyer had said his job, the presidential mandate to organize the Bank, was done. McCloy said the Bank was now in business: the reconstruction phase was largely over, and the development phase was already in process. This somewhat congratulatory statement gave the impression that his mandate had been simply to put the show on the road. The Bank had indeed started, both to borrow and to lend, basic policies and procedures were in place, and the organization had been fleshed out. Initial troubles had been dealt with, and the basis had been laid for the routine management of an ongoing institution; so the international troubleshooter was leaving the institution.

Indeed, McCloy's role in the building of the Bank as a sound institution had been crucial. Although he was not the first president, he was the one who breathed life into the organization and created the structure characteristic in many respects of the Bank today. The most important of his contributions may well have been his insistence on a clear delineation of responsibilities between the management and the board before he agreed to take the job. But the start of lending and borrowing operations and the development of key policies must rank as significant achievements. They vindicated his insistence on the sweeping powers he claimed for the presidency. The source of his success was above all his energy, his ability to "handle more tasks and balance more responsibilities than any six men would normally undertake."[82] As throughout his career, he did not stand out for his intellectual brilliance; his strength was an uncanny sense of what needed to be done to move things along, and this made him particularly effective at this initial stage in the Bank's evolution.

Yet, for all his success, he remained remarkably uninvolved in the day-to-day business of the Bank and the problems it was meant to address. There is little trace of the impact of his personality. Staff members who served in the Bank during those years remember him as a matter-of-fact and somewhat impersonal boss, "a very magnetic personality in whom everybody had confidence"; they do not remember him as the "builder of the early days of the Bank."[83] His manner was gruff, forthright, and unpretentious. He did not stay long enough to form the attachment to the Bank and its people that his successor enjoyed, and there was little evidence of the warmth and personable nature that his biographers ascribe to him.[84]

McCloy was not close to his senior staff, especially to his vice president. We were "not on the same wave length," Garner later wrote in his memoirs.[85] Garner was a stickler for details and orderly procedures, qualities that McCloy appreciated but did not share. So Garner was left to manage the Bank, an arrangement that normally worked well. It worked less well when McCloy occasionally, and probably inadvertently, crossed into Garner's territory, or when Garner's bluntness, especially in dealing with the executive directors, caused complications.

There were also factors that tended to frustrate McCloy in his job. His relationship with the executive directors was tense and uneasy from the start. His insistence that their role in running the Bank and determining the selection of projects be sharply limited had been accepted—but only grudgingly. He did little to let the executive directors forget their resentment because he never accepted the need for a full-time board. Morton Mendels, the Bank's first and long-time secretary, put it diplomatically: "McCloy was so completely wrapped up in the work of the Bank, in which he was acquitting himself extremely well, that he might have been guilty of scant reporting to the board; he might have been guilty of letting the board go by default once or twice."[86] Relations became "explosively bad" when McCloy in 1948 attempted to restructure the board into a part-time body of high officials stationed in their home countries.[87]

The principal reason for McCloy's detached attitude, however, may have been his understanding of his role. He looked at the task of turning the IBRD into a viable institution as a job that had to be done to realize the United States' vision of a peaceful, prosperous postwar world under its dominion. The problem of getting the Bank started, and particularly of finding a competent person to run it, had not only raised doubts about the concept of internationalism in financial matters but had become an embarrassment to the U.S. government. Leading the Bank thus became a challenge to McCloy's commitment to public service. He regarded this challenge as important enough to interrupt his private career once again. Motivated by a sense of national duty, he accepted the job once he had determined the parameters for success and defined his conditions accordingly. For McCloy the task was not open-ended. He never intended to devote more time than necessary to the Bank. His job was to get the Bank started, and once that was accomplished, he would move on.

McCloy had an extensive network of friends and connections, which benefited the Bank and helped to make it known and trusted. His service in the government and his close relationship with leading political figures helped him draw attention to problems the Bank encountered. Although he understood the special nature of his position as the head of an international organization, he considered his work to be in line with his strongly held commitment to patriotic duty. For this reason he had no difficulty, when testifying before Congress on matters related to the Marshall Plan, in drawing on his experience in the World Bank. (His successors in the decades ahead would consistently refuse requests to testify formally as being inconsistent with their role as international officials; if they testified before the U.S. Congress, they could be asked to testify before the legislatures of all other member countries, which was clearly not practicable.) In the introduction to his testimony before the Senate foreign relations committee, he described his position: "I am here, I suppose, in a somewhat indiscriminate capacity as an American citizen, as President of the Bank and an officer of the Bank."[88]

His close ties to the "American Establishment" also reflected his deep interest in the affairs of the U.S. government. Once the Bank started to work, McCloy was happy to spend more and more of his time on non-Bank activities, particularly those involving the U.S. role in world affairs. In the spring of 1948 he thus became a member of a task force to study the growing intelligence bureaucracy. The work on this task force extended through much of 1948 and provided "a virtual refresher course in the status of intelligence matters at a critical moment in the cold war."[89] He was also involved in planning the airlift in response to the Berlin blockade, and through his close contacts with fellow wise men—Dean Acheson, Robert Lovett, Averell Harriman, Charles Bohlen, and George Kennan—he participated in the shaping of many of the country's key foreign and military decisions. All this "increased his itch to leave the Bank . . . . From his seat at the Bank, McCloy felt left out"(304).

When President Truman asked him to be high commissioner for occupied Germany—a position he had earlier refused—he was ready to go. As he had done when offered the World Bank presidency, McCloy had a number of conditions designed to ensure the success of his new mission. One of those conditions, however, was to safeguard the World Bank. McCloy's note on his meeting with Truman on April 30, 1949, refers to this condition and reveals his first choice of a suitable successor: "I talked to him about the Bank, its continuity and the importance of not permitting it to drag as it had after Mr. Meyer's resignation, with all of which he agreed. He said we should not take anyone from the Bank until a successor was named. He asked me whom I would suggest and I unhesitatingly said Bob Lovett." True to his establishment background, McCloy had selected another wise man—a powerful New York investment banker with extensive experience in Washington, D.C.—a man just like McCloy, and someone he had worked closely with in the War Department. Truman apparently "said he agreed if we could get him. I did not suggest any other names."[90]

We must presume that Lovett, who had just returned to his investment business with Brown Brothers Harriman & Co. following a tour as undersecretary of state, declined the offer. But McCloy would not leave the Bank until he was satisfied that a suitable successor had been found. He was aware of the concern about continuity and professionalism at the helm of the Bank. Investors in the Bank's paper would often say: "Well, Mr. McCloy, we like you fine, but what's going to happen when you leave the Bank? Who's going to be the next President of the Bank? Suppose you put some damn politician in there, what's going to happen then?"[91] It was somebody close to home whom McCloy picked as his successor.

CHAPTER THREE

Eugene Black

Bringing the Developing World to Wall Street

When Eugene R. Black became the third president of the World Bank in July 1949, he took over an institution that had just started to function. In the three years since its doors had opened, only ten loans had been made—eight to principally war-torn countries of Western Europe. Two bond issues in New York and a small borrowing in Switzerland had raised some $250 million to fund the Bank's lending operations. The Bank had 408 employees representing 21 nationalities. It was relatively unknown, even to the politically and economically sophisticated public. Its mission—lending to countries whose credit standing did not enable them to borrow in international markets but whose economic prospects were favorable enough to service the debt essential to their economic revival—was understood by few; those familiar with the Bank regarded it as an interesting but risky experiment. Even inside the

Bank there was not as yet a vision of its role and potential. The Bank was just beginning to focus on the issues associated with lending to developing countries; the challenge of economic development in the poor countries of the world was only dimly perceived at the time.

An Institution in Search of Its Role

In his thirteen years as the Bank's president, Black led the Bank from these tentative beginnings to broad recognition as an important, well-functioning, effective, and profitable development institution. He established the Bank's credit in the capital markets of the United States, ensured the acceptability of its bonds to the country's institutional investors, and obtained the highest commercial ratings for its paper.

By the time Black left in 1962, the Bank had raised $4 billion through seventy-seven borrowing operations in the United States and all major European capital markets. He assembled and led a growing, international staff—the staff numbered 833 from 55 countries when he left—who brought to the Bank not only experience but also the imagination to tackle the demands of the expanding membership of the organization. Lending increased rapidly, and at the end of 1962 a cumulative total of $6.8 billion had been committed for 330 projects in 60 countries. Lending covered virtually all sectors relevant to economic progress, including infrastructure, industry, agriculture, and education. In response to the changing needs of the membership, the organization became more differentiated; the Bank's major affiliates, the International Finance Corporation (IFC) and the International Development Association (IDA), came into being on Black's watch.

Eugene Black had been deeply involved in the Bank's business before he became its president. A major factor that had led to Eugene Meyer's unexpected resignation and that made the job so unappealing was the unsettled relationship between the president of the Bank and the board of executive directors, particularly the U.S. executive director. The respective roles of the management and the board had not been defined, and this turned virtually every transaction into a contest between the president and the U.S. executive director. In McCloy's view, the Bank's weakness was "too much politics, too little finance."[1] McCloy insisted that the U.S. executive director had to be a person with whom he could have close rapport and who was well acquainted with the marketing of securities and sensitive to the obligations represented by them. Black recalled later that he himself had stressed the importance of a supportive relationship between the president of the Bank and the U.S. executive director.[2] When McCloy decided to accept the presidency of the Bank, it was with the proviso that Black would be appointed executive director. The Chase National Bank agreed to grant Black a two-year leave of absence, and he joined the Bank's board on the day McCloy became president.

When McCloy decided to leave the Bank, and there was talk of Black becoming his successor, Black resisted. He recalled later that there had been some talk that he might be offered the presidency. "I was in Europe, and I sent word back that under no condition did I want my name to be put up. I tried every way in the world not to take it. I made various suggestions of other people. I did everything on earth to prevent my taking the job. I didn't want it. I wanted to make my career in Chase Bank" (51f.). As soon as he returned from Europe, Black was pressured to accept the presidency, and the Chase National Bank was pressured to release him. After several days of hiding in his house in Princeton, New Jersey, without answering the telephone, he agreed to accept. He would not regret his decision. Looking back in 1961, he said, "I became very interested in what I was doing, and I found that there was more inner satisfaction in doing this than there was in making money. . . . It's been among the most interesting years of my life, because you do get a great kick out of what you can do for these countries" (52).

Black's work in the Bank and his observations in the course of extensive travels in the Bank's member countries helped him to develop a conceptual framework and a clear sense of priorities for the Bank's mission and policies. His firm belief that common sense must prevail and his skills as a diplomat made him a person whose advice was sought by both recipient and donor members and by creditors and debtors alike. The competent international staff, which he helped assemble and which responded with respect and affection to his leadership, was an essential source of his effectiveness.

What kind of a person was he? Why did he, a successful, conservative banker, want to get involved with such a questionable experiment in international finance? What did he bring to the Bank?

A Conservative Southern Gentleman

Eugene Robert Black was born on May Day, 1898, in Atlanta, Georgia. His mother's father, Henry Grady, had been a famous spokesman for the South in the Reconstruction era, a journalist who argued eloquently that the South needed to follow the example of the North and overcome its backwardness. Black inherited his personal charm, though not his gift as a fiery public speaker. Black's father, after whom Black was named, was a leading southern banker who became head of the Federal Reserve Bank in Atlanta and, in 1933, chairman of the Federal Reserve Board. Black resembled his father closely, and his father's example inspired him to think of a career in banking.

Black graduated Phi Beta Kappa from the University of Georgia with a major in Latin. He enlisted in the U.S. Navy, after the army turned him down because of a heart murmur. He spent the war on convoy duty in the North Atlantic, apparently seasick much of the time. Upon his return to civilian life he spent several months in New York City with Harris, Forbes & Co., an investment firm, and later opened the first southern office of the firm in Atlanta. He traveled widely selling bonds, meeting bankers and investors, and eventually became a partner in the firm, in charge of its operations throughout the South. There is no indication that he was particularly affected in his work by the Great Depression; it was a difficult but not an impossible situation, and it was easier to market bonds than equity shares. In 1933 he joined the Chase National Bank, which had at one point owned Harris, Forbes & Co., as a vice president and moved to New York. Black eventually became a senior vice president of the Chase National Bank, handling its large investment portfolio. Along the way he had become a seasoned investment banker and a well-known and respected figure on Wall Street. Going through the letters he received when he became executive director and later president of the World Bank is like going through an edition of *Who's Who* of the financial world of the United States at that time.

Black cannot be exclusively defined by his work and his financial expertise. He was a man with diverse interests. He was fascinated by Balzac and his interpretation of human motivations. Since his college days he had cherished a passion for Shakespeare. He was a familiar figure in Shakespearean scholarly societies and instrumental in the creation of the Shakespeare festival in Stratford, Connecticut. He knew Shakespeare's plays intimately and loved them with an enthusiasm that to James Morris reflected "his greatest asset: his gift of apparent simplicity."[3] Black had little formal professional training; his affection for Shakespeare and Balzac did not make him a towering intellect. He knew that he had to rely on others for analysis and ideas. He was a good listener and was able to absorb and condense complicated subjects into terms of ordinary relevance. His mind remained uncluttered, his thinking had a distinct practical bent, and his decisions were guided by an instinctive grasp of what was sensible and likely to work.

Part of Black's charm was his gift as a storyteller. He could be entertaining, both because he wanted to put those around him at ease and because he appreciated the humorous side of life. While he was not unappreciative of the respect he enjoyed as an international financier, he appeared to be aware of his own weaknesses and was capable of making fun of himself. Unlike his grandfather, who was a renowned orator, Black was a poor public speaker. "Mr. Grady's is an example I cannot hope to match. . .," he said in an address to the University of Virginia; "like Mr. Jefferson I have no appetite for public speech."[4] He had never done any public speaking before he came to the Bank, and decided that he might be a little less nervous if he tried doing a lot of it. This he did, both as executive director and as president of the Bank. Yet his effectiveness as a speaker apparently had more to do with his personal charm than with his rhetorical impact. It is said that, in one U.S. state, a puzzled Irish-American politician listened to Black for forty-five minutes and finally said, "Mr. Black, I haven't the faintest idea what you're talking about. But you look like an honest man; and I'll help put through a bill to make your bonds legal for investment in this State on one condition—that you never lend a ——— nickel to Britain."[5]

Black spoke English with a slight southern flavor and liked to show his southern background, presumably because it was not common to find southerners in international governmental finance. In good French restaurants he sounded quite southern when, putting aside the elaborate menu, he asked the sommelier for bourbon and the waiter for fried chicken. Davidson Sommers found that the southern flavor would become more pronounced when Black felt under pressure.[6]

The respect he enjoyed was a recognition of his experience and judgment in financial and economic matters; his popularity was a reflection of his personality. He did whatever he did with a distinct sense of style. His style was evident in the way he dressed: always in a formal Saville Row business suit, and, when outdoors, always wearing his black Homburg from Lock's of London. It was equally apparent in the generous way he entertained. He retained in his "slow and rather stylized courtesy much of the fabled Dixie charm."[7] His graciousness was not a pose, and this proved effective, especially with the Yankees; his graciousness sprang from a genuine interest in people, all kinds of people, and a desire to interact with them, satisfy his curiosity about them, or negotiate with them.

Black had a vast number of friends, and he made new friends all the time. He kept in touch with all of them and was not hesitant to seek their help, often on behalf of others. Every trip he took was carefully planned not only to serve its business objectives but also to meet many old friends en route for old time's sake—and yet always to assist in his professional pursuits, if only by giving him more information or another point of view. The large number of faithful friends reflected his interest in people and his charm. As a leading banker, and certainly as president of the World Bank, he had to say no more often than he could say yes to all kinds of requests. He was able to say no and convey a sense of sincere appreciation for the request and the person who made it, and the petitioner, rather than leaving disappointed, would leave impressed with the sense that he had just met a gracious and understanding person.

His background, his work as a banker, and his style marked Black as thoroughly conservative. This was also apparent in his political views. Without sharing any of the anticommunist fervor of the postwar era, he was deeply concerned about the threat of spreading communism and its impact on the restoration of a functioning global, capitalist economy. This concern is reflected in many of his speeches, as is his pragmatic understanding of the social and economic conditions that make communism so appealing in many poor countries.[8] Black was a firm believer in the democratic values represented by the United States; economic prosperity was for him the essential prerequisite for political freedom and democracy. It was for this reason that he was personally committed to the objectives of the Bank: improving the living conditions and economic prospects of its members, especially of the poorest among them. These views made him choose work in the World Bank over a career in the Chase National Bank; they gave his firm capitalist beliefs the liberal flavor of internationalism. This also meant that his conservatism did not dictate his political affiliation. He was at home with Democrats and Republicans alike. It was during the Truman administration that he was appointed, first as executive director, and then as president of the Bank. But he was equally close to the Eisenhower administration, which had no hesitation in recommending his appointment to a second and a third five-year term.

The picture that emerges is of a man who was uniquely qualified to lead the Bank from its tentative, experimental beginnings to recognition as a significant global institution. He was able to lead the Bank and to focus on the right issues because he had the right instincts in matters of economic development and a good sense of what could be accomplished. Black's background as a banker, the respect he enjoyed in the banking community, and, in particular, his expertise in the marketing of securities were essential for the Bank to raise the resources it needed and establish its credit. Because of his familiarity with the financial community, he was less timid about its reactions than McCloy was. His contacts and the trust and confidence that he personally inspired soon became identified with the organization he led. Above all, his dedication to the role that the Bank was meant to play as a link between industrial and developing, rich and poor countries, allowed him to give leadership and direction during a period characterized by experimentation and innovation.

The Bank's Credit and Its Money

The Bank's challenge, as seen by the *Economist* in 1947, was "to find not borrowers, but lenders prepared to accept reasonable terms."[9] Because the Bank had only a small amount of usable capital, borrowing in the financial markets, and in the United States in the first place, was essential.[10] Yet the Bank had no credit in those markets. When McCloy, Black, and Robert Garner—who joined as vice president on the same day—came to the Bank, the Bank had not raised a penny. When Black became president some two years later, a beginning had been made; the Bank had sold two bond issues in the U.S. market for a total of $250 million and had completed a small private placement in Switzerland equivalent to about $4 million.

Black became involved in the effort to market the Bank from the moment he joined as executive director. Mindful of Eugene Meyer's difficulties, McCloy had insisted on clarifying the responsibilities of the president and the board. From the moment McCloy took office, Morton Mendels, the Bank's secretary at the time, later reported, the initiative in both procedural and substantive terms was with the president, no further doubt about that.[11] "The word 'management' came into the jargon of the Bank after McCloy came in."[12] Notwithstanding the agreed division of responsibilities between management and board, however, McCloy insisted on involving Black closely in the business of the Bank. McCloy relied heavily on Black for advice and support, and he recognized that he needed him especially to mobilize the resources required for the Bank's operations. Along with McCloy and Garner, Black devoted much time to the task of promoting the credit of the Bank and its access to the U.S. capital market. Through his extensive contacts in the financial community, he was able to acquaint influential people with the Bank, its evolving objectives, and its operating policies. It was very important, for instance, for bankers and insurance companies to understand that the Bank was not giving money away and that the Bank was going to ensure the security of its loans.

An initial and major obstacle to the Bank's fund raising in the United States was the lack of enabling legislation.[13] National banks could not invest in the Bank's bonds without congressional legislation; more important, insurance companies, savings institutions, pension funds, and fiduciary trusts could not invest in the Bank's paper without the authorization of their state legislatures. Black therefore spent much time persuading members of the U.S. Congress and of state legislative assemblies to pass the requisite laws. Although the Truman administration backed the Bank's efforts, this support was of little help in the states. Black had to conduct a lengthy crusade against the prejudice associated with foreign lending and against the memories of financial losses, which had given rise to legislative supervision of institutional investors in the first place. There were setbacks, but there was also slow progress. The acceptance of the Bank as a creditworthy institution is a tribute largely to Black's patient efforts and to his persuasiveness.

The investment community was suspicious of the quality of foreign loans. The foreign lending experience of the 1930s was still on everybody's mind; as already mentioned, well over a third of U.S. investors' holdings of foreign government securities was in default at the end of World War II. Why would anybody invest money in an organization supporting foreign countries in economic trouble, especially if investments in U.S. government paper would provide comparable yields? The initial approach followed by McCloy, Black, and Garner was to familiarize potential investors with the Bank's capital structure, specifically the extent of the U.S. shareholding in the Bank, the availability of the unpaid part of the U.S. subscription, and the significance of this arrangement in securing the Bank's bonds. Investors attached considerable importance to the executive directors' confirmation that each individual shareholder would be liable for the Bank's debts up to the full amount of its subscription, irrespective of the action of other shareholders. In the context of 1947, this arrangement effectively extended the Bank's credit to the amount of the U.S. shareholding in the Bank. In due course, the subscriptions of other shareholders with convertible currencies, such as the United Kingdom, France, the Netherlands, and Germany, would be accepted in the Bank's borrowing base. In 1959 a doubling of the Bank's subscribed capital was deemed necessary to provide additional headroom, that is, the room needed to ensure that outstanding loans did not bump up against the statutory limit of the Bank's subscribed capital.

Two measures of the Bank's success were the growing amount and increasing frequency of borrowings in the U.S. market and the credit ratings that the Bank enjoyed. The Bank was favored by the rating services from the beginning. It was given AA and A ratings by two of the three services in 1947; as time went on, the ratings gradually improved and included ratings by Moody's, which had not previously rated financial institutions. From the mid-1950s, the Bank's securities enjoyed a AAA rating by all three rating agencies. This rating epitomized the success of Black's personal effort to establish the Bank as an eminently sound and creditworthy institution.

The concept of the Bank as an international institution included not only widespread international membership and foreign lending but also widespread international mobilization of funds. At first, however, the U.S. capital market was the only source of convertible, globally usable resources. Except for two small private placements in Switzerland with heavy involvement of the Bank for International Settlements (BIS), the Bank raised all its funds in the United States until 1951. In those days of dollar shortage, the Bank's borrowers demanded dollar funds that could be used to finance imports from the United States or anywhere else. From the start, however, the need to establish the Bank as a borrower in other capital markets was on Black's mind. As soon as Europe's capital markets showed signs of revival, he was negotiating World Bank access, albeit on a modest scale, to those markets. Initially this access took the form of the sale of dollar bonds abroad. In his speech to the board of governors in 1949, Black urged members to enhance the international character of the Bank by taking legislative or administrative action to make the Bank's bonds eligible investments. The Paris and Amsterdam stock exchanges started trading the Bank's dollar bonds in 1950. A growing number of banking institutions abroad, in both industrial and developing countries, were authorized to invest in the Bank's dollar-denominated securities. In 1951 the Bank was able to enter the London market with a £5 million issue; this was followed in 1954 with a first issue of Dutch guilders in the Netherlands. By the mid-1950s, the principle of the Bank's presence in the international capital markets was established, although the predominance of the United States as a source of funds continued into the 1960s.

Still another aspect of internationalizing the Bank's fund raising preoccupied Black: the release of the so-called 18 percent portion of members' subscriptions—the part of each subscription that could be paid in the members' own currency. Black tackled this issue head on at the first annual meeting he addressed as president. He said then, "I am sorry to say that we have not succeeded to the extent we had hoped in broadening the international character of the financial resources at the disposal of the Bank. I refer in particular to our efforts to obtain additional consents to the use in our lending operations of the 18 percent local currency part of the Bank's capital." At that time only the United States had agreed to the full release of the 18 percent portion; others, such as the United Kingdom, Canada, Denmark, and Belgium, had made partial releases totaling some $12 million. Because he felt that the credibility of the Bank was dependent on the support of its membership, Black saw the release of these funds as an important test of the international and cooperative character of the organization. "Unless," wrote Black in February 1950 to the executive directors, "some greater liberalization of the use of the non-dollar 18 percent, or consent to the Bank's borrowing in their domestic markets, is conceded by the governments of the Bank's member states (other than the United States), the Bank will increasingly take on the pattern of a 'dollar bank.'"[14]

The issue assumed some importance when the Bank planned to help borrowers whose needs consisted of imports from the nondollar area but which might have no dollar earnings and would not be creditworthy for loans repayable in dollars. Despite Black's eloquent appeals, only very hesitant progress was made in persuading members to allow more generous releases. He eventually forced the issue by making assistance to Yugoslavia contingent on the availability of 18 percent releases. Yugoslavia's import requirements from the various member countries were identified in advance, and those members then agreed to make 18 percent funds available to cover expenditures in their territories. As this practice became fairly widespread, it gradually increased the amounts available to the Bank. Eventually, the European postwar recovery and the accumulation of large dollar balances outside the United States in the late 1950s made it possible for a growing number of members to agree to the fully convertible release of their 18 percent subscriptions.

Another increasingly significant source of funds in the 1950s was the sale of participations in Bank loans or of part of the Bank's loan portfolio. For Black this was less important as a means of stretching the resources available to the Bank than as a way of introducing the Bank's borrowers to the international capital markets.[15] Initially, sales were made with the Bank's guarantee; starting in 1950, however, participations and portfolio sales without that guarantee increased and eventually prevailed. In 1962 participations reached a peak of $319 million, or 36 percent of the level of commitments in that year.[16] The significance and volume of portfolio sales later declined, mainly as a result of the considerable rise in interest rates.

Establishing the Bank's reputation as a financially sound institution with an impeccable credit record was Black's most important achievement. He made a significant personal contribution to the introduction of the Bank into international financial markets. In the process he showed great political skill, particularly in seeing through the passage of critical U.S. legislation. The energy he brought to the task showed how much he enjoyed being a banker-diplomat. In persuading politicians in Washington and in Europe that the Bank was being run on business principles, he relied on Garner, who applied himself with single-minded determination to the operations of the Bank and refused to accept the idea that public and private organizations could not be run by the same standards.

While gaining the trust of its creditors, the Bank was establishing its reputation in the developing countries as the gatekeeper of the international financial markets. Black contributed to this achievement because he came to personify access to those markets and to the people who controlled them. He convinced the Bank's borrowers that the Bank was not just like any other creditor: this institution was an important arbiter in financial matters—an arbiter whose endorsement was essential to attracting other foreign credit or investment. The Bank thus came to be seen by leaders of all political persuasions as the creditor that must be repaid, irrespective of the sacrifice involved in meeting the obligation. This perception of the Bank as a preferred creditor remains intact today, and the Bank has never suffered a loss. It was the financial turmoil in the wake of the debt crisis of the 1980s that caused a number of the Bank's smaller borrowers to fall behind in their payments and persuaded the Bank to make explicit provisions to cover possible losses.

The Bank's Operational Principles

Apart from the financial backing of the Bank's securities, Black emphasized the apolitical nature of the Bank's business and the professional care it exercised in selecting sound, economically justified investments for financing. From the moment he became president, his strategy of marketing the Bank involved an effort to convince investors of the soundness of the Bank's lending activities. Interestingly, he did not refer to the Bank's experience as a supporter of reconstruction investments but instead focused from the outset on the task the Bank was facing in developing countries. A speech to the annual convention of the Savings Bank Association of the State of New York in October 1949, for example, dealt in detail with the situation in India and the work of the Bank in that country, endeavoring to give "a more vivid picture of the way in which we conduct our business by taking one particular loan application and describing the sequence of events until a contract was finally signed."[17] On other occasions Black would talk about the Bank's work in Latin America. He would convey to his audiences both the careful and conservative approach followed by the Bank and the importance of the Bank's work for the future of the free world.

The confidence of investors in the Bank depended ultimately on the Bank's ability to get its money back. The backing of the subscriptions of major shareholders and the conservative gearing ratio—the ratio between borrowings and equity capital—allowed the Bank to get started, but only sound lending could help the Bank sustain its operations. Mindful of the risks and failures of foreign lending, the founders of the Bank had given this aspect much thought.[18] The Articles of Agreement contained provisions to guide the conduct of the Bank's lending. One of those provisions restricted the Bank to making or guaranteeing loans "except in special circumstances" for "specific projects of reconstruction or development."[19] This provision was meant to ensure that the resources provided by the Bank would be used for productive purposes and, by adding to the borrower's economic strength, contribute the resources needed to service the loan. Ironically, the Bank's early loans for reconstruction in Europe were all of the program type, that is, not aimed at specific projects; it was when the Bank started to lend to developing countries that the project focus in the Bank's operations became the norm.

Black became a strong proponent of the project concept in the Bank's lending. The Bank's annual report for 1949–50, the first year of his presidency, spelled out the Bank's principal policies, including the rationale for the specific-project provision. According to the report, written by Richard Demuth and Ben King, "if the Bank were to make loans for unspecified purposes or for vague development programs . . . there would be danger that the Bank's resources would be used either for projects which are economically or technically unsound or are of low priority nature, or for economically unjustified consumer goods imports." Financing a slice of a national development program was not then considered an adequate basis to judge "whether financial investment will in fact be translated effectively into the concrete substance of development."[20]

The Bank's project concept was criticized as a device for selecting relatively safe investments.[21] In fact, from the outset the Bank insisted on evaluating project proposals in the context of the borrower's economy. It emphasized the analysis of the economic benefits of the investment as the centerpiece of its assessment, and the methods of calculating those benefits were steadily refined. It was the Bank's and Black's particular concern to ensure that the projects taken up by the Bank were economically of high priority and that the resources devoted to a Bank-supported project did not come at the expense of other, more essential projects. It is true, nonetheless, that the choice of projects by the Bank was influenced by "the assumption that the eyes of the capital markets of the world were fastened not only on the Bank's financial position and the creditworthiness of its borrowers but on the outlook for future income from specific projects."[22] This constrained the Bank's enthusiasm for exploring new avenues for investment, especially in projects that were not self-liquidating.

To identify the appropriate national economic context for project investments, Black put strong emphasis on the need for carefully prepared development plans. Black and his advisers felt that it was essential for governments to establish a sensible order of investment priorities so that the limited resources—both domestic and foreign—available for investment would be used where they could best support the progress of the national economy. He told the Bank's governors in Paris in 1950 that "we have been concerned to assure not only that the prospective gain to the borrower overbalances the burden of the debt obligation, but even more important, that the project financed has been accorded proper priority in the borrower's development plans."[23] Black was adamant that the Bank's money should be used for projects of the highest priority. He said, "The Bank does not fling money into an economic void. We do not plant steel plants in the desert; we do not help put street railways in a country whose first need is for port development."[24]

This concern about planning may seem at odds with Black's professed capitalist views. However, many of the Bank's senior staff members had worked in the U.S. or European governments during World War II and had come to believe that government needed to play a strong role in the management of the national economy. Moreover, indicative planning and resource allocation were generally accepted as complements of market forces and private initiative even by those who, like Black, believed in a leading role for the private sector in the economy.

The importance attached to well-informed economic planning led to the Bank's early foray into the field of technical assistance. Countries that did not have a clearly worked-out set of economic priorities were encouraged to come to the Bank for assistance. Under Bank stimulus, a number of countries asked the Bank to carry out comprehensive economic surveys as a basis for a responsive investment program. Black, and in particular Garner, attached great importance to these general surveys because they represented to them a logical way to ascertain the economic priorities of a country. There was some opposition to this approach by those who were concerned that assistance in preparing an investment plan would imply that the Bank was prepared to finance it. However, Black and Garner accepted this implication and welcomed the opportunity to support sound development programs.[25]

The first mission of this kind was sent to Colombia in 1949, and its work established the basis for a close and enduring relationship between the Bank and that country. Eventually, other countries requested the Bank's economic surveys. Altogether, there were some two dozen of these missions up to 1964, when the last one went to Morocco. In the late 1950s such missions frequently preceded independence and Bank membership for former colonies; they were significant in the start of an operational relationship, especially in many African countries with a poor planning base. In the evolution of the Bank the survey missions—although for practical reasons initially consisting almost entirely of experts not on the Bank's staff—represented a step in the transformation of the Bank into a development institution. The Bank realized that care in the use of the Bank's money was not sufficient to ensure developmental impact. As Demuth recalled, "Basically we weren't a bank just in terms of wanting to lend money and get repaid with interest, but we were interested in the effects of our operations on the development of the country" (63).

The Bank's choice of projects was affected by another consideration imposed by the Articles of Agreement: the stipulation that the Bank's loans were essentially to cover the foreign exchange cost of the projects it supported. Black and particularly Garner were at first rigorous on this issue, apparently believing there was something inherently unsound in borrowing foreign exchange to cover domestic expenditures.[26] Yet the Articles of Agreement already recognized that domestic expenditures incurred for a project could well give rise to the demand for additional imports;[27] therefore in "exceptional circumstances" it might be appropriate to cover these "indirect" foreign exchange requirements as well. The Bank's fifth annual report spelled out the conditions that would allow the financing of local expenditures: (a) the project, even though not involving foreign exchange expenditures, must be of very high priority; (b) the local funds required for the project could not be raised domestically; or (c) the local funds required would be inflationary without the provision of additional imported consumer goods or raw materials.[28]

Thus the Bank and Black recognized early that the economic difficulties of the developing countries could not always be effectively addressed by relying exclusively on financing the foreign exchange needs of projects. Freely usable foreign exchange resources at times could be more effective than specific projects in supporting development. Program lending or the financing of local expenditures were the available alternatives. There was much debate in the Bank about the respective merits of these two alternatives until Black came down "pretty strongly in the direction of financing local expenditures rather than getting away from the specific project approach."[29]

Of course, whether the Bank was prepared to lend to a member country depended on the assessment not only of the country's creditworthiness but also of its economic policies. On a number of occasions the Bank refused to lend because the borrower's policies were thought to affect adversely the country's creditworthiness or the success of the proposed investment. Black's own impressions, based on his contact with the political leaders in the Bank's member countries, were presumably an important part of this assessment. At the annual meeting in 1956 he admitted, "We have made no secret of the fact that we sometimes refuse to lend to countries which are pursuing unsound policies or to borrowers who, because of governmental restrictions on rates, are unable to maintain a sound financial position . . . . When we lend we want our money to contribute to the growth of local savings and to stimulate their application to productive purposes. We do not think it is the Bank's role to help governments postpone the difficult decisions needed to mobilize local resources."[30] Accordingly, Black rejected any suggestion that the Bank's lending should not set conditions on such matters as a balanced budget or adequate electricity tariffs.

The enunciation of the Bank's major operational policies in the fifth annual report—which, in addition to the definition of projects and the issue of local currency financing, covered such items as the processing of loans, lending to private enterprises, loan charges, loan supervision, and technical assistance—was a signal that the Bank was becoming an established institution. The policies represented a creative effort to build on the experience of the institution in a new and uncertain environment. While trying to safeguard the institution and its creditors, the Bank was also trying to learn more about the needs and problems of the Bank's borrowers—a complex subject that was not well understood. Black had traveled widely in Europe during his work for the Chase National Bank and had a clear understanding of Europe's reconstruction needs. His tenure as executive director had allowed him to expand his vision of the emerging nations and the very different problems they faced. He recognized the importance of analyzing and addressing these problems.

Black's Bank

The most striking feature of the Black presidency is the extent to which Black came to personify the Bank. His tenure of office was so long, the stamp of his personality on the institution so strong, and his responsibility for its evolving pattern so clear that the Bank became widely known as Black's Bank.

This was first and foremost a reflection of his personality. Black had a wonderful way with people. From the outset he had excellent relations with the executive directors. McCloy, a hard and energetic worker, had had little patience with the formalities represented by the board of executive directors. Not surprisingly, by the time he left, considerable resentment had built up among the executive directors.[31] This changed quickly when Black became the chairman of the board. He took the time to cultivate the board members—socially to some extent, but also by being available to listen to them and by conveying a sense of appreciation. In board meetings he was able to make the executive directors feel that the ultimate authority was theirs without giving them any more power than they had previously been accorded. This made it much easier to gain the board's approval with fewer questions and less discussion.

Black was a much-liked, popular CEO to the Bank staff. Although he considerably expanded the staff, he knew practically everyone in the Bank and took a personal interest in their families. Christmas parties, bowling tournaments, and annual picnics in Rock Creek Park with softball games were regular occasions for Black to interact with the staff and their families. His judgment of people was reflected in the buildup of the Bank's senior staff: Robert Garner, the Bank's vice president; William Iliff, Black's assistant (who, in 1956, became vice president along with Davidson Sommers, the general counsel, and J. Burke Knapp, the director in charge of Latin American operations); Richard Demuth, assistant to Meyer, McCloy, Black, and later Garner; and Harold Graves, who looked after public relations and wrote many of Black's speeches. They were all men of talent and devotion. Black relied on them and on the Bank's professional staff for support. In allocating responsibilities, he displayed an appreciation of his associates' strengths and weaknesses and used their talents effectively.

Black's geniality and style were accompanied by a distaste for administration. He left the responsibility of running the shop to Garner and, in Garner's absence, to Sommers. When Sommers complained, Black responded, "Well, someone has to do it. You don't think I'm going to, do you?"[32] According to Garner, Black strongly disliked desk work, organization, and the reading of reports. He was an interested and very good listener, as well as a good observer. This, of course, did not mean that he was soft and unwilling to make tough decisions. Quite the contrary. Beneath his "charming exterior [was] a lining of steel and he would not be pushed around."[33] Garner, a man with a predilection for organization and operation, willingly and effectively played the role of the faithful manager and disciplinarian, allowing Black to rule the Bank as the understanding father figure. Black was, James Morris wrote in 1963, in his time by far the most interesting employee of the Bank. "The Bank depended upon him like an army upon its marshal."[34]

Black's diplomacy relied on personal interaction. One of his principles was, "never write a letter, when you can use the telephone, and never use the telephone if you can meet face to face."[35] He enjoyed direct contact with people, was able to approach them without prejudice, and was confident of his judgment and his persuasive powers. This also meant that he appreciated meeting people whom he could respect for their personal qualities and achievements. His conservative outlook and his preference for capitalist prescriptions for dealing with economic problems did not affect his admiration for Nehru, the prime minister of India, or his jovial relations with Nasser, president of Egypt, and Marshal Tito of Yugoslavia. He drew the line, though, with Sukarno, the president of the Dutch East Indies, whom he met in 1947 in the course of a lengthy visit to that country. Sukarno, Black thought, was "an opportunist, a glib charlatan, a spellbinder."[36] Black's sympathies were with the Dutch administration, and he expected that Sukarno would create economic chaos and allow the communists to move in.

Black's talent for dealing with people had an important practical dimension: his knack for bargaining. Bargaining and negotiating were neither a chore for him nor an acquired skill; they were part of his nature, a gift. He knew how to gain the confidence of those he encountered and to obtain their agreement. He was well aware of this talent and would often say, "I'm not a policy man, I'm a deal man."[37] His skill as a negotiator shaped his success as a banker and his reputation as a bond salesman. His experience with selling bonds turned out to be critical for marketing the World Bank and establishing its creditworthiness. And because of his skill as a negotiator, he earned an international reputation as a mediator of wise judgment and absolute integrity.

Black had concluded early that countries in default on their international financial obligations could not expect to attract fresh foreign loans. It would also be difficult for the Bank to sell its own securities if it made loans to defaulting countries. Thus, it became a prerequisite for Bank lending that member governments make reasonable efforts to settle claims arising from financial defaults or the nationalization of foreign properties. Black was a strong proponent of this policy from the moment he joined the Bank.[38] As a result, many defaults that had bedeviled relations between developing countries and the world's financial centers since the 1920s and 1930s were successfully resolved. The Bank did not usually get involved in the settlement negotiations, but it watched over the process carefully. The Bank, and Black personally, thus acquired a reputation for expertise in resolving complicated financial disputes.

Black's curiosity about people and their motivations explained both his propensity to negotiate and his success as a negotiator. What had been a gift that facilitated his career as a commercial banker and bond salesman made him a consummate diplomat once he joined the World Bank. Black enjoyed this aspect of his work, and it seems fair to assume that the diplomatic challenge of the World Bank presidency had much to do with his decision to take the job.

The Bank's concern about unresolved financial disputes and Black's reputation as a reasonable man with extensive experience in financial matters led many parties to ask the president to mediate their disagreements. Black was ready to be helpful and accepted requests for his intervention. One condition for the Bank's involvement was that both parties to a dispute had to agree to the Bank's role. Black claimed that he did not solicit requests for the Bank's help in settling disputes, which required substantial and time-consuming efforts. He was aware of the Bank's limitations; unless the problem was primarily a financial one, he would not agree to become involved (41).

Nonetheless, there was at least one major dispute that he actively sought to mediate despite its extensive political ramifications: the allocation of water resources between India and Pakistan. Black saw that this issue, if left unresolved, would hamper the exploitation of the subcontinent's irrigation potential and contribute to food shortages and that it could easily lead to military conflict. The Bank's own ability to effectively assist India and Pakistan would be limited unless an understanding between the two countries about sharing the water resources in the Indus Basin could be reached.[39] Stimulated by an article by David Lilienthal in *Collier's* magazine proposing a technical solution to the division of the rivers flowing into the divided Punjab, Black approached the leaders of India and Pakistan with the suggestion that the Bank could provide technical assistance in resolving their long-standing quarrel. Both eventually accepted, and the Bank went to work. The mediation, which extended over nine years and resulted in the conclusion of a treaty between India and Pakistan, brought Black and Iliff, who had principal responsibility for the negotiations, international acclaim. Black regarded it as one of his most important accomplishments. In his oral history interview Black concluded, "It's the most important thing the Bank has ever done, by far."[40]

He was often personally involved at the crucial stages of a mediation; in fact, a number of cases turned on his personal role. His success in winning the confidence of President Nasser of Egypt was instrumental in the settlement of claims and counterclaims arising from the nationalization of the Suez Canal. But there were also failures. The Bank's effort to achieve an agreement between the Iranian government and the British shareholders of the Anglo-Iranian Oil Company, following the nationalization of the company, did not succeed. It appeared that the parties to that conflict were not really interested in an impartial settlement at that time.

Black did not see his own and the Bank's role in the field of international mediation as an activity isolated from the Bank's ordinary business. It was to him very much a part of the Bank's service to its membership. He accepted the Bank's role as mediator of long-standing economic and financial disputes as a continuing responsibility. In a wider sense, the effort involved in the settlement of disputes was an extension of the need to persuade governments and economic leaders to adopt reasonable business and financial practices. Black saw this task above all as a diplomatic challenge. Toward the end of his association with the World Bank, he reflected on his experience in a series of lectures for which he chose the title "The Diplomacy of Economic Development."[41]

Black concluded that the relationship between aid donors and aid recipients and between the Bank and its borrowing members called for new ways of interaction. Development diplomacy was the new art form needed in the affairs of nations whose specific aims and objectives had yet to be fully understood. Black thought that

> the development diplomat must fill the gap between the conventional diplomat and the trader and the investor. His aim should not be commercial or strictly economic; but neither should he be concerned with the narrow political objectives which sometimes overburden the regular diplomat. The development diplomat should be a man with a vocation, rather than a man with immediate terms of reference. As an artisan of economic development he should use the tools of economics and other disciplines as best he can to place in perspective, to shed light on and to illuminate the choices before the decision-makers in the underdeveloped world (24).

The key problem for Black was the allocation of resources, and it was important to achieve economic rationality in this critical area of decisionmaking. Yet for Black "the strength of the development diplomat lies in illuminating choices, not in trying to impose solutions" (36). It would seem that the imposition of explicit economic policy conditions had no place in his concept of the interaction between the Bank and its members.

The dialogue of development diplomacy, if it was to succeed, had to be based on professional values. The task called for people with a vocation, not with an ideological mission. To be effective, they had to be able to interact with "men and women [in the developing countries] to whom the right kinds of development decisions are an integral part of their own professional outlook; contacts with men and women who speak the language of economics without the taint of ideology" (36). In other words, Black thought that institutions like the Bank needed to be informed of and sensitive to the situation in the developing countries, yet insistent that the solution to their problems be realistic.

The Challenge of Economic Development

The problem of underdevelopment, as it was then termed, as a phenomenon requiring special attention was only dimly perceived when the Bank opened for business. European reconstruction was the principal preoccupation and the subject of the Bank's first lending operations. Developing member countries had approached the Bank with requests for assistance, but these requests raised primarily questions of creditworthiness rather than curiosity about the reasons for their economic backwardness. Chile, for instance, applied in 1946 for a loan that was eventually approved in 1948 after the crossing of the principal hurdle: the agreement that the government of Chile would negotiate in good faith with the holders of its prewar bonds. This agreement represented a departure from Roosevelt's version of the Monroe Doctrine, which had treated the indebtedness of Latin American countries with indulgence. Yet with this new toughness came also an appreciation of the special problems developing countries faced.

It was after Black became president that the Bank started to focus on the new challenge of economic development. There was no further lending for reconstruction because the Marshall Plan had come into being and provided the support still needed by Europe. Whatever lending to European members took place was for specific, development-related projects. "Black, with his own panache, was able to give a kind of glamour and prestige to the bank which attracted very able young men. No one could accuse them of being woolly-minded do-gooders; [after all] the bank never had any bad debt."[42] A number of the very able economists working in the Bank—John Adler, Antonin Basch, Andrew Kamarck, Benjamin King, Paul Rosenstein-Rodan, John de Wilde, to name just a few—were looking at the problems of developing countries and beginning to come up with remedial prescriptions. Black was not an economist, but he followed the evolution of the staff's economic thinking closely and had refined his own understanding of the development process. This understanding allowed him to determine the basic direction for the Bank's work, while the details of policy and administration expressed in his speeches were framed by his staff.

Clearly the business of the Bank in economic development would have to be quite unlike the ordinary investment banking business. It would, of course, have to be conducted in the context of a comprehensive assessment of the economy of the borrowing member country and take into account the broad variety of elements that contribute to development. The nature of those elements was much less obvious then than it is today, fifty years later. Black shared some of the common perceptions of the time, which saw the lack of development as being caused by the lack of modernization, or essentially in technological terms. In his address to the governors in 1954 he presented a vision of progress projecting "tractors working on land that before had only known the bullock. . . small factories working where industry had never appeared before . . . (mountain) streams being harnessed to produce energy . . . hundreds of miles of pipe bringing natural gas . . . . Down in the villages . . . grain being milled by machinery, instead of being pounded out by hand, and electric light replacing the oil lamp."[43] Yet it is striking how well Black's speeches and writings, and the reports of the Bank at the time, foreshadow today's agenda of development issues. There was already discussion of the need for policy reform, for structural change, and for improved governance; the importance of the population problem, of education, of institutions, and of effective public administration was being recognized. In short, there are few elements of today's diagnoses that the Bank did not envisage even then as part of the development problem.

Although Black appreciated the contribution of the Bank's economists, he did not allow them a major role in the running of the Bank. Decisionmaking was left to the generalist-practitioners, and the design of specific lending operations, the conditions attached to them, and the determination of whether and when to go forward with particular projects were heavily influenced by project staff. This caused much frustration among the economists and led to the early departure of Rosenstein-Rodan. In fact, the economics department, which had been a key element in the organization, was abolished in 1952 in the one major reorganization presided over by Black.

Black could see early on that it would be time-consuming and difficult to step up the rate of lending for development. He saw it as no accident that the early loans to developing countries

> have been mainly to countries where considerable economic and technical advance has already taken place . . . . The greater the progress a country has already made in development, the easier it is for it to progress further; and by the same token it is almost always easier to expand a going concern than to start a new one from scratch. Yet the essence of successful economic development, and therefore the essential task of the Bank, is precisely to bring new enterprises into being and new techniques into effective use in economically retarded areas— and the more retarded the country the more urgent and challenging is our task.[44]

That and the unpredictable task of identifying and preparing suitable projects for investment led Black to dismiss the idea of predetermined lending targets. In a 1952 article in *Foreign Affairs* describing the Bank's work he wrote that "the volume of lending cannot be fixed at some predetermined, hypothetical level. The

Bank and its borrowers must base their joint operations on projects and programs which are soundly conceived and have real economic value."[45]

Black had a vivid sense of the meaning of economic backwardness and deprivation. Extensive trips to the Bank's member countries allowed him to see firsthand the living and working conditions of the people the Bank was supposed to help. Compassion and curiosity made him take full advantage of the opportunity for extensive field visits, disregarding the discomfort and health hazards associated with such trips. He could tell the Economic Club of New York in 1953, "I have seen at first hand some of the underprivileged millions who are continually faced with the specter of hunger—who have never known what it is to have decent shelter, decent clothing, adequate medical care or the elements of an education."[46] However, his compassion never tempted him to see foreign aid as a panacea. He was critical of those who "recognize, in theory, the need for internal changes and local effort but, in practice . . . place all the emphasis on outside assistance . . . ignoring the fact that the insufficiency of financial and other resources, as often as not, is itself the product of political and social evils within the countries themselves"(5).

Black sought to convey to his audiences a sense of the disparity between rich and poor countries and of the tensions created by the ever-widening gap in incomes between industrial and developing countries. A particularly moving example is his commencement address to the University of Chattanooga, Tennessee, in June 1951, which he used to illustrate how privileged the young graduates were.

> To understand how fortunate you are, let's go back to the year 1930, when many of you were born. Let's take 50 of you at random and suppose that instead of being Americans, you had been born in prewar India. . . .The chances are that only one of you would be receiving a college degree in this or any other year—only one of you. Of the others only two would be able even to read and write. About 20 more could aspire to earnings, for a year's labor, about equal to what many of you, as beginners, will make for less than two weeks' work. That

leaves just under 30 of our original 50 to be accounted for. None of that 30 among you would be alive today. Many of you would have died in infancy; the rest of you would have died of hunger or disease by the time your contemporaries in America were half way through high school.[47]

Black felt a compelling need to speed the development process; he recognized the impact of "the revolution of rising expectations."[48] "Millions. . . have been made aware that their poverty is not inevitable, not divinely ordained. And from these millions leaders have emerged, dedicated to the task of telescoping into a few short decades all the material and social change that evolved elsewhere only over a century or more."[49] Yet he saw that the very success of development tended to make the task more, not less difficult: falling death rates and accelerating population growth meant that more children had to be cared for and educated, that less savings were available for the investments needed to raise the living standard. Although the Bank in his time shunned the promotion of population planning as a subject too sensitive to include in the policy dialogue, he personally recognized the importance of the subject and played an active role as a member of the Population Council after he had left the Bank.

Black's perspective on the development problem and on the Bank's mission was shaped strongly by his firm belief in the ideals he felt the United States embodied: individual freedom, democracy, free enterprise, and the perception of the threat of communism to those ideals. "For those of us who enjoy the great blessings of freedom, it is often difficult to understand the appeal of an ideology which in practice denies to the individual the right to govern his own destinies. But for those less fortunate, freedom means little when it is freedom only to live out their lives in misery and want."[50] Economic development and prosperity were seen as means to achieve political stability. "I want to press on you again the view that development is an urgent task. We cannot build a stable world out of nations whose populations are engaged in a tooth-and-nail struggle merely to keep themselves alive."[51] The same thought is reflected in the 1952 article in *Foreign Affairs,* which describes the Bank's work in response to this fundamental political challenge.[52]

Black was critical of the rationalization of foreign aid as a means of combating communism by buying friends. He knew that what mattered was not how much money was spent but whether the money was effectively used.[53] He was concerned that foreign aid provided in pursuit of military and political objectives would be ineffective in promoting the economic and developmental goals of that assistance. "The government of an underdeveloped country is likely to feel it has fulfilled its part of the bargain when the treaty is signed or the vote in the United Nations taken. That government is not likely to take very seriously any protestations of concern about economic development—or pay much attention to what is said on the subject."[54]

For Black, "a major test of any project the Bank is asked to finance is whether, directly or indirectly, it will increase production."[55] Black believed in the rational and sensible use of capital because he felt strongly that tangible benefits must justify the Bank's activities and because he saw the productivity of Bank-supported investments as an essential safeguard for the recovery of the Bank's loans. To establish appropriate priorities, Black considered the formulation of a "properly balanced development program" as the first, essential prerequisite for effective external assistance.[56] This would ensure not only the proper sequencing of investments but also investment expenditures that were within a country's capacity to carry out, including the capacity to borrow externally. Black did not underestimate the difficulties posed by resisting informal political pressures for monumental showpieces, the power of vested interests, and the need to satisfy different regions of the country and different communities; he saw the Bank as playing a critical role in providing "tactful but firm support" to member governments to cope with these pressures.[57]

Black recognized the limitations of foreign aid and external advice. "At best, outside aid can provide only a margin over and above what a people are doing for themselves. It can be the margin between failure and success, but only when there is substantial local effort. And there can be such an effort only when a nation has a will to develop—when there is a drive within the country itself to improve the living standards of its people, and a government which reflects that drive."[58] It was obvious to Black that the bulk of the resources required for investment in the developing countries would have to be mobilized at home by the countries themselves.[59] This implied the adoption and vigorous execution of appropriate fiscal policies to avoid the distortions associated with inflationary budget deficits and the introduction of tax systems and expenditure policies that would leave a greater share of domestic resources for development purposes.[60] Black also recognized the importance of a "fairer" distribution of income as an important prerequisite for successful growth "to provide ordinary people with both the means and the motive to increase their productive output" (7).

The vision of progress that Black conveyed reflected his own interest in tangible evidence of change and the belief that, ultimately, technical advance would make the difference. This view and his sensitivity to the problems of economic backwardness were no doubt influenced by his own upbringing in the southern United States, a relatively backward region in his youth. He often referred to this experience, sometimes telling the stories his grandfather used to illustrate the need for the South to catch up with the economically advanced North.

Underlying this commitment to economic progress was Black's compassion for the people whom he saw suffering in misery—a compassion rooted not in abstract humanitarian interest but in his keen interest in people and his compelling way of dealing and interacting with them. As he put it in his last address to the board of governors, "the Bank's work is not to be assessed in terms of the building of cold monuments of stone and steel and concrete; it has had a deeper purpose—to enlarge the riches of the earth, to give men light and warmth, to lift them out of drudgery and despair, to interest them in the stirring of ideas, in the grasp of organization and techniques toward the realization of a day in which plenty will be a real possibility and not a distant dream."[61]

Broadening the Institutional Frame

Greater awareness of the plight of the developing countries and the search for a more differentiated approach to helping them exposed some of the narrow rigidities of the original concept of the

Bank. The Bank's ability to support the emerging private sector, for instance, was constrained by the requirement of government guarantees for its lending. It also turned out that the Bank's lending terms and interest rates, although reflecting its own favorable credit rating, were not appropriate in all cases. The poorer member countries could not afford to meet their external borrowing requirements on the terms offered by the Bank. The rational, market-based approach to development finance was not consistent with the urgency of accelerating economic growth; the investment requirements and the growth prospects, especially of the poorer countries, did not match. It was not always possible, even with perfect economic management, to achieve adequate growth while keeping a country's indebtedness within prudent limits. Furthermore, the importance of major investments in health and education was recognized, but lending for projects that were not clearly productive remained unacceptable. In short, as the Bank's experience with economic development in different countries grew, the limitations inherent in the conventional banking concept became more obvious and called for a broadening of the institution's scope.

The ideas inspiring the creation of the Bank assumed a strong role for the private sector in the international economy; one of the institution's principal purposes was the promotion of private foreign investment.[62] The Bank, however, was a public institution, owned by governments that looked to the Bank for assistance in solving their financial problems, and the bulk of the Bank's lending understandably was for the benefit of the public sector. Nonetheless, Black and Garner believed in the central role of private initiative and investment.[63] They considered private ownership and management particularly appropriate in the industrial sector, and refused to lend to public sector industries and financial enterprises. This remained the Bank's policy until the late 1960s, despite strong pressures from a number of the Bank's developing member countries to assist government-owned financial institutions and enterprises. But the requirement of a government guarantee for any Bank lending presented problems for both governments and private business; governments did not want to be seen to favor some investors, and businessmen did not want to involve governments in their business. Although the creation of private development finance institutions as retail distributors of the Bank's loans allowed the Bank to support private entrepreneurs at least indirectly in a number of countries, the Bank could do little to assist directly those economic actors regarded as crucial to economic progress.

This dilemma attracted the attention of the NAC in the spring of 1948. The council proposed that Congress authorize an extra $500 million for the Export-Import Bank to support the growth of private enterprise. Black, who was then executive director, vigorously opposed the idea of providing further funds and additional responsibilities to the Export-Import Bank because he felt that this would deprive the fledgling international bank of an important opportunity for action. The sense that Black was trying to protect the Bank's turf is evident in this instance, and this defensive attitude was a persistent theme in the relations between the Bank and the Export-Import Bank in the early years of his presidency.[64]

When Black became president, the idea of an affiliate organization to stimulate private investment, domestic and foreign, in developing countries for productive purposes had been suggested by Demuth and supported by McCloy. Black continued to pursue the idea, while Garner and Demuth became the prime movers of what was to become the International Finance Corporation (IFC). For Black, the IFC was not just another investment bank, it was an international institution for tackling the problems of private investors generally and promoting their activities. In a speech to the Economic and Social Council in April 1955, he outlined his expectations:

> I believe that the Corporation will have an importance going far beyond the sum of its investments. It will, we trust, serve as an effective clearing house to bring together investment opportunities, private capital and experienced management. The IFC will necessarily be concerned with the same problems that affect private investors generally. We are hopeful that it may be able to do much to improve the general climate in which those problems must be solved. I think that the IFC, as an international institution working impartially for the welfare of all its members, will be in an unusually good position to encourage the adoption of governmental policies favoring the expansion of private investment.[65]

Following the founding of the IFC, Black elaborated further on the context of these developments in his annual address to the governors in September 1956:

> The Bank was originally conceived solely as a financial institution. But as it has come to grips with the problems of development, it has evolved into a development agency which uses its financial resources as but one means of helping its members along the whole broad front of economic progress. . . . I see the Bank becoming a still more effective agent for promoting capital flow into the less developed countries, and perhaps the most persuasive external means of encouraging these countries to adopt policies and attitudes conducive to sound economic growth. . . . There is continuing need for flexible and imaginative approaches to all the problems of development. One such approach is the International Finance Corporation, for which we in the Bank have high hopes.[66]

Yet, despite these high hopes, it took seven years for the IFC to be created, and then only in a form so weakened, compared with the original proposal, that its initial role was severely hampered. The main reason for the slow progress was strong opposition in financial circles in the United States. The objections related to the use of public funds for investment in the stock of private enterprises. Everybody was in favor of the growth of private enterprise in the developing world, but the notion that public institutions should become owners of private companies seemed inconsistent with the spirit of free enterprise. Presumably, narrower concerns about the IFC as a competitor may also have influenced the position of the investment banking community. Black rejected these concerns and enlisted the support of an unusual ally, the United Nations. Massive pressure brought on the U.S. government eventually persuaded the Eisenhower administration to proceed with the proposal: a sharp reduction in the amount of the affiliate's capital and initial acceptance that the corporation would not invest in equity were the concessions needed to ensure congressional approval. The latter limitation severely handicapped the IFC in its early days but was soon removed.

It was ironic that Black had to seek the support of the United Nations to establish an affiliate that by design and nature corresponded more closely, if anything, to the economic and financial concepts of Wall Street than the World Bank itself. The Bank, especially under McCloy, had been very careful to distance itself from the United Nations and to establish its autonomy and independence from any mandates issued by the United Nations, precisely to demonstrate that economic, not political, principles determined its decisions. Although Garner never had much time for the United Nations, Black was more pragmatic. Furthermore, it suited him to work cooperatively with the United Nations on the proposed IFC because it allowed him to deny his cooperation in a matter close to the heart of the United Nations, the establishment of a concessionary lending facility under U.N. control.

If the IFC was welcomed as a venture that promised to respond to a need considered important by the more conservative exponents of the Bank—the need to provide effective support to the private sector—the attitude toward the International Development Association (IDA), the Bank's soft-loan affiliate, was initially much more cautious. Black, Garner, Demuth, and many others were concerned that their painstaking efforts to demonstrate the Bank's sound, business-like, hard-nosed approach could be undercut by the introduction of lending on other than market-based terms.

As in the case of the IFC, the origins of IDA go back to the early days of the Bank. At the instigation of the developing countries, which were looking for ways to mobilize capital funds on terms less onerous than those the Bank could offer, the U.N. Economic and Social Council initiated a succession of studies, all of which resulted in the recommendation to establish a financial assistance agency under the auspices of the United Nations to provide funds on "liberal" terms at "nominal" interest rates. The enthusiasm of the industrial countries for entrusting the United Nations with the handling of financial development assistance was limited. The Bank took the position that this was a proposition beyond its scope as an institution linked to the capital market. Demuth, representing the Bank's management, told the U.N. Economic, Employment and Development Commission in May 1951:

We regard the development task as urgent. We believe that, in some countries, the rate of development cannot be accelerated substantially if the only external capital they receive is in the form of loans which have a reasonable prospect of repayment. If additional assistance is to be given to these countries, we believe strongly that it should be in the form of grants, rather than in the form of quasi-loans, and that the grants should preferably be administered through international channels. But the decision whether to make grants available for this purpose is one which only the more advanced countries can make in the light of their own national policies, resources and the totality of their commitments. On that point, therefore, the Bank cannot appropriately express any view.[67]

Demuth rejected the suggestion that the Bank had not adequately observed its mandate of promoting economic development as an "assertion made without factual demonstration. . . .All of us in the Bank regard the promotion of economic development as our primary task. To the achievement of that goal, all the energies of the Bank have been directed" (30).

The U.S. International Development Advisory Board under the chairmanship of Nelson Rockefeller recognized that much of the basic investment required in developing countries could not be financed on a loan basis. It recommended the creation of an international development authority to be managed by the World Bank. The management of the Bank accepted the need for close coordination between the Bank's lending and the assistance to be provided by the proposed development authority and, hence, the desirability of a management link between the two organizations. However, Black and his associates were concerned that the strenuous efforts to gain the confidence of the investment community in the financial soundness of the Bank could be undermined by the Bank's association with any lending on terms other than those established by the market and to countries whose economic condition would not allow them to service conventional Bank loans.

Thus, in his address to the U.N. Economic and Social Council meeting in Santiago, Chile, in March 1951, Black acknowledged that some developing countries might not be able to develop without concessionary assistance. He warned that this should not be provided "in the form of very long-term low interest rate loans. . . Although easier terms reduce the element of risk, they do not come near to eliminating it. In the end, although some loans will turn out well and will be repaid, others will bring in their train, first, severe strain on the economy of the borrower and, finally, default. . . . The effect of such defaults is to destroy credit generally and to wither the integrity of all orthodox lending."[68] For this reason, Black felt, if there was need for concessionary assistance, it should be provided in grant form. Black took the same position in a statement to the second committee of the General Assembly in December 1951 but added that "the grants should preferably be administered through international channels, and that, to the fullest extent practicable, the technical facilities of existing international agencies should be utilized for such administration."[69] Black remained strongly opposed to all proposals of giving aid in the form of long-term, low-interest rate loans. "Loans of this kind are, in essence, part loan and part grant. They have the inherent fault that they are not always apt to be regarded as serious debt obligations. Like all other 'fuzzy' transactions, they therefore tend to impair the integrity of all international credit operations. And they accomplish nothing that cannot be accomplished equally well by an intelligent combination of real loans and real grants."[70]

This is where the matter rested until February 1958, when Black warmly welcomed Senator Mike Monroney's proposal of an International Development Association to function in cooperation with the Bank as a proposal he was willing to explore. The reasons for his change of mind became apparent when Black addressed the governors at the annual meeting in Delhi in October 1958. Prime Minister Nehru had made it clear that he considered grants to be insulting and thus encouraged Black to change his attitude toward soft loans. Black found that "some of our rapidly developing member countries, . . . for reasons not directly attributable to poor financial and economic management, are approaching the limits of their present capacity to assume additional obligations. . . ."[71] Indeed, countries such as India and Pakistan would find it next to impossible to squeeze more out of their domestic economies and would have had to lower their development sights considerably. The newly independent African countries similarly would be very bad off. The potential for the Bank to assist especially the neediest among its members was therefore becoming increasingly constrained. Black concluded that "there *is* need for new supplies and sources of international development capital, and I believe that international organization can be the practical, twentieth century way of meeting that need" (11).

The creation of IDA signaled the transformation of the Bank into a development institution. It was now able to assist all its members regardless of their income level and debt-servicing capacity; it was also in a position to support all the activities relevant to the long-term economic advance of its members irrespective of their potential for revenue generation. To be sure, the formal integrity of the Bank as a market-funded financing institution was preserved by incorporating IDA as a separate fund. Amending the Articles of Agreement of the Bank to provide for the accommodation of the IDA fund could have been simple; but it would have been hazardous as well, for it would have provided opportunity for other amendments. Above all, the separate identity of IDA served to "emphasize to the world, especially to the investors in Bank bonds, the completely different financial status of the two institutions [and to] assure investors in Bank bonds that their interest in the Bank would not be diluted by the diversion of funds into the softer IDA channels."[72]

The acceptance of IDA into the Bank's fold represented Black's acknowledgment that there was a legitimate need for concessional assistance and that the Bank could provide this assistance without compromising its strict standards of sound country performance and projects. Black's concern about the financial integrity of the Bank and its acceptance on Wall Street was now matched by his concern about the effectiveness of the Bank in supporting the poorest among the developing countries.

The creation of IDA had important implications for the institutional autonomy of the Bank. Up to now, the Bank could operate as a financial institution guided by standards appropriate to its line of business. Its income amply covered its administrative budget. Political considerations affected the Bank's behavior mainly as they reflected the Bank's reputation in the financial markets. The creation of IDA, with its need for periodic replenishment of resources by the member governments, changed that and forced the Bank in time to pay increasing attention to the views and priorities of the parliamentary bodies that had to appropriate those resources.[73] A meeting between Black and Robert Anderson, the U.S. secretary of the treasury, foreshadowed this change. As Davidson Sommers recalls, Anderson announced that the United States was ready to support the proposal to establish IDA and told Black, "We've let you be very independent in the Bank with your borrowed money; but in IDA, where we have to appropriate the funds, we'll expect you to be more flexible." Black replied, "Well, I might be a little flexible, but I ain't gonna be plumb loose."[74] Clearly, he felt awkward and under pressure. But although he may have been able to shrug off the implications for the Bank of the creation of IDA, it was obvious that the U.S. government would pay much closer attention to the way the Bank used its resources and conducted its business.

An Era Ends

Black's presidency lasted thirteen years. In that time the Bank was transformed from an unknown institution with a potential for making a modest difference in the world to one that had already begun to make a recognized difference. Its clientele increased. Its financial resources expanded. Its basic policies were put in place. The capital it provided, although small in relation to demand, grew substantially. Its economic management advice began to loom as important, if not as prominent, as its capital. The institution changed from a bank in which the borrowers' capacity to repay was the ultimate basis for a credit, to one in which the potential for increasing the capacity to repay was essential as a justification for providing capital. It became accepted as an institution that carried on its core business in a professional and nonpolitical way and could mediate hot situations in the world in the same manner. Professional values and a technocratic outlook were sought in the recruitment of personnel at all levels and were reinforced by in-house training and management.

All this took place under Black's guidance and by his example. He was an active, not an absentee CEO, a son of the American South who could turn his attention to a much larger south and understand its problems. He led the Bank with his vision, and the Bank was the instrument to turn his vision into reality. Black's departure from the Bank signaled the end of an era, an "era of good feeling." The era had been dominated by Black's personality, his leadership, his graceful style, and charm; it was also an era during which the Bank enjoyed universal respect and acclaim. The leaders of the industrial countries—Eisenhower and Kennedy, British Prime Minister Harold Macmillan, and Chancellor Ludwig Erhard of Germany—felt good about the Bank. So did the financial community and its leaders, the Rockefellers, Hermann Abs of Germany, and others. The leaders of the developing world, such as Nehru and Nasser, Ghana's President Nkrumah, and Tito felt good about the Bank; they respected the principles for which the Bank stood, even when they disagreed with them, because they recognized the financial and technical integrity of the institution.

That "era of good feeling" had a cost. No one could or would undervalue the human and financial base of Black's Bank or the contributions to development it made possible. The pervasiveness of the "good feeling," however, and the human establishment and operational orientation developed in the era, brought certain rigidities in their wake. The very concept of "Black's Bank" linked the institution to a man and a time and thus implied a certain static quality. And that in turn implied, however unintended, a conservative reaction to change. The need for change was inevitable, indeed it had already begun in Black's time, as new political and economic circumstances emerged and as the Bank's own experience unrolled.

Black's successors would not have to create a bank as Black had done, to give substance to an idea. They would have to shake up a bank that had acquired an enviable reputation and naturally tended to value the way things were. They would have to open the institution to meet the challenges posed by a sharp increase in Bank membership, by the emergence of a less supportive view of economic assistance among donor countries, by the new understandings of the meaning of development, and by inevitable, although gradual, generational changes in staff and management.

Chapter Four

George D. Woods

Transforming the Bank

Georgia D. Woods became president of the Bank on January 1, 1963. This time it had not been difficult to find a candidate willing to take over the job. Black had vowed not to leave until he was satisfied that the Bank would be in good hands, if only because he had "an obligation to the bond buyers." He could be confident, however, that there would be capable people ready to step into his shoes. In 1961 he observed, "In the old days, nobody would take the presidency. Now there will be plenty of them who'll be glad to take it."[1] Indeed, the people Black was thinking of as his successors—Douglas Dillon or David Rockefeller—belonged to the elite of the social and financial establishment. George Woods, although Black knew him well, was not at the top of his list.

Yet George Woods was in many ways the ideal candidate. He was an experienced investment banker, chairman of the First Boston Corporation, with a solid professional reputation on Wall Street, and, perhaps more important, he had devoted much time and thought to the problems of the developing world. Where Black's expertise was the marketing of bonds, Woods's strength was in the underwriting, the buying side of the investment business, which gave him an unequaled understanding of corporate finance.[2] He was inclined, therefore, to focus less on raising resources and on the Bank's reputation on Wall Street and more on the use of the funds the Bank provided. This focus was appropriate because the Bank Woods took over was a well-established financial institution. Questions about the right strategy for economic development and the choice of appropriate priorities were now raised with growing insistence, replacing the earlier concerns about the Bank's image on Wall Street.

A Familiar Figure

George Woods was no stranger to the World Bank. The First Boston Corporation had managed, along with Morgan Stanley, the Bank's bond issues. They had been picked "because they had a very fine system for retail distribution."[3] Woods, who in 1951 had become the chairman of First Boston, had therefore come into contact with the Bank practically from the beginning of its operations. His involvement with the Bank's efforts to raise capital sharpened his interest in the institution's lending work, and he had been more than willing to help as an adviser with problems that intrigued him.

The first such occasion was a mission to India in 1952 to develop a program for the expansion and modernization of the private steel industry. As a result of this mission, the Bank supported investments in India's private steel industry through several loans. For Woods, the mission represented the beginning of an intense relationship with a country that fascinated him. He met many of India's leading businessmen in the course of this first visit and was clearly charmed by their sophistication and personal warmth. He kept in touch with most of them throughout his life; with a few, such as G. D. Birla and J. R. D. Tata, he maintained a close personal friendship. He was to revisit India on many occasions.

As a column in the *New York World-Telegram and Sun* noted in 1957, "George Woods has been to India several times since that first visit in 1952 and has come to be recognized as an authority on the economics of that country."[4] In February 1954, Woods again went to India for the World Bank to explore the feasibility of establishing a private development finance company. His earlier contacts with Indian business leaders enabled him to put together a group of prominent businessmen who drafted a charter and who subsequently joined the board of the Industrial Credit and Investment Corporation of India (ICICI). The corporation was supported by a number of foreign investors and by a Bank loan. Woods was later instrumental in creating similar financial institutions, also supported by the Bank, in Pakistan and in the Philippines. When the ICICI later encountered problems—originating from serious disagreements among influential board members and weak management—Woods was called back to deal with the situation, and he successfully reorganized the corporation's board and management.

Woods was also associated with one of the Bank's major mediation exercises, the settlement of the claims of the Suez Canal shareholders by the Egyptian government. Black, who had been in close touch with President Nasser of Egypt, asked William Iliff, one of the Bank's vice presidents, to handle the negotiations and suggested that he work together with George Woods. Iliff later recalled, "He and I worked together on this thing throughout most of the negotiations, and I must say . . . that we made a very happy team." Iliff relied on Woods because "a good many technical issues here were technical issues of corporate finance, and of course nobody in the United States or anywhere else knows more about corporate finance than Mr. George Woods does, and apart from that, he's a man of a very keen diplomatic sense."[5] The negotiations were difficult and involved extensive shuttling between Cairo, Rome, and London. Finally, on July 13, 1957, the parties signed an agreement that allowed the Bank in due course to assist with the rehabilitation and expansion of the Suez Canal. Woods's assistance appears to have made a critical contribution, especially during one of the last meetings with the Egyptians. As Iliff recalled:

> The Egyptians had been very difficult on this particular morning, and they had been chiseling a lot at certain proposals that we had put up to them as, in our view, an appropriate approach to this problem. Mr. Woods had listened to them very patiently for about three quarters of an hour, and he

suddenly got up from the table where he and I were sitting, and he walked over into a far corner of the room, and he put his hand underneath the lapel of his coat and he scratched his shoulder, in a very characteristic gesture of his which always indicates that some devastating remark is about to come out. He came back to the table and he sat down, and he looked at the Egyptians on the other side of the table and he said, "Look here, gentlemen, don't you realize that you have made the greatest steal in history since the Dutch bought Manhattan from the Indians for 20 bottles of gin? Stop your chiseling!" And the Egyptians did stop their chiseling. That was one of the breaks that we had in this particular situation (47).

Apart from being the Bank's banker and at times its diplomatic representative, Woods served (as of February 1962) on the IFC's international advisory committee. This group of prominent investment bankers included Hermann J. Abs, Deutsche Bank; Viscount Harcourt, Morgan Grenfell; André Meyer, Lazard Frères; and Baron Guy de Rothschild, Rothschild Frères. The group met from time to time with Black to review the IFC's investments and policies.

Although Woods remained an effective chairman of the First Boston Corporation, he devoted an increasing share of his time to development issues. The diversity and extent of his involvement with the Bank reflected his growing interest in the problems of the developing countries. In an address to the Society for International Development Woods later recalled his first contacts with developing countries:

My exposure to the subject matter, international development, . . . has been a pretty long one. Back in the 1920s, the investment house for which I was working unleashed me against the mainland of China and a number of other foreign parts in a search for clients overseas. For me, it was a wonderful education: I got to see not only China but other parts of the Far East and a good deal of South America as well—much, in fact, of what we now call the underdeveloped world. But it never occurred to me that the day would come when help to this world would become a matter of high national policy in the industrial countries. In those days, things had a simpler look: we left development pretty much to the businessman, and to the laws of providence and Adam Smith.[6]

His advice in development matters was not only sought by the Bank. When President Kennedy developed his plans to revitalize the U.S. foreign aid program, he invited George Woods along with other corporate leaders to "discuss application of concepts involved in new approach to foreign assistance" and to obtain the support of the business community for his program.[7] Subsequently, Woods became a member of the president's task force on foreign aid and established close relations with the people involved in the foreign assistance program.

In the summer of 1961, Kennedy's assistant, Ralph Dungeon, was beginning the search for a suitable candidate to run the newly renamed bilateral aid organization, the Agency for International Development. According to Arthur Schlesinger, "Dungeon was looking for someone conservative enough to reassure Congress but liberal enough to carry forward the program—a business image, as it was put, without a business mentality. He finally hit upon George Woods, a progressive-minded investment banker."[8] Woods was ready to accept the job. On August 24, 1961, Woods cabled to Harry Addinsell, his mentor and predecessor as First Boston's chairman, "Since your departure I have been under extremely heavy pressure to take number one post in foreign aid administration. As of today would say chances are about fifty-fifty that I will accept."[9] A week later he cabled, "odds instead of fifty-fifty are now eighty-twenty in favor of my taking assignment."[10] But then the odds shifted. The idea of Woods's appointment met with strong opposition among liberal Democrats in Congress because of the involvement of First Boston in the so-called Dixon-Yates affair during the Eisenhower years. Woods had no desire to face a protracted and painful struggle for confirmation and removed himself from further consideration for the appointment.

Within nine months, however, he faced a new proposition. Eugene Black had decided to resign from the presidency of the World Bank. George Woods was available and ready to take over the leadership of the institution whose work he had followed closely for so long. The appointment would arouse no opposition.

A Self-Made Man

George David Woods was born in Boston on July 27, 1901, the son of a worker in the Navy Yard who had a drinking problem and died when George was three years old. George grew up with his mother and a sister in constrained circumstances in Brooklyn, where his father had moved before he died. George's mother supported her family by sewing and mending clothes. The two children contributed by handling chores, including sweeping the sidewalk and babysitting. George's childhood appears to have been well protected and happy. His sister later recalled, "We were never affluent, but my mother was a very happy woman. She adored her children and that kept us from being underprivileged."[11] His mother seems to have been particularly fond of her son, and they were very close until her death in 1954.

The circumstances of his childhood turned Woods into a determined person who understood early that it was up to him to make his own way through life. But the financial constraints he experienced as a youngster did not lead him to be overly concerned about making a lot of money. Nor was he prepared to do just any work as long as it provided a decent income. All along, he did what he did because he enjoyed doing it and because he was good at it. Even as a child he was unathletic, perhaps even physically lazy—someone who wouldn't walk if he could ride. He was not physically competitive, and lack of athletic achievement seems not to have been a reason for him to try harder but, rather, to recognize his limitations. Despite his distaste for physical exercise and his appreciation of fine food, he managed to stay slim, perhaps because he was a heavy smoker until a serious heart attack in 1954 forced him to quit.

Woods liked to be with people whom he considered interesting. He could be warm and charming, and he cared about his friends. But he was a listener rather than a talker, and he was not gregarious. Instead, he tended to brood and keep his emotions to himself. He did not like debates or confrontations because he did not like the commotion associated with them. This did not mean that he could not be combative. He was sensitive, particularly if he felt slighted, and would react with unrestrained resentment to any perceived attack. He was sensitive about not having gone to college and suspicious of those who had, especially those who had gone to elitist schools. He did not have a notable sense of humor and was liable to misunderstand what might have been said as a joke.

George Woods's mother wanted to provide her children with the best education she could afford, and so George went to Commercial High School in Brooklyn. There was no money for college, and when George graduated from high school, he went to work. At 17, he was hired as an office boy at Harris, Forbes & Co., a leading underwriter of municipal and utility bonds. He proved to be ideally suited for work in the underwriting business. He had a quick mind and was very good with numbers, as is evident from many anecdotes remembered by his friends.[12]

The senior executives of Harris, Forbes & Co. liked the young man. Harry Addinsell, one of the vice presidents and later chairman of First Boston and a lifelong friend of Woods, recalled, "I knew Woodsie was a man of destiny from the moment I saw those eyes of his lookin' at me from behind the desk. He's always saying I brought him up, but that's not so; he brought himself up."[13] His mentors persuaded the young Woods to go to night school and to study the theory of banking and finance. They followed his progress with interest. To their dismay, Woods often played hooky—to work overtime at the office on prospectuses.[14] Woods appears to have shown keen interest and a real talent for anything that had to do with money and investing. He was given a desk in the buying, or underwriting, department, where he drafted prospectuses, did statistical work, and drew up contracts. He never worked in the trading department and had no interest in the selling of securities.

In 1927, at age 26, Woods became a vice president and was entrusted with major projects. In 1928 his bank sent him to Japan to organize the financing of the Nippon Electric Power Company with a $9 million bond issue. Arthur Dean, a young attorney who later became a partner at Sullivan and Cromwell and was eventually the first U.S. disarmament negotiator, went along on this trip and became a lifelong friend. Woods had become a major player in his investment banking firm and contributed significantly to its success.

As business declined during the Great Depression, Harris, Forbes & Co. was acquired by the Chase Bank in 1930. Woods not only survived the merger but was made vice president of the new firm. With the passage of the Glass-Steagal Act in 1933, however, banks belonging to the Federal Reserve System had to separate themselves from their securities affiliates. Stockholders of the Chase Bank and of the First National Bank of Boston were offered rights to subscribe to a new securities company called First Boston Corporation. First Boston offered a unique variety of services. The securities affiliate of the First National Bank of Boston had done little in the way of underwriting but was the leader in trading government and municipal bonds, a business that thrived throughout the depression. The Chase, Harris Forbes side contributed its reputation and talent to the creation of an underwriting department, which became important once the underwriting business revived after the depression. George Woods was a major part of the talent that was transferred as part of the deal. He became a vice president and a member of the board of First Boston.

Woods's reputation in finance increased steadily. As a young man in the 1920s, he had seen at close hand the buildup and the collapse of corporate giants; in his prime "he had a hand in utility expansion on a scale beyond the dreams of the giants [of the 1920s]" (9). He played a personal role in building First Boston into what, by the time he left, was probably the largest U.S. investment banking firm in terms of overall operations. He put together some of the biggest and most successful bond issues for California's public utilities. Arthur Dean described Woods's thoroughness and creativity: "After George arranges for financing, he discusses the long-term problems. His study of a company's prospects is creative. After advising about the issuance of stocks he takes a continuing interest in the results."[15]

Among the more imaginative and creative ventures he undertook was the financial blueprinting of the Henry J. Kaiser industrial organization. He took on Kaiser when nobody else on Wall Street would touch him because of the large debt Kaiser had incurred. Woods worked out a deal that got the company out of debt and put the steel and aluminum enterprises on a firm financial footing. Woods's close involvement with Kaiser and with the members of the Kaiser family grew over the years; Kaiser became the contractor in the rehabilitation of India's private steel industry and a key partner in the Volta River hydroelectric project supported by the World Bank.

The only distraction Woods allowed himself from a life otherwise committed to hard work was his keen interest in show business. It was he who saved Ringling Brothers and Barnum & Bailey Circus after a disastrous fire in Hartford, Connecticut, in 1944 in which many spectators lost their lives. He worked out a plan to compensate the victims, then reorganized the company to keep it from collapsing. For several years he served as treasurer and director of Ringling Brothers. Woods used his skill as a financier to help the troubled circus company turn around its performance, but he was primarily motivated by his love of the circus. He was a well-known buff. "The clowns all know him. And the jugglers know him, too. The bareback riders call him by his first name" (23). To the stars and the show girls on Broadway he was an "angel." As a Broadway angel, Woods backed an impressive number of hits—often against the advice of his Wall Street friends. He was not a dilettante; he would not back a show unless he was convinced that it had a chance of success, and his keen interest and deep involvement gave him a remarkable sense of which shows would succeed. Invariably, he made a lot of money with his investments on Broadway. Later, his interest in the performing arts involved him in the creation of the Lincoln Center, of which he was a trustee and, for a number of years, treasurer.

Woods saw himself as a creature of First Boston, but it is obvious that First Boston became increasingly his creation. He was the key figure in working out a deal that brought the Mellon dynasty into the picture in 1946.[16] The Mellons wanted Woods to become president of Mellon Securities; instead, Woods persuaded them to combine their securities business with First Boston. This addition complemented First Boston's predominant position in the utilities field with important industrial accounts, which Woods took over and nourished. From this point, Woods's progress to the top of his firm was simply a matter of time. In 1947 he became one of two executive vice presidents, in 1948 chairman of the executive committee, and in 1951 chairman of the board.

Woods occasionally made mistakes, but when he did he went to great lengths to recover his losses. In 1954 Woods agreed that First Boston should take an equity position in an oil refinery in Puerto Rico, but this time he failed to take into account the peculiarities of the chemical business. As Woods said, "We were in the chemical business, and we didn't know a damn thing about it."[17] When the refinery began to lose money, Woods joined the board of the company and assumed personal responsibility for its affairs. For more than a year he devoted 80 percent of his time to restructuring the refinery's management and financing, and in due course the company's performance turned around. It was important for Woods to recover First Boston's investment in the company, but what really mattered to him was that "a lot of nice people, who shouldn't have been in the thing bought those debentures—Methodist missionaries and folks like that" (246).

A major disenchantment that left "its stamp on the 'thoughtful side' of George Woods" was his involvement in the so-called Dixon-Yates affair.[18] The incoming Eisenhower administration had pronounced itself against the further expansion of the Tennessee Valley Authority (TVA) and in favor of private power generation; Woods, who shared this conviction, had offered his advice with enthusiasm. In his Senate testimony in 1955 he explained, "I wanted to throw my hat in the ring to get the government out of business and to slow down, and perhaps stop, unessential expenditures of government funds."[19] As a result, Adolphe H. "Dad" Wenzell, a director and vice president of First Boston, was sent to work with the Bureau of the Budget in Washington, and prepared a report on power development in the Tennessee Valley. One option was construction of a power station by a consortium of two private utilities (headed, respectively, by Edgar H. Dixon and Eugene A. Yates) to supply power in the TVA grid for the Atomic Energy Commission and the city of Memphis. First Boston was assisting Dixon-Yates in putting together the financing of the project. As soon as the Democrats, the traditional backers of the TVA, found out about Dad Wenzell's role in advising the government, they cried foul. Estes Kefauver, the formidable Democratic senator from Tennessee, charged Wenzell—who by then had retired from First Boston and joined the World Bank—with "serving two masters" in a way bordering on "violation of the Criminal Code."[20] The administration backed away from the Dixon-Yates proposal, and the deal collapsed. Woods denied any suggestion that he had sought involvement in this project with any profit motive in mind; he was guided, he said, by his belief that private capital could be persuaded to finance much of the needed power investment. Woods had decided not to charge Dixon-Yates any fee because of First Boston's earlier involvement with the U.S. government, but Woods testified "that he had been in the investment banking business since 1918 and never before had been associated with a project where the fee was declined."[21] Although Woods was exonerated from any responsibility, he was marked as a Republican by many Democrats on Capitol Hill; when, years later, President Kennedy suggested him as head of the U.S. Agency for International Development, they objected strenuously.

In his long career as an investment banker and with First Boston, Woods had tended to gravitate toward activities he liked and was good at—he had found others to deal with aspects of the work in which he had little interest. His love was corporate finance; corporate financial structures fascinated him, and he worked exclusively on the underwriting side of the investment banking business. He had no interest in the marketing end of the business, and the nuances of trading bored him. He had no taste for administrative and managerial responsibilities and was glad to leave those to his longtime friend and colleague James Coggeshall, who became president of First Boston when Woods became chairman. Woods and Coggeshall had a happy, symbiotic relationship—"one of the most remarkable I've ever run into in the business world," observed Edward Townsend, who worked closely with Woods for many years.[22] Yet, they were very dissimilar. Woods worked on the financial problems of companies with "jewel-like precision," while Coggeshall did the "going out and seeing people."[23] Coggeshall would nurse contacts with bankers and insurance executives, form the underwriting syndicates, and line up the dealers. It was not that Woods was a recluse or uncomfortable dealing with people. On the contrary, he liked to discuss problems and explore solutions, and he could be a superb negotiator; but he had to be interested in the matter at hand and convinced that the people he was dealing with could contribute something of interest. This stubborn insistence on focusing only on what he found challenging was a luxury that he could no longer afford when he took charge of the World Bank, and it became a factor that affected his performance there.

It is not clear how Woods became interested in issues of economic development. His own background and his personal experience of economic hardship may have had something to do with it. There is much evidence to suggest that he was motivated in his work as a banker by a sense of social responsibility. The experience of the Great Depression had given him a good sense of the widespread impact of financial decisions on the life and welfare of people. The interests of the workers, customers, shareholders, and savers whose lives would be dependent on the success of First Boston's financial transactions were on his mind. There are numerous examples of his devoting large amounts of time trying to solve some financial problem for a friend, with no reward but the satisfaction of helping someone in need and perhaps solving an intriguing problem.

A provision in Woods's contract with First Boston allowed him to take time off for public service, and he made frequent use of this opportunity, especially in accepting the various assignments he performed free of charge for the World Bank. It seems reasonable to assume that it was through these assignments that his interest in economic development problems emerged. His contacts with India, in particular, seem to have given him a sense of the dimensions of these problems, as well as of the opportunities waiting to be exploited.

Transforming the Bank

Few people expected energetic and innovative leadership when Woods arrived at the Bank in January 1963. He was past 60 and, after a serious heart attack in 1954, not in very robust health. There was concern that he had sought the presidency of the World Bank as a prominent, high-profile position to cap his career as an investment banker. In fact, he came full of vigor and with strong views about the changing role of the Bank.[24] He would not be the president of Black's Bank but would transform the Bank by putting his own ideas to work. In the process, he became one of the Bank's most innovative presidents, one who reinforced the Bank's role as a development institution and prepared it for the major role it was to play.

The Bank was ready for new initiatives in 1963. Black had given the Bank considerable momentum, but toward the end of his long tenure he had become more detached. He spent much time in New York and did not address some of the more difficult issues—such as the implications of the creation in 1960 of IDA. There was thus a sense that the Bank was coasting along, "waiting for a new initiative from a new president" (2).

Woods came to the Bank with a clear sense of the important role the Bank would have to play in the development field. He recognized the development problem as a generic economic problem, not just as an issue that had to be addressed within the context of the East-West conflict. The emergence of many new nations, especially in Africa, represented a challenge that Woods understood. He recognized that "the need to quicken the tempo of economic growth is now more urgent than ever, simply because aspirations for progress are now so universal." [25] Traveling to India and Pakistan or to the Middle East and Latin America, he had been impressed by the economic potential of the developing world. Just as he could visualize and focus on a problem of corporate finance, he could appreciate the opportunities for economic development. Woods had become an acknowledged master of corporate finance because he was innovative and not limited by conventions in dealing with the problems he had been asked to solve. This was the spirit in which he came to the Bank and the reason for the apparent paradox that one of the most accomplished investment bankers of his time should readily accept that the Bank was more than a bank.

In his first public speech as president of the World Bank he drew attention to the worsening financial position of the developing world:

In the past year, the ability of a number of the less developed countries to undertake new borrowing on conventional terms has continued to weaken: in fact their commercial debt increased more than it had in the previous year, while their capacity to earn foreign exchange did not improve. In consequence, we face an urgent problem: If the pace of development in these countries is to be maintained without overloading them with external obligations, then ways must be found to assist them more and more with grants or with credits carrying lenient financial terms.[26]

Woods did not see the need for concessional lending terms as a compartmentalized problem to be dealt with in isolation by the Bank's soft-loan affiliate but as a responsibility for the entire Bank Group.[27] In his address to his first annual meeting in 1963 he proclaimed, "We should take the fullest possible advantage of the strong financial position in which the Bank now finds itself. We should not hoard our strength, we should use it." He proposed that the Bank modify the terms of its lending "so that they will be more suitable for the new kinds of clients and the new kinds of projects that must begin to concern us."[28] What he had in mind was extending the grace period and the maturity of loans to better match the requirements dictated by extended implementation periods and slow attainment of capacity of projects in the poorer developing countries.

In the same spirit, he persuaded the executive directors to consider using part of the Bank's net income for the benefit of its membership rather than automatically transferring surplus to the Bank's reserves, as had been the practice. Even before Woods's arrival at the Bank, the Bank's management and the executive directors were embarrassed that the Bank was "piling up profits at an almost indecent rate."[29] Reserves were growing rapidly and were approaching $1 billion. There was some concern that this level of reserves would attract attention; indeed, there had apparently been suggestions in the U.S. Congress that the Bank cover certain deficits of U.N. organizations (121). The Bank's staff prepared a paper proposing that part of the Bank's profits be channeled to IDA, either through a direct transfer or indirectly, by declaring a dividend.[30]

Woods was not concerned that the distribution of part of the Bank's profits would affect the Bank's reputation for financial prudence. He felt strongly that, as the funds were earned from the borrowing member countries, the members should have the benefit of these resources.[31] Initially, he favored the idea of a Bank dividend, to uphold the principle of having no financial link between the Bank and IDA, but the executive directors were clearly opposed to the idea of dividends. With the encouragement of the United States and Germany, Woods introduced in 1964 the practice of transferring to IDA a portion of the Bank's net profit, equivalent to what "we might prudently have declared as dividend."[32] The *New York Times* warmly endorsed the transfer because the Bank's credibility as a development institution would be threatened "if it simply sat on its money bags." The *Times* concluded, "In recognizing that its riches and experience must be put to use, the bank is living up to its original concept as the dynamic generator of economic development."[33] The decision reversed the no-financial-links policy, which Black had established to avoid anything that could give rise to what he had called "fuzzy loans."[34] It epitomized the shift in the character of the Bank from an institution governed strictly by banking principles to one that focused on development.

Actually, the new policy of profit transfers became a source of problems for Woods. After the Bank, during 1964–66, transferred some $200 million to IDA, it encountered problems raising funds, especially in the United States, and was threatened by a shortage of resources. In the circumstances, Woods at first recommended that there be no transfer to IDA in 1967. When this proposal encountered opposition, he recommended a token transfer of $10 million to maintain the established principle. Although the transfer was approved, it earned him the displeasure of both the Part I (industrial) countries, which opposed the idea of transfers at that time, and the Part II (developing) countries, which felt shortchanged because the amount was insignificant.[35]

Woods observed the factors that had tended to make catching up more difficult for the developing countries. He saw that their export earnings and opportunities were limited because of trade barriers, that the structure of their external debt was often unsound, and that their economic and financial policies failed to support effective resource mobilization and allocation. These problems formed for him the background against which the Bank Group had to formulate its policies. They suggested "that the time has come when the Bank will have to add new dimensions to both its lending and technical assistance activities."[36] In his address to the first United Nations Conference on Trade and Development (UNCTAD), Woods declared that the Bank had embarked on a program of critical self-analysis: "The first consequence of this re-examination had been a decision to expand the scope of our financing."[37]

Woods believed that the Bank needed to intervene earlier in the development process but that it should also "follow development into its more advanced stages" (7). Intervening earlier meant to Woods a much more serious involvement in agriculture, the sector that in most developing countries predominated both as employer and as a source of demand. Another reason for concern about agriculture was a growing preoccupation with the need to supply adequate food to a sharply increasing population. Woods thought that the scale of the Bank's involvement in the sector had not been commensurate with its importance and that the Bank had to move beyond financing large-scale investments in irrigation, flood control, and land clearance to activities that had a direct impact on agricultural operations, such as credit, storage facilities, and extension. The idea was welcomed with enthusiasm by the small agricultural staff of the Bank, who had been arguing for years that the Bank should play a more active role in promoting agricultural production. Demuth recalled that when he informed the head of the agriculture division of Woods's decision, "his normally dour face burst out into a smile a mile wide."[38]

The logic that had persuaded Woods of the Bank's need to become more active in agriculture also led him to call for a larger Bank role in the financing of education. He saw education both as an important end in itself and as a critical factor in developing the skills needed to achieve economic progress. His initial focus was on secondary and vocational schools, which "can have a fairly rapid impact on development by providing the middle-level manpower as well as the specialists in administration, agriculture and other subjects that are so important in economic growth" (7). Apparently Woods had a problem with university education; he resisted Bank financing of universities or university programs. Demuth thought he was skeptical "because he'd been on some university boards and he'd seen how they moved the monies around from one program to another" (4).

Despite his belief that the Bank had to intervene upstream in the development process, Woods saw an important role for the institution in advancing the transformation and modernization of the developing economies. Woods thought that the Bank needed to help its members diversify their economies by financing industrial investments in a more flexible and versatile manner. "The need to help the developing countries escape from their overdependence on the export of primary goods," he declared at the first UNCTAD meeting, "appears to me incontrovertible."[39] The Bank, in his view, should promote new industrial activities that could form a nucleus for further growth. He recognized that the Bank's insistence on government guarantees for its loans tended to impede more active support of private enterprise, and he was willing to explore how the Bank could become more effective. He was convinced that the IFC needed to play the central role in supporting industrial investments by the World Bank Group, and for this reason he transferred the industrial projects staff of the Bank to the IFC. But the IFC also needed to play a much larger role financially. Woods could recall his attempts to help India's private steel industry, whose needs exceeded what the fledgling national development finance companies or the IFC might be able to provide.

Eventually Woods concluded that the most effective way to give the Bank Group a larger role in financing private enterprise was for the Bank to lend the IFC capital, which could then be re-lent to private enterprises without government guarantee. Woods believed that the IFC "should not only continue its present types of activity on an increased scale, but that there is a considerable area of additional operations it could undertake. With additional resources, IFC could make much larger commitments in individual transactions than its present resources permit and, in those cases where appropriate, it could provide finance in the form of direct loans without equity features."[40] At the same time, the IFC's own capital would be freed for investment in much-needed equity.

India must also have been on his mind when he suggested that the Bank should consider providing long-term financing for the import of "individual pieces of equipment, components and spare parts . . . in cases where full use cannot be made of existing industrial capacity because there is no foreign exchange with which to buy such equipment from abroad."[41] The question—which had been so hotly debated in the early days of the Bank—of whether the Bank should confine its assistance to specific development projects or should try to address the needs of its membership more pragmatically through general program loans—was thus raised again and would become a contentious issue during the Woods presidency and beyond.

Woods understood that the Bank Group could not make a significant financial contribution to the development of industry in the developing world. He saw that the amount of investment which the Bank and the IFC could offer to private industry was dwarfed by the potential contribution of foreign private investment. His background as an investment banker persuaded him that the mobilization of private flows would have to be the key at least to the industrial part of the developmental transformation. However, fear of expropriation or other arbitrary acts by governments discouraged private investors' ventures in developing countries. This consideration led him "to wonder whether the Bank could not in some way make use of its reputation for integrity and its position of impartiality to help in clearing up this impediment to private investment."[42]

The Organisation for Economic Co-operation and Development (OECD) had studied proposals to adopt a binding code governing the treatment of foreign investment and to set up a multilateral investment insurance scheme. However, support for schemes involving politically sensitive commitments was scant, especially at a time when many governments of newly independent countries had come to power on the promise of reducing every form of foreign influence. Aaron Broches, the Bank's general counsel, told Woods of a more modest idea that he had been pursuing: to establish facilities, linked to the Bank, that would be available to foreign investors and host governments for bringing investment disputes to conciliation or arbitration. Woods embraced this idea with an enthusiasm that reflected his interest "in exploring all possible ways in which the Bank can help to widen and deepen the flow of private capital to the developing countries."[43] He saw the proposal through to the establishment in October 1966 of the International Centre for Settlement of Investment Disputes.

Although Woods, like his predecessors, saw the Bank as an institution firmly based on the principles governing private investment banking, he had less difficulty than his predecessors in acknowledging its role as a specialized agency of the United Nations. He understood that the developing countries had become a major political force in the United Nations and that for them the growing North-South disparity replaced the East-West conflict in importance. In his periodic reports to the United Nations Economic and Social Council, Woods tried to convey the relevance of the Bank's work in this changing context. But it was the creation of UNCTAD, with its agenda of contentious issues, that he saw as "an opportunity to exhibit a thoroughly cooperative attitude on relations with other international agencies."[44]

Once he had made the decision that the Bank would expand its activities into lending for agriculture and education, Woods felt strongly that the Bank needed to work closely with the specialized agencies active in those sectors—the Food and Agriculture Organization of the United Nations (FAO) and the United Nations Educational, Scientific, and Cultural Organization (UNESCO). There was, however, opposition from staff members who felt "that the 'normal' way for [the Bank] to expand its lending in a new field would be to hire the necessary experts and proceed with the same independence it had shown in the fields of electric power and transportation."[45] Woods accepted the rationale that had led the international community to establish separate functional agencies but insisted on cooperative arrangements with these agencies at least in the preinvestment stage. In fact, the arrangements worked out with the FAO and UNESCO allowed the Bank some influence over the staffing and operations of specific units created for collaboration with the Bank and committed the Bank to cover a major share of the cost involved.

Woods's more forthcoming attitude was appreciated by functionaries of the United Nations and the specialized agencies. No wonder that Philippe de Seynes, the under secretary general for economic and social affairs, compared George Woods with Pope John XXIII, presumably because of his compassionate concern for the fate of the developing world.[46]

Strengthening the Bank's Analytic Work

Indeed, the underlying theme in Woods's approach to reorienting the Bank was his concept of development as a specific economic phenomenon. He saw the developing countries as suffering from many common problems. Their vulnerability to changes in the terms of trade, their heavy burden of external debt, their lack of diversification in the structure of production, the weakness of their institutions, and shortages of skills were manifestations of economic problems, which he clearly perceived and believed needed to be tackled. Although Woods accepted that the Bank's principal medium of operation was through supporting specific projects, he saw the justification of the project in the context of the country's economy. In his encounters with the emerging African nations, he tried to identify the natural resources that could be exploited as a first step on the road to development of a particular country.[47] He promoted the concept of aid coordination to provide more effective targeting of foreign assistance available to a country from various sources. The concept of country-focused assistance called for analysis that extended beyond the concern about creditworthiness and required the collection of data and information that would allow a more accurate assessment of progress.

Woods was thus persuaded that economists needed to be given a larger and more prominent role in the Bank. In a memorandum addressed to Aaron Broches he wrote, "The operations of the Bank with respect to economic matters have been at a low ebb for a long period . . . . I am anxious to lean over backwards to change this situation."[48] He selected Irving Friedman, who had spent many years in the IMF, as his economic adviser and head of a rapidly growing economic staff. As Friedman later recalled, Woods told him, "I think that you can't have a development agency unless it has as its fuselage the loans which are being made, but one wing has to be project work and the other wing has to be economics."[49]

Of course, the Bank had many able economists on its staff, but most of their work was related to the Bank's lending operations in a supporting role. Friedman noted, "What I found when I came to the Bank was that the Bank had the notion that you only knew about a country if you expected to make a loan to it and only to the extent that you needed information for the loan" (9).

The expansion of the Bank's role in the emerging field of development economics was supported by important outside advisers as well. Edward Mason, professor of economics at Harvard University and a close observer of the Bank, wrote a lengthy memorandum in December 1964 to Woods suggesting a larger role for economists in the Bank. Willard Thorpe, in 1963 the chairman of the Development Assistance Committee of the OECD, thought that the Bank needed to do more analysis of the issues affecting the performance and prospects of the developing world. This was also the time when a number of problems, such as the debt problem and the terms of trade problem, were perceived as manifestations of an unfair system. UNCTAD, convened in 1964, provided a prominent forum for these issues. It was natural that the Bank would be called on to examine the concerns and suggest remedies.

Friedman was Woods's personal choice and had his full support, especially as Woods perceived resistance to Friedman's appointment among the Bank's establishment. The Bank was a bit of a closed shop, and senior positions generally had been filled from within the organization. Attempts to bring in people at higher levels had been rare and had usually failed. Friedman's previous service with the IMF probably burdened his integration into the Bank with the strains that characterized the relationship between the two Bretton Woods institutions.[50] His insensitivity to his new colleagues and to his new competitive environment did not help matters. He was suspicious of his senior colleagues in the Bank and believed that the establishment in the Bank rejected him as an agent of the changes Woods sought to bring about.[51] "Irving's got a lot of assets, but one of his liabilities is that he wants his own turf," was the way Demuth characterized it.[52] To distinguish himself from others and to emphasize the special relationship he felt he had with Woods, Friedman insisted that he should have the title "The Economic Adviser," which became a joke in the Bank.[53] This limited his effectiveness in engendering the dialogue with Bank economists to produce the change he and Woods felt was needed.

Nonetheless, the Bank's capacity in economics was significantly upgraded. During Woods's presidency a large number of economists were hired, in part through the Young Professional Program; many of them had more up-to-date training than some of the older staff members. With the active encouragement of Woods, Friedman revitalized the staff economic committee and tried to gain some influence on the decisionmaking process in the operational field. He also pushed hard to make country performance a criterion for lending and to establish regular consultations, similar to the IMF's consultations, for pursuing an active policy dialogue with the Bank's borrowing members.[54] The time to recognize explicitly a more general role of the Bank in the field of development policy and planning had not yet come, but a greater degree of policy focus was introduced into the Bank's economic work, and the core was created of a staff that, under Hollis Chenery, would establish a much more significant role for the Bank in development economics.

An innovation of the Woods era that proved important for the reshaping of the Bank was the introduction in 1963 of the Junior Professional Program, later renamed the Young Professional Program. In its early years the Bank had relied on recruiting experienced personnel in midcareer. The civil service of major member countries had been an important source of qualified professional staff; in particular, many people from major metropolitan countries came to work for the Bank when their services as colonial administrators were no longer needed. In the early 1960s, as the Bank's staff grew in numbers, it became increasingly difficult to find midcareer staff willing to relocate to Washington and work for the Bank. Furthermore, the changing perception of the development problem and the growing emphasis on economic analysis required different skills. Under the leadership of Richard Demuth the Bank had therefore begun to look for ways of recruiting graduates of leading universities, who would have recent academic training in fields relevant to the Bank's work and who would gain the needed practical experience while in the service of the Bank. Woods endorsed this idea with enthusiasm; it suited his view of the need for change in the Bank. He could hardly have anticipated how important the program would become in time as a source of candidates for the middle and senior management cadre of the Bank and as a vehicle to buttress the preeminence of economic thinking in the Bank's work.

The Pressure of Population and Debt Service

The optimism of the 1950s about the achievements and prospects of the developing countries gave way to a much more critical attitude in the 1960s. Backed by the evidence assembled by his economists, Woods spent much time emphasizing the difficulties faced by the developing member countries of the Bank. In an informal address to the Council on Foreign Relations, he said, "It will not come as news to you if I say that the economic position of most of the underdeveloped countries is not favorable. Their food production per head is not higher today than it was ten years ago. . . . In terms of overall growth, some countries are standing still; too many others are creeping forward at rates of per capita income growth far below what they could and they must achieve."[55]

Woods considered the growth of population one of the major obstacles to economic improvement, but he stopped short of claiming a role for the Bank in this field:

> Looming over many of the underdeveloped countries is the problem of population growth. At the present rate, the population of the world will double in less than forty years; and most of this increase will take place in the underdeveloped countries. India alone adds to her population every two years the equivalent of a country as big as Canada. Simply to maintain their present low levels of nutrition, housing and facilities for education and public health, the less developed countries will have to double their rates of production. Something like two-thirds of all the new investment they can afford to make must be devoted to the needs of new population rather than to lifting living standards. Each country, within the framework of its own culture and its own social values, must decide for itself whether and if so by what means to control population growth. The importance of this issue can hardly be overemphasized.[56]

Woods saw the burden of external debt service as a major difficulty for the developing countries. He saw the problem less as the result of excessive borrowing—"as long as a country needs net capital inflow and can use it productively, there is nothing inconsistent between growing indebtedness and growing economic strength"—than as one due to the interest rates and the structure of the debt.[57] At the UNCTAD meeting of March 1964 he observed that the public indebtedness of the developing countries had increased two-and-a-half times during the preceding seven years, while debt service payments had risen by almost four times over the same seven-year period.[58] Appeals to the industrial countries to soften the terms of their assistance and exhortations to the developing countries to shun the onerous terms of suppliers' credits thus became important concerns of his presidency.

As a banker, Woods had a keen sense of the financial position of the developing countries and recognized that the number of countries able to meet their investment needs by borrowing on conventional terms was steadily diminishing. "If the pace of development in [the poor] countries is to be maintained without overloading them with external obligations, then ways must be found to assist them more and more with grants or with credits carrying lenient financial terms."[59] This also strongly affected his view of the importance of IDA assistance. In his first formal address as president of the Bank, he was ready to conclude that "within the World Bank group of institutions, it is clear that in the normal course of things, an increased proportion of the total of our development financing should come from IDA" (14). His emphasis on a greater role for IDA was also a reflection of his belief that multilateral assistance would work more efficiently than bilateral assistance and that an international organization would be more sensitive to the subtlety and complexity of the issues involved in development.

Although Woods remained emphatic about the need for more aid on better terms, he understood that the flow of external capital was only part of the solution. As sources of foreign exchange for developing countries, export revenues were four times larger than investment and aid flows, and so export activities were a significant source of further growth. For this reason Woods felt that international action to stabilize and increase the export trade of developing countries was imperative and an essential complement of meaningful development assistance.[60] Consistent with this view, he took a close personal interest in the studies the Bank undertook as the result of the first UNCTAD conference on schemes to stabilize commodity prices and particularly on the so-called supplementary finance scheme, which envisaged Bank assistance somewhat comparable to the IMF's Compensatory Finance Facility.[61]

Above all, however, Woods believed that successful development depended on the actions of the developing countries themselves. The industrial countries could provide more generous financial and technical assistance, they could establish a more favorable trade environment, but "the development process itself is essentially a matter of domestic effort, for which no amount of external help can be a substitute."[62] Woods knew the impediments frequently created by politics or narrow self-interest in the governments of developing countries. He called for policies and conditions that would be conducive to productive investment. Political and financial stability was obviously a basic prerequisite. Reform of the system of land tenure or the tax regime might be needed to provide incentives for productive investment. At the very least, Woods thought, rational and sensible policies could stimulate domestic saving and prevent the flight of domestic capital resources.

Finding the Necessary Resources

When Woods took charge of the Bank, the resources available to IDA were almost all committed. Contrary to the expectation at the time when IDA was established—that the funds would be sufficient for at least five years—they were exhausted after only three years, as a consequence of both the difficulties encountered by the Bank's established members and the needs of the growing number of new members, particularly in Africa. Black had initiated discussions about a replenishment of IDA's resources. Woods took up the issue with vigor when he joined the Bank, and by the end of 1963 he could note with satisfaction that, under the lead of the United States, the principal donors had agreed to replenish IDA's resources roughly in the amount of their original subscriptions.

This first replenishment benefited from the generally positive attitude toward foreign aid, which had led to a steady increase in aid flows throughout the 1950s and into the 1960s. There was much optimism about the prospects of the developing countries. The United Nations designated the 1960s as the development decade, with the implication that by the end of that decade the task of development would be substantially accomplished. Woods's presidency started on this optimistic note. However, the mood soon changed. In 1965 Woods noted that the net flow of long-term capital from the industrial to the developing countries was stagnating at about $6 billion despite a significant rise in the income of the industrial countries. At the same time the absorptive capacity of the developing countries had steadily increased as their institutions strengthened, skill levels improved, and the portfolio of well-prepared projects expanded. Woods had asked his economists to come up with an estimate of additional aid requirements based on the Bank's assessment of individual country needs. This estimate suggested that the developing countries could productively use an additional $3 billion to $4 billion a year. This convinced Woods that "the present level of finance is wholly inadequate, whether measured by the growth rate which the advanced countries say they are willing to facilitate or in terms of the amount of external capital which the developing countries have demonstrated they can use effectively."[63]

His conviction led Woods to propose a much more ambitious target for IDA's second replenishment, which he started to negotiate in 1965. He thought that the amount should be quadrupled so that IDA would be able to commit $1 billion annually, "a good round figure."[64] But the environment had changed, and it proved impossible to generate the support necessary to carry through his ambitious proposal. In particular, the United States was reluctant to support such an increase in IDA funding because it was by then running a consistent balance of payments deficit and was otherwise preoccupied with poverty programs at home and with the Vietnam War abroad.

The size of Woods's proposal and his method of negotiation were partly to blame for the failure of the IDA negotiations—or at least for the long delay of the second replenishment. Instead of the envisioned $1 billion per year, the second replenishment provided $400 million per year. That was still a substantial increase over the preceding level, but the second replenishment did not become effective until July 1969, three years after the first replenishment resources had been fully committed. Whereas the earlier negotiations had been conducted by the United States—by far the largest contributor—Woods thought it would be more appropriate for the Bank to take the lead in the current negotiations. This may well have reflected the wishes of the U.S. Treasury, which must have felt reluctant to play a leading role in an exercise that posed difficult domestic issues for the United States. One problem, for example, was that the U.S. share of IDA-funded procurement at that time fell far short of the amount of the United States' 40 percent contribution to IDA. The more troublesome aspect of the replenishment negotiations was the way Woods went about dealing with the principal contributors.

Woods followed his experience in negotiating complex financial deals by bargaining separately with the various partners and keeping the overall picture to himself. Instead of calling a meeting of the donors and presenting them with his plans for IDA, he decided to tackle the donors one by one "as though he was fighting a battle."[65] He decided to concentrate first on the United States as the largest contributor and as one that, despite balance of payments problems, would be sympathetic to the proposal of a substantial increase. He followed up with the Germans, British, and French. The *Economist* commented, "It seems curious that a regular committee procedure has not been adopted to thrash this matter out. Indeed, it seems incredible. Mr. Woods apparently believes in multilateral giving but bilateral asking."[66] Woods felt that the *Economist*'s "petulant" complaint was uncalled for and asked John Miller, the head of the Bank's Paris office, to explain that there had been a meeting of donors but that the absence of budgetary decisions by some major donors made further meetings futile: "In the interim I was doing the 'one-by-one' meetings, which I still think laid a useful groundwork."[67] Woods did not appreciate the working of bureaucracies. He concentrated on trying to persuade key, largely political individuals who he thought were sympathetic to his views. In the process he alienated the responsible staff, who felt that Woods was "trying to run around them."[68]

In the end, Woods's tactics did not succeed, and he had to delegate the task to vice president Burke Knapp. Knapp called a meeting of the representatives of the donor governments and put in place a process of close consultations that eventually led to an agreement. It became clear that the amount proposed by Woods was far more than donors could be persuaded to contribute at the time. Woods had, indeed, achieved a sizable increase, from $250 million to $400 million per year, but the agreement might have been concluded a year or two earlier.[69] The delayed replenishment meant that IDA commitments, instead of rising, actually dropped sharply to $107 million in fiscal year 1968, the final year of the Woods presidency. IDA was able to function in the interval thanks in large part to "extraordinary support" given in the form of voluntary contributions by Canada, the Netherlands, the Nordic countries, and Switzerland. [70]

Woods's problem of mobilizing resources was not confined to IDA. The balance of payments difficulties of the United States, which made the United States reluctant to increase IDA contributions without such safeguards as tying the use of funds, also affected the U.S. Treasury's response to the Bank's requests to raise resources in the U.S. capital market. When the Bank wanted to borrow in New York in 1965, the Treasury, responding to strong congressional concerns about the Bank's impact on the U.S. balance of payments, refused to grant the required permission.[71] Woods's strained relations with Treasury Secretary Henry Fowler did not help matters.[72] Raising the funds required to support the operations of the IBRD thus became another major concern for Woods.

Attempts to diversify the Bank's sources of capital beyond the modest beginnings made by Black proved only partly successful. "Tight money conditions disappointed our expectations that we would enter several European markets during the year," Woods reported to the governors in 1966. "A banker without money is like a doctor without pills. . . . with the widespread shortage of capital, the World Bank and IDA are facing a serious financial problem."[73] A year later the situation had not improved. "For the second consecutive year," Woods told the annual meeting in Rio de Janeiro, "I must report to you that finding finance for the operations of the Bank and IDA is a dominant continuing problem."[74]

In the circumstances, it is not surprising that Woods began to worry "that the Bank might not be able to borrow the funds it needed to meet its obligations to its borrowers."[75] In fact, Bank annual commitments declined from a peak of over $1 billion in fiscal year 1965 to around $850 million in the following three years. Richard Demuth, a member of the president's council and a close observer, thought that Woods's self-confidence was affected by these developments so "that at one point he put a stop to all Bank lending . . . . which was a rather remarkable step for a president to take."[76]

Impatience with India's Development

The difficulties Woods encountered in raising resources for the Bank and IDA were due only in part to the financial strains experienced by major donor governments. They also reflected a growing skepticism about the progress the developing countries had achieved as a result of the support provided by the Bank Group and bilaterally. The optimism about the economic prospects of the developing countries that had spurred the industrial countries to ever greater generosity in the 1950s had given way to impatient questions about the length of time and further assistance required to bring the developing countries to the "takeoff" stage. Such questions were asked with particular insistence about India, which had been a focus of attention for the Bank from the beginning. "No country has been studied more by the World Bank than India, and it is no exaggeration to say that India has influenced the Bank as much as the Bank has influenced India."[77]

India had a special place in Woods's heart and mind. Since his first visit in 1952, he had been fascinated by India—by its potential, its people, and its history; he felt challenged by its problems, its poverty, and its size. Woods had come to know India well in the course of a number of business and private visits. He had established warm and friendly relations with many of India's leading businessmen and their families, and he had met and established rapport with Prime Minister Nehru and many of his ministers, especially Morarji Desai, who was deputy prime minister and finance minister in the mid-1960s. The active correspondence he carried on with many of them into his years in retirement conveys a sense of affection, a willingness to be helpful, and a feeling of committed friendship. He once remarked, "If the only thing I do while I am president of the Bank is to turn India around, I'll be happy."[78]

In his efforts to help India, Woods pushed the Bank to innovative approaches. He was persuaded that output in India suffered from shortages of raw materials and spare parts, which India could not import because of its lack of foreign exchange. Lending for new facilities would not help in this situation, so the Bank began to provide funds for raw materials and spare parts to India through a series of annual program loans. Woods strongly favored Bank-IDA lending policies that would allow what he called "maintenance import loans." In the financial policy committee of the executive board he argued, "We should be prepared, in addition to normal project loans, to make available, in appropriate cases, long-term financing for the import of components and spare parts for industry generally or for some particular segment of industry of special importance to the given economy."[79] The major shareholders of the Bank accepted this departure from the established project-lending concept with considerable hesitation, and each program loan presented to the Board for approval became an occasion to reexamine in detail the justification for an exception from the norm.

Even more controversial was Woods's decision that the Bank should participate in a debt relief exercise. Although India was never in danger of defaulting on its debt, debt service absorbed a substantial portion of its export earnings and deprived the economy of critical free foreign exchange. In addition to program and commodity assistance, Woods considered arrangements that would ease the burden of debt service, as a particularly effective form of assistance. To induce India's official creditors to grant debt relief, he decided that the Bank, as one of India's major creditors, should make a contribution. While discussions with the members of the India Consortium proceeded, he decided that the Bank would place up to $50 million from India's debt service payments for 1967–68 on deposit in the Reserve Bank of India.[80] Subsequently, the Bank participated in the debt relief agreement negotiated with the consortium members for the four-year period starting April 1, 1967, in the amount of $15 million per year. This remains the only case in which the Bank participated with other official creditors in general debt relief. Both arrangements proved controversial. A number of executive directors questioned the legality of the deposit scheme and the wisdom of becoming involved in debt relief. But Woods persisted, and the executive directors adopted his recommendation "on participation in Indian debt relief action" less than two weeks before he left the Bank.[81]

Woods failed in his ambition to "turn India around." In fact, his motives were questioned by influential Indian policymakers and the media in India. His attempt to help India achieve a decisive breakthrough coincided with a downswing in the relations between India and the Bank. Mason and Asher captured the change in the relationship:

> Underlying the history of Bank relations with India has been the broad trend of "fashionable" thinking about the subcontinent. As it gradually became involved, the Bank—like other external sources of assistance—was appalled by India's poverty, dazzled by its size and by the prestige of being active there, and impressed by the articulateness of its political leaders and top-level civil servants and by the high priority they accorded to economic development. . . . A decade later the mood had changed to one of disenchantment—with planning, with India, with infrastructure. . . . What had previously been viewed as technical excellence in India was characterized as doctrinaire arrogance. Partly as a result of the overblown expectations of an earlier period, India was seen as a bottomless pit, absorbing vast amounts of aid with little or no visible results. [82]

Since 1958 India had received substantial assistance through the India Consortium chaired by the Bank. The consortium had been organized to address an acute foreign exchange crisis, but once established, it continued to serve as a convenient coordinating mechanism backed by a tacit commitment to underwrite India's foreign exchange needs. The early years of India's third five-year plan (1961–65) represented a high point in the workings of the consortium. Members pledged well over $1 billion per year in development assistance, with 20 percent of that amount provided by the Bank. This favorable situation soon changed, however. Bank missions in 1962 and 1963 reported that India's income growth was disappointing, falling well short of the plan's targets. The reports blamed the management of the Indian economy.

Against this background and the desire of the major donors to be reassured about the Indian government's program, the Bank decided in 1964, with the less-than-enthusiastic agreement of the Indian government, to carry out a comprehensive review of the country's economy. The Bell mission, named for its leader Bernard Bell, recommended many policy changes, including simplification of the elaborate control system and steps to facilitate the introduction of intensified agricultural production. In return, the mission supported India's request for additional assistance, especially quick-disbursing assistance. The role of the mission thus foreshadowed the approach the Bank followed fifteen years later in its support of structural adjustment. The focus was on the balance of payments, specifically on the need to devalue.

There is some evidence that Woods was initially opposed to any Bank discussion of the exchange rate. Benjamin King, the Bank's resident representative in India at the time, recalled making the case that the Bank should examine the exchange rate: "He [Woods] was quite tough in his arguing against it but he did concede at the end that the Bank did have a legitimate reason for discussing exchange rates."[83] Woods accepted the recommendations of the Bell mission that a liberalization of the control system and a devaluation were essential. He informed the Indians that they could not expect the high level of assistance—especially quick-disbursing program aid, which they counted on for the fourth five-year plan—unless they undertook the recommended policy reforms. The IMF agreed that the devaluation was essential, and the United States lined up with the Bank and the IMF to press for devaluation and import liberalization.

In response to the pressure exerted by the Bank-led consortium, and in the expectation that the Bank would persuade consortium members to provide $900 million a year of commodity aid in addition to project and food aid, the Indian government devalued the rupee by 36 percent in June 1966. However, the devaluation failed to have the desired impact on the economy. S. Boothalingam, the responsible secretary in the ministry of finance at the time the decision to devalue was taken, thought the pervasive control system had quickly neutralized the impact of the devaluation and concluded that the devaluation "was not allowed to work."[84] The devaluation was too small to stimulate a major shift into export production, and it coincided with a succession of two serious droughts, which required massive food imports and induced a sharp recession.

The consortium provided the promised assistance for one year, but a sharp decline in U.S. aid and the hiatus in the replenishment of IDA led to a drop in aid commitments. Although the responsible officials and ministers saw the need for economic reform, the Indian political establishment and the press were furious (134ff.). They had deeply resented the criticism of their performance and the pressure for reform. The need for devaluation was seen as a price to pay for the necessary foreign assistance, and when this assistance failed to materialize, many Indian officials and politicians and the press cried foul. They held Woods responsible for the debacle and "never quite forgave Woods."[85]

The event that many in India took as confirmation of Woods's negative disposition toward India was the speech he gave at the second UNCTAD meeting in Delhi in February 1968. In it he described the staggering problems of the developing countries, with some criticism of their political and economic performance, but he also emphasized that there is need for "greater modesty and realism in expectations" on the part of the aid donors. The principal message of the speech was a call for an "improvement in the amounts and terms of capital transfers" to the developing countries. What was heard most clearly in India, however, and caused much fuss, was the following paragraph in the introduction:

> We must be frank to say that in many parts of the world, the situation is discouraging, even disturbing. Here in our host country, the home of one-seventh of all the human race, after twenty years of independence many millions of people have

yet to experience more than the feeblest manifestations of progress. Those who believe as I do that India is engaged in a task of deep meaning for all the developing countries, must be gravely concerned by the uncertainties that cloud her national life. India is an exceptionally dramatic case because of its size and its location on the troubled Asian continent; but it is by no means the only country where hope has dwindled toward despondency. [86]

This candid exposition of the state of affairs in India did not go down well in a country that was sensitive to criticism in normal circumstances and certainly on an occasion that was meant to underline its leadership role in the world. Woods was quite willing to accommodate requests by his friend Deputy Prime Minister Desai to tone down the most offensive passages in the published version of the speech. But the damage was done. He had become a very unpopular man in India.

Tensions under Woods

Just as Woods's involvement with India was clouded by disappointment, his role as president of the Bank was overshadowed by tensions. Richard Demuth thought he saw a sharp distinction between the first and the second half of Woods's tenure. He saw the first years as "a time of real decision making" and "good initiatives" and the last two years as a "calamity."[87] The Bank's historians, Edward Mason and Robert Asher, came to the same conclusion: "Frustrated and often suffering from nervous exhaustion during the latter half of his tenure, he became progressively more irascible and undiplomatic."[88] His failure to achieve agreement on a second IDA replenishment, which he had himself turned into a central theme of his presidency, and his inability to assist effectively in achieving the transformation of the Indian economy were no doubt important factors contributing to the change. Some also attributed the change to Woods's health problems; he had had a severe heart attack in 1954 and major surgery at the end of his first year in the Bank. However, this factor was dismissed by those who had known him for a long time; to them Woods had been "always that way."[89]

Much of Woods's behavior had its roots in his personality. He had a notable temper, and a number of able people in the Bank came to grief because he held them responsible for some matter which had displeased him.[90] Woods would react vindictively to anything he perceived as a slight. Airlines and hotels could become the targets of his wrath if he was bumped off a flight or denied a room. His biographer, Robert Oliver, describes how Woods vented his anger where he was relegated to economy class by an airline on a flight to Manila.[91] Woods attributed a similar incident in Africa to a lack of attention by American Express, the Bank's long-standing travel agency; he canceled the contract with American Express and insisted that the Bank handle travel arrangements on its own.

Part of Woods's problem was that he always saw himself as an outsider in the Bank. His strengths were his intelligence, his broad vision, and his forcefulness. Despite his long and close links with the Bank, however, he was not successful in dealing with its entrenched establishment. When he was tough, he generated resentment and opposition, not compliance.[92] Woods worked hard to understand how the Bank functioned. At the end of his first year in the Bank, he wrote to Davidson Sommers, the Bank's former general counsel, who had advised him, "Thinking over the year, it seems to me that one of the important accomplishments, if not the most important, has been my education on the strengths and weaknesses of the staff of the Bank, how it functions and how its activities are interrelated."[93] Although the Bank was familiar to him and he had known many of the senior staff even before he became its president, he did not have the involvement in the Bank that he had with First Boston, a bank that he knew intimately because he had grown with it. He was missing colleagues whom he knew he could trust and who, like Coggeshall, complemented him and would handle the aspects of the job that he found uninspiring and that tested his patience. Notwithstanding his firm belief in the importance of support to the developing countries and the superiority of multilateral assistance, he was skeptical about the capacity of the World Bank and the commitment of its staff. He complained to Irving Friedman about the "country club atmosphere" in the Bank and the lack of dedication of the staff.[94] He reflected a view that was quite common in the late 1950s and early 1960s among outside observers in the United States, especially in the U.S. government, who compared the volume of the Bank's lending with the institution's size and importance and concluded that the Bank was "long on public relations, but short on performance."[95]

Tension was growing between Woods and the executive directors, so much so that Edwin Dale of the *New York Times,* in his report on Woods's last annual meeting, referred to "unpublicized friction."[96] Woods was not accustomed to spending long hours with his board of directors, and he lacked a taste for political and procedural nuances. He tended to become irritated by the amount of time wasted on what he regarded as trivia. In the circumstances, it was not surprising that Woods found it difficult to deal with a resident board of directors that did not consider its role limited to policymaking but sought to extend it into the day-to-day activities of the Bank.

Woods "argued aggressively with board members. He was very blunt and outspoken."[97] This aggressive and involved style reflected his nature, his "jagged, powerful mind," which stood in marked contrast to the "elegant, rounded features" of his predecessor's personality.[98] His arguments with the board were sometimes "not really so much on policy issues or what he wanted to do, but on personality issues, and the Board meetings . . . became contests between the different Directors and the President."[99] "There were directors who disliked him and whom he disliked, and this was well known. You could see the sparks flying across the room."[100] As his frustrations about IDA and India grew, the level of tension increased and began to characterize the atmosphere in the board room. "It got so bad his last year," Broches recalled, "that when McNamara came every Director told him, 'Whatever you do, don't act like Woods. Don't have confrontations.'"[101]

Woods had a relationship of mutual respect with the Cuban director Louis Machado, the dean of the board, who had served on it since 1946. He also had high regard for Pieter Lieftinck, the Dutch director, and his views. Woods invited Lieftinck to head a major study of the water and power resources of Pakistan—an unusual task for a sitting member of the board. Lieftinck appreciated this challenge and was grateful to Woods for the assignment.[102] Lieftinck did not remember the Woods years as a period of tension and growing confrontation; his view was that there may have been more debate because there was greater awareness of the importance of development financing. He thought that Woods ran the board in an open, democratic fashion: "I had the highest regard for Gene Black, but it was considered a little unusual to go against Gene Black, to quarrel with him. George Woods did not give the impression of a man who would take it amiss if you expressed a different opinion, so I do think that discussion may have been more lively under George Woods ... but I don't remember more intense discussions or more differences of opinion appearing under George Woods than Gene Black" (16). Although Lieftinck's memory may have been colored by the sharp contrast he saw in the roles of the executive directors during the Black and Woods years and the subsequent McNamara era, his recollections would seem to confirm that Woods's problems with the board were essentially caused by his bluntness. He was ready to accept that the members of the board played an important part in establishing the policies of the institution, but he also recognized that they had their own axes to grind, and he thought it was his role "to resist these self-serving interests of the Board and to keep his eye on the overall good of the membership."[103]

The disappointment over the second IDA replenishment also affected Woods's relations with the U.S. government, with which Woods stayed in close touch. He had regular contact with the treasury secretaries, especially his old friend Douglas Dillon. He was also on fairly close and personal terms with President Johnson, who occasionally sought Woods's advice and wrote to him acknowledging that "the advice and counsel that you pass along to me are always received with high favor and gratitude."[104] Lieftinck observed that Woods tended to be sensitive to the views of the U.S. government. "When he got a signal from the U.S. government that he should not make a loan. . ., he was ready to respond—perhaps more than staff wanted."[105] He was particularly anxious to avoid anything that could affect U.S. support for IDA. This is why he curtailed the staff's first-class travel privileges and why he rejected managing director Pierre-Paul Schweitzer's invitation to join the IMF in creating the Bretton Woods recreation center for the staff. All the greater, therefore, was his disappointment that the U.S. administration and Congress did not support his proposals for the second IDA replenishment. Toward the end of his tenure, Woods was often at odds with the U.S. director over the approach to IDA and the U.S. government's criticism of the Bank's staff "as a band of happy Sybarites living on the public purse."[106] Woods felt betrayed by the Johnson administration; his feelings about the secretary of the treasury, Henry Fowler, were said to be "unprintable" (17).

Woods came to the Bank with sensible ideas about reforming the institution's management style. He tried to replace the exclusive reliance on the president's office for decisionmaking that had been a hallmark of the Bank under Black with a more participatory approach, and to this end he established the president's council. The council's membership included, apart from the two vice presidents, the senior department heads in charge of the key aspects of the Bank's work. This was a much-needed broadening of the Bank's top management in response to the growing size and complexity of the Bank.[107] Woods used the council, which initially met every morning, to keep informed and as a forum to test his ideas before making decisions.[108]

Although the president's council reflected Woods's desire to reach out and to bring a collective perspective to leadership and decisionmaking, the atmosphere in the council was evidently less than friendly and harmonious. Rainer Steckhan, Woods's discreet personal assistant in his last two years at the Bank, reports, "Woods could be very harsh with people." (5). Burke Knapp agrees: "George could be severe with people to the point of being rough."[109] This roughness and his tendency to bring a personal edge into his arguments proved difficult for many and shaped his reputation. But to Woods this was a way of testing people. He did not take it amiss when people contradicted him, and it was not unusual for him to yield in an argument after first having disagreed vigorously—and sometimes unpleasantly. Many of his colleagues thought that Knapp, who worked most closely with Woods, must have had a difficult time. Knapp admits that his relationship was not as easy as it had been with Black but remembers that he was "happy" in his work "feeling that I had a boss who understood what we were trying to do together" (11).

Woods tended to develop strong views about people on the basis of his opinion of their intelligence. He "liked people to stand up to him" and "didn't like it when people were not sort of straight with him."[110] "If he had confidence in you," Roger Chaufournier—whom Woods had promoted to deputy director of the Western Hemisphere department—thought, "it was very good to work with him."[111] Many staff members who came in touch with Woods remember his personal warmth and understanding. For example, the resident representative in India failed to meet Woods at the airport, and Woods's personal assistant caused him to be late for a crucial meeting with the Indian prime minister. These incidents might have produced anger in less sensitive people, but Woods dismissed them as understandable accidents and told the two staff members not to worry.[112]

In the end, however, the tensions associated with Woods reinforced the disagreeable image created by his blunt and abrasive behavior. He had no talent for popularity, and perhaps no desire to be popular. He lacked the ability to be pleasant to people whom he disliked and with whom he fundamentally disagreed. He regarded as wasteful the time spent establishing who would be credited for success. As a result, his important achievements in the Bank and in the cause of development have been too little recognized.

Woods's Grand Assize

Woods's presidency was a period of unusual ferment in the field of economic development. The sluggish economic performance of the developing countries in Asia and Latin America contrasted sharply with the postwar prosperity in Europe and Japan. In addition, the claims of the newly independent countries in Africa made more apparent the true dimensions of the development challenge. The significance and focus of development assistance changed in response to these trends, and the Bank had to adjust to remain relevant. Woods had a clear sense of the changes that were taking place and encouraged the necessary adjustments.

The Bank had already started to change in the direction of a broader-based and more development-oriented institution during Black's presidency. This shift became more pronounced and explicit under Woods. The horizons of the Bank's activity expanded, the IFC was given a push, economic analysis took on a central role, and aid coordination through a growing number of consultative groups enhanced the Bank's role and the strategic focus of its own assistance. Where Black had welcomed the creation of IDA with considerable caution, Woods recognized that concessional assistance was critical to the Bank's mission.

Woods saw the need to accelerate economic progress in the developing world as one of the important challenges of his time. "It is certain," he concluded his address to the Bank's shareholders in 1966, "that the last third of the twentieth century belongs to the problems of the two-thirds of mankind which are economically the least well situated. There is plenty in the record to show that these problems *can* be met; but meeting them will require strenuous efforts and new thinking by developed and developing countries alike."[113] This challenge is what had brought him to the Bank and inspired his eloquent appeals for development assistance.

In the process he attempted to define the complexities of the development process and emphasized, in particular, the burden resulting from the accelerating growth of population. He attempted to estimate the capital requirements the developing countries needed for reasonably rapid progress and to relate this estimate to his proposals for additional contributions to IDA. It was his misfortune that his appeals for more generous assistance fell into a period of budgetary constraints in the principal donor countries and growing skepticism about the effectiveness of foreign aid. When President John F. Kennedy proposed at the 1961 General Assembly meeting of the United Nations that the 1960s be declared the first United Nations development decade, there were high hopes that the relatively modest targets for growth in the developing countries and for the transfer of resources from the rich to the poor countries could be met. By 1967, however, the momentum of the development decade had evaporated. Nobody was more aware of the diminishing interest in development matters, and nobody was more concerned about it, than George Woods.

He was, therefore, happy to accept an invitation by Lord Boyle, the chancellor of Sussex University, a former treasury minister and minister of education, to spend a weekend with like-minded people who had expertise in the development effort and commitment to it. The gathering, organized by William Clark in April 1967, included Woods's friend Barbara Ward, who had just been appointed by Pope Paul VI to the Pontifical Commission on Justice and Peace, and René Maheu, the director-general of UNESCO. The weekend discussions concluded that the most promising way to revive the flagging cause would be to establish a commission of authoritative experts to examine the state of development and propose to political leaders and to the public at large the steps necessary for maintaining hope and progress.[114]

Woods took up the proposal with enthusiasm and agreed that the Bank would support it with the needed staff and financial resources. He decided that an address that he had agreed to give to the Swedish Bankers Association in October 1967 would be an appropriate occasion to present the proposal. The address, written with the assistance of Barbara Ward, was one of his finest. It spelled out his belief that "the plight of the developing peoples—of the two-thirds of humanity who are striving to cross the threshold of modernization—is *the* central drama of our times" (2).[115] He saw the East-West conflict diminishing and the disparity between the rich countries in the North and the poor countries in the South becoming "the basic threat to our world" (9). The main reason why the problems of development cannot be resolved by relying "on the 'normal' methods of international trade and investment" was, in his view, that "the spurt of population [growth] is taking place *ahead* of the means of feeding and absorbing it" (6). He attributed the declining enthusiasm for support to the developing countries not to the fiscal and balance of payments problems of the donor countries but to "discouragement and skepticism about the general effectiveness of aid to development" (8). In the circumstances, he felt it was essential to disperse "the gray fog of suspicion and discouragement" (4) and to show "that in fact the record of the developing nations is far better than the popular image suggests" (8). For this purpose he proposed a "grand assize" on development: the donor governments would "invite the dozen or more leading world experts in the field of development to meet together, study the consequences of twenty years of development assistance, assess the results, clarify the errors and propose the policies which will work better in the future" (9).

Although Woods did not stay long enough to see his proposal materialize, it epitomized the visionary quality of his leadership of the Bank. He had presided over the transformation of the Bank from an essentially conservative financial institution into a development institution by redirecting its focus and resources to the analysis of the development phenomenon and the support of more relevant economic activities. He had emphasized the importance of IDA as a critical source of assistance for the growing membership of the Bank, especially in Africa. He pressed for a sharp increase in the Bank's volume of activity. His proposal of the "grand assize" represented a claim for a larger, global role of the Bank in correcting the disparity between rich and poor, North and South. It was left to his successor to elaborate further the scope of the Bank's activities and to enlarge the size of the Bank to assume this global position.

CHAPTER FIVE

Robert S. McNamara

Champion of the Developing World

A s George Woods approached the end of his term as president of the World Bank, he turned to his predecessors, Black and McCloy, for advice on finding a suitable successor. They told him it was up to him to find somebody to relieve him. Woods reflected on the qualifications required by the job for the following five to ten years and concluded that "it might be well to look away from the investment banking and the banker fraternity."[1] He recognized that the task confronting the Bank involved a great deal more than making loans and that "the problems of economic development, which [was] the Bank's principal business, [were] one of the two or three most important influences which will determine the course of international events over the rest of this century" (4). The man Woods thought would be ideally qualified to run the World Bank—although he was doubtful about his availability—was Robert S. McNamara. "Secretary McNamara has for a long time had a deep interest in these [economic development] problems and he will bring to them qualities of creative imagination and leadership which are unexcelled" (3).

Woods and McNamara knew each other slightly before they both came to Washington; once in Washington, they maintained contact. It was McNamara's address before the American Society of Newspaper Editors in Montreal in May 1966, in which he equated security and development, that impressed Woods and led him to think of McNamara as a possible successor. He broached the subject with McNamara over lunch in April 1967. McNamara listened and expressed curiosity and interest but remained noncommittal.[2] Following the meeting in April, Woods and McNamara kept in touch. Woods sent McNamara copies of important reports, illustrations of the Bank's activities, and speeches he was giving; there were occasional meetings and social occasions, which kept the dialogue going.

In the summer of 1967 McNamara indicated to Woods his interest in the job but maintained that he could not predict when he might be released from his responsibilities as secretary of defense. Because of this uncertainty, Woods negotiated with the executive directors an extension of his five-year contract by one year or until his successor would be found. He expected that McNamara would be available toward the end of 1968, after the U.S. presidential elections, so that this arrangement would provide a suitable bridge.[3]

A Very Different President

McNamara's interest in the presidency of the World Bank increased along with his disenchantment with the Vietnam War. The World Bank seemed to be an attractive challenge following the exhausting years in charge of the Defense Department. The Bank, with its focus on conditions in developing countries, also seemed to be the right place to put into practice the conclusions reflected in his Montreal speech—that those conditions represented a potential threat to peace and stability. It was left to President Johnson to make the decision that McNamara would go to the Bank. McNamara had mentioned his interest in the Bank to him, and Johnson could not help but notice his disenchantment with the Vietnam War ("he's gone dovish on me," Johnson said).[4] So, in mid-November Johnson instructed his treasury secretary to propose McNamara as the candidate to succeed Woods.

In a press release on November 30, President Johnson informed the surprised American public, "Some time ago, Mr. McNamara reported to me that Mr. Woods had talked to him about succeeding Mr. Woods as president of the Bank. Mr. McNamara said that he was interested in the World Bank post as an opportunity for continued service. He assured me of his willingness to remain as Secretary of Defense so long as the President considered it to be necessary, but he believed the service would benefit from the appointment of a fresh person."[5] There was much speculation about how much this change of jobs originated with McNamara and how much it was based on President Johnson's decision to put somebody else in charge of the crucial defense portfolio. McNamara said, "I do not know to this day whether I quit or was fired. Maybe it was both."[6] It seems obvious that his departure reflected a mutual recognition of the need to part.[7]

On November 30, following an embarrassing premature announcement of his appointment in the *Financial Times,* the executive directors unanimously elected McNamara to succeed Woods. However, a date for his move to the Bank had yet to be set. Eventually it was agreed that McNamara would leave the Pentagon following the preparation of its next budget on February 29, 1968, and would become president of the Bank on April 1.

Woods had overseen the enhancement of the Bank as a development institution. But McNamara eschewed the cautious, Wall Street–oriented approach to development finance, adopting instead an aggressive mission that emphasized the claims and expectations of the Bank's developing member countries. The needs of the developing world became paramount in determining the volume of the Bank's activities, as well as the kind of assistance it was providing. For McNamara, the Bank had no intrinsic significance as an efficient organization that evoked loyalty. To him, the Bank was a tool for achieving the important ends he visualized. Its credit rating, the capacity of its staff, and even its preservation were of concern only in relation to that mission.

McNamara shaped the evolution of the Bank as no one before or after him. He came to the Bank brimming with energy, forceful, active, pushing to get things done. He brought with him the firm belief that the problems of the developing world could be solved. What was needed was clear analysis of those problems and determination in the application of appropriate remedies. The results could not fail to materialize. This can-do creed marked McNamara as the quintessential American. "No one would ever mistake McNamara for a European; he was American through and through, with the American drive, the American certitude and conviction," David Halberstam wrote.[8] This optimism became the dominating theme guiding the institution and, inevitably, turned it into "McNamara's Bank."

The Whiz Kid

Robert Strange McNamara was born on June 9, 1916, in San Francisco and grew up across the bay, in Oakland. His father, the son of Irish immigrants, had worked his way up to become the sales manager of a wholesale shoe firm. Family circumstances and economic pressures had not allowed McNamara's father, or his lively and intellectually curious mother, to have much formal education. They were fiercely determined to provide their children with the educational opportunities they had been denied. "Their resolve shaped my life," is how McNamara put it.[9] The McNamaras were representative of the first-generation American family striving to succeed and living vicariously through the achievements of their children.[10]

McNamara's parents recognized early that Bob was an unusually gifted child. McNamara's sister is quoted as saying, "We had a very happy home life. The only thing nontypical about it was Bob. Even as a little boy my brother was terrific. He was something special. All of us knew he'd grow up to be something special, and I believe he has."[11] His progress through school and at the University of California at Berkeley, where he majored in economics, reflected his unusual talents. He received perfect grades and was elected to Phi Beta Kappa in his sophomore year. He was bright, with an intense intellectual curiosity. Above all, he was a compulsive worker and perfectionist.

McNamara's intelligence, his grasp of logic and mathematical concepts, was matched by his sense of purpose and diligence. His ability to concentrate and his remarkable energy carried him to the top—what one of his friends from high school called "coming to the surface" (31)—wherever he was. McNamara was reserved and did not like to show off; he was serious and firmly guided by his intellectual interests. Yet he was neither a "nerd" nor a loner. He was an emotional, warm person who always felt constrained to control his emotions through a tough regime of self-discipline. He became socially active and was a popular student, an active member of the student government, a fraternity member, and a member of the most prestigious honor societies. He was also active in sports. Although not well coordinated, he was tenacious and relied on his restless energy to prevail in competitive sports. Because he did not have to work too hard to maintain his excellent grades, he had time to pursue intellectual interests extending well beyond his formal courses. His economics professor regarded him as a "genuine intellectual" and expected that he would become a teacher (31).

His vivid experience of the Great Depression and the atmosphere at Berkeley shaped McNamara's liberal social outlook. However, his middle-class background and the belief that the right effort would be rewarded tempered his liberalism and "kept him from flying emotionally into causes" (32). His concern about economic and social issues, about unemployment and poverty, originated in and reflected a thoughtful awareness of the world that surrounded him; his insistence on thinking problems through and coming up with realistic solutions led him to reject extremist views.[12]

Rather than follow his intellectual interests by going to graduate school to pursue a career in academe, McNamara looked at practical considerations—such as the need for a sure route to a high-paying job—and enrolled in the Harvard Business School in 1937. It was there that he acquired the management techniques that became characteristic of his style, and there that he was taught to plan, set goals, consider options, and project consequences. There, too, he learned the principles of accounting and statistical control. "Even the name of this new field suited McNamara's emerging personality. . . . In all variants, the word that had the most meaning for the stiff, cautious McNamara was control."[13] The concept of management based on the accumulation and analysis of quantitative data appealed to his disciplined mind and provided him with a tool for exercising control in uncertain conditions. McNamara had always been uncomfortable with spontaneity, improvisation, and uncertainty. He was put off by messiness and inaccuracy. Through diligent preparation he avoided the element of surprise. Statistical methods extended the range of predictability in an uncertain life; well-organized meetings suited him, but impromptu press conferences and cocktail parties made him uncomfortable.

After completing his master's degree and working for a brief spell with Price, Waterhouse & Co., McNamara returned to the Harvard Business School as an instructor. His academic career was interrupted by the outbreak of war, but the army gave him opportunities to apply his brand of management techniques and statistical methods to the movement of men and matériel. While in the military he spent six months in Calcutta to plan the flow of supplies across the Himalayas into China. There he saw firsthand, in the aftermath of the Bengal famine, the great extremes of poverty, hunger, and deprivation.

McNamara planned to return to the Harvard Business School and resume his academic career after the war was over. Instead, his friend and mentor in the military, Tex Thornton, persuaded him to join a group of wartime colleagues who intended to do for private industry what they had successfully done for the military: apply statistical controls to save money and increase efficiency. The group decided to offer its services to the Ford Motor Corporation, which was outmoded and ailing and had fallen well behind its principal competitor, General Motors. Over the opposition of more traditional automotive executives, the group of bright young people—nicknamed "whiz kids" by the weary Ford executives—introduced their new management methods and accomplished what Henry Ford II had hired them to do. The company grew rapidly, won back a large share of the market from General Motors, and saw the value of its stock soar. Despite the internal struggles, McNamara "found ways to work with [his] associates, and received a series of promotions because [he] produced results."[14] In November 1960 he became president of the Ford Motor Corporation. "If McNamara had set out specifically to seek high office in the company, no one ever learned it. He was ambitious, but his approach was rather one of dedication to the success of the company first: the rest would follow."[15] Challenge was what inspired him and what he needed most: an objective whose achievement could engage both his energy and his analytical ability. It was discipline, concentration, and relentless work that made his success inevitable. But it was his keen understanding of organizational dynamics that enabled him to prevail in an intensely competitive environment. He liked to be in charge, and he enjoyed both authority and responsibility. He understood the importance of power, and at Ford, and later in the Defense Department, he proved to be an expert in its use.

McNamara became president of Ford on November 9, 1960, the day after John F. Kennedy was elected president. A little over a month later, Kennedy introduced McNamara to the press as his secretary of defense. "After much thought," McNamara told the press corps, "I came to the conclusion that personal considerations must be subordinated to the responsibility to the President of the United States and to serve the public when requested to do so" (10). The personal considerations were considerable. He gave up a substantial salary and large unexercised stock options. What outweighed these concerns was the attraction of a new challenge: to make the national defense program more effective and develop a coherent nuclear strategy.

When McNamara took up his assignment, his mandate was to bring the military under civilian control. He would do that through the application of modern management techniques, which would also bring about improved efficiency and provide "security for the nation at the lowest possible cost."[16] The central element of McNamara's new approach was the planning-programming-budgeting system, which he used to analyze defense requirements and produce long-term, program-oriented defense budgets. "McNamara's tendency to take military advice into account less than had previous secretaries contributed to his unpopularity with service leaders."[17] His system was especially suspect among the military because it was civilian controlled and seemed to rely heavily on impersonal quantitative analysis. McNamara was undaunted by either the task or the opposition of the military. He dismissed as absurd the notion that the military was "some sort of ungovernable force." He was confident, as he later put it, that his experience as a manager allowed him to force organizations—if necessary against their will—"to think deeply and realistically about alternative courses of action and their consequences."[18]

Although McNamara had been appointed to his new job because of his managerial expertise, he quickly became involved in the substance and the politics of government administration. President Kennedy, and later President Johnson, sought his advice not only on matters related to the nation's defense but also on issues of foreign policy and international relations. Soon, however, the escalating Vietnam War claimed much of McNamara's time and energy. In the eyes of the public, he became the leader most directly responsible for the conduct of the war. His quantitative methods of assessing its progress were seen as heartless. His faith in dubious numbers fed to him by the military appeared to be the source of his upbeat pronouncements about the progress of the war—pronouncements that bore less and less resemblance to the reality portrayed by the media. In fact, McNamara had started to doubt whether the war could be won by military means. He resisted proposals to deploy more troops and to escalate the bombing, pushing instead for negotiations. Disagreements with President Johnson over the prospects and aims of the war eventually could no longer be ignored and led to his departure from the Pentagon.

His exit from the government seemed to mark the failure of the methods he had introduced. "Nobody should be under any illusions as to what his departure means," wrote Joseph Kraft in the *Washington Post*, "it expresses a failure in the managerial faith, ... a faith in manipulated settlements that went beyond old-fashioned conflicts, in arranged solutions that took all interests into account. It was faith in the manager."[19] Yet, McNamara's faith in reason and logic was not affected: as another reporter at the time concluded, "He leaves with what he came, a continuing faith in reason and logic and the processes of objective analysis."[20] Indeed, the management system he introduced in the Department of Defense became part of his lasting legacy.

The Vietnam tragedy affected McNamara deeply. The bloodshed and suffering caused by the fighting, and the futility of the war, troubled him a great deal. His methods and systems and the outcome of the war brought him for the first time a major personal defeat. Many years later, reviewing the lessons of Vietnam, he concluded, "We failed to recognize that in international affairs, as in other aspects of life, there may be problems for which there are no immediate solutions. For one whose life has been dedicated to the belief and practice of problem solving, this is particularly hard to admit. But, at times, we may have to live with an imperfect, untidy world."[21]

The awareness of his failure did not cause him to despair, nor did it affect his eagerness to take on new challenges. He was able to suppress whatever qualms he had and to concentrate single-mindedly on the task ahead. For many years, he refused to talk about the Vietnam War, and when, at the World Bank, he referred to his managerial experience, he would talk about the Ford Motor Company, not about the Pentagon. At a press conference in 1980, Lew Simons of the *Washington Post* asked McNamara whether he had gone to the World Bank "as some sort of self-imposed penance" for his contribution to the Vietnam War. He replied, "Baloney. Maybe some thought it should have been. I didn't consider it such. I considered it a marvelous opportunity."[22]

A Global Vision

President Johnson's decision to nominate McNamara as president of the Bank did not meet with immediate and unanimous approval. The executive directors had impressed on their American colleague Livingston Merchant their desire to be given a list of several names, and he had promised that they would have some choice in the matter. When the time came, however, they were given only one name, McNamara's. President Johnson, when reminded of his earlier promise, is reported to have told Secretary of the Treasury Fowler that he would agree to provide a list of candidates, as long as there was only one name on it, that of Robert McNamara.[23]

McNamara came with impressive credentials as a successful corporate executive and manager, but he had been deeply involved in politics, and his association with the controversial Vietnam War raised awkward questions. As if to confirm the doubts about his ability to remain politically impartial, he appeared on television within days of his taking over the Bank with an eloquent endorsement of his friend and former colleague Robert Kennedy for the U.S. presidency. There was consternation among the executive directors and senior staff. Apart from the principles that had been violated, the chances of getting the IDA replenishment through Congress were hardly helped by the entry of the Bank's leader into the U.S. political arena. McNamara was appropriately contrite. He told the members of the president's council that "he was sorry that he was a cause of publicity about his position at the Bank. He had turned down several offers to write about his years at the Pentagon, particularly the most recent years which were inevitably a part of current politics. But what he had had to say about the exercise of power at the time of the Cuban missile crisis was not. He had felt compelled to say it, and he had therefore said it."[24]

This was an important reminder that politics in the international arena was played according to different, more subtle, rules. It also illustrated that McNamara felt unconstrained by these rules. The incident did not dampen his enthusiasm to get on top of his new job. Indeed, he was well prepared for his task at the World Bank. For him, there was a direct link between concerns about military security and economic development. He had spent much time in the Pentagon reflecting on the threat to the security of the free world. Stimulated by presidential adviser W. W. Rostow, he recognized that without economic prosperity, military security would be a fragile accomplishment. Gaining the allegiance of the developing countries through the provision of economic assistance had long been an accepted practice. For McNamara the threat of violence and warfare was not just an aspect of the cold war; it was above all a consequence of the widening gap in incomes between the industrial and developing countries and the resulting economic insecurity. In his Montreal speech in May 1966 he came to a poignant conclusion: "In a modernizing society security means development. Security is not military hardware, though it may include it; security is not military force, though it may involve it; security is not traditional military activity, though it may encompass it. Security is development, and without development there can be no security. A developing nation that does not, in fact, develop simply cannot remain secure for the intractable reason that its own citizenry cannot shed its human nature."[25]

McNamara had been led to the World Bank by the logic of his reflections as secretary of defense. He hit the ground running; within the first few weeks he revealed the plans that he had for the Bank, that he pursued consistently throughout his tenure. To him the World Bank was "an innovative, problem-solving mechanism . . . to help fashion a better life for mankind in the decades ahead."[26] In setting his objectives, he did not feel constrained by the Bank's tradition of financial prudence. The daunting problems faced by the world required daring and risk-taking. In his first address to the governors he proclaimed, "The parable of the talents is a parable about power—about financial power—and it illuminates the great truth that all power is given us to be used, not to be wrapped in a napkin against risk."[27]

McNamara believed firmly that the Bank was an institution with the potential to reduce the global tensions and the long-term threat to security that he perceived. The determining consideration for him was the needs of the developing countries. It was obvious to him that the developing countries needed more assistance than they had been receiving. Accordingly, he set out "to create in the Bank a critical mass of power, both financial and technical, sufficient to accelerate the rate of development in the poorer countries to a high but sustainable level."[28] He recognized that the Bank could not handle the job by itself. "I do not believe," he told the Bank's governors in 1968, "that the Bank can go it alone and do the job of development that needs to be done around the world by itself; but I do believe that it can provide the leadership in that effort, and can show that it is not resources which are lacking—for the richer countries amongst them have resources in plenty—but what is lacking, is the will to employ those resources on the development of the poorer nations."[29]

Throughout his tenure in the Bank, he struggled to gain a clear understanding of the problems the developing countries were facing. This was a personal challenge. In order to extend his knowledge, he talked eagerly with everybody who seemed to be able to offer insights and solutions. He traveled extensively to see for himself what was happening. There were many people outside the Bank who influenced his thinking. Among them, Barbara Ward and Maurice Strong played a particularly prominent role. L. K. Jha and I. G. Patel in India and Julius Nyerere, the charismatic president of Tanzania, were among the people in the developing world whose advice he sought. Inside the Bank he respected the experience of Burke Knapp and Peter Cargill, his senior vice presidents. Ernest Stern would eventually occupy a special position as intellectual foil and as the lieutenant to whom he could look to implement his plans. Most of McNamara's initiatives could be traced to interaction with particular individuals rather than to the organized institutional process. His visits to practically all the Bank's developing member countries were occasions to educate himself and to test his conclusions in discussions with leaders, officials, and ordinary people. He insisted on spending time in the field, visiting schools and population clinics, talking to farmers and extension workers. He had little time for ceremony and preferred the company of an informed, intelligent junior official to that of a senior but inarticulate government minister.

The evolution of McNamara's views was thus an intensely personal process. Pushing the Bank to be more inquisitive was also an important aspect of his leadership. The expansion of the Bank's economic research capacity under the leadership of Hollis Chenery became an important part of the institutional response to this quest for better understanding and for more effective solutions. The collection and processing of data were central aspects of the effort and were designed to allow him to make better decisions and lead more effectively.

McNamara knew that economic development was a multifaceted, multidimensional process. Yet he seemed always to be looking for some single key to this important problem. At least, he believed that some aspects of the problem were more important than others, so that the complex reality of the developing world could be brought down to a few actionable parameters—the lack of investable resources, or population growth, for instance. His analysis of the plight of the developing countries, and the way he presented new insights to the world—typically, to the assembled shareholders of the Bank—had the flavor of a search for definitive answers. This search was reflected as well in the sequence of dominant themes in the work of the Bank during the McNamara period.

Underlying McNamara's search for the right answer was his firm conviction that every problem can be solved through the application of reason and hard work. "There is no cause for despair. . . ," he concluded in his first address to the board of governors. "As we lift up our eyes from contemplating our troubles, who can fail to see the immense prospects that lie ahead for all mankind, if we have but the wit and the will to use our capacity fully. I am not despondent about the difficulties that lie ahead because I have faith in our ability to overcome them" (13f.).

The preoccupation with the economic prospects of mankind did not keep McNamara from noticing the manifestations of acute need. His observations in the course of project visits or encounters with people would stimulate his problem-solving instincts. Whenever he came across an obvious problem, he would seek to bring the Bank to address it. Whether the Bank was indeed the actor best qualified to deal with the problem was of little importance to him; its weight as an institution and its financial resources would make the difference. The successful campaign against riverblindness, which he initiated following his first visit to West Africa, is a good illustration of his personal impact on the solution of a serious problem affecting the lives of many African farmers.

A Bigger Bank to Address Global Problems

McNamara spent his first days at the Bank reviewing the record of past lending. He was surprised to find "how small and patchy the effort had been compared to the obvious need."[30] The Bank had to grow to meet the global challenge McNamara had accepted. The members of the president's council, the group of senior Bank officers formed by Woods to assist the president in running the Bank, described to him the financial, political, and economic constraints that limited the Bank's level of assistance. He listened but was not impressed. He concluded the meeting by requesting department heads to list all those projects the Bank should be financing, regardless of these constraints. He used this to outline the first five-year lending program, the centerpiece of his way of managing the work of the Bank.

The exercise started innocently. It was taken up with puzzled enthusiasm by the Bank's staff, most of whom had been frustrated by Woods's cautiousness during the latter years of his presidency. The financial vice president, Simon Aldewereld, seemed to understand best what was intended and was most eager to do it. He was put in charge of developing a five-year program of operations for the Bank by the middle of June. He was able by April 17, 1968, to present a proposed plan of action specifying in detail the process that would lead up to the desired result. The five-year lending program became the Bank's organizing principle. The Bank's funding, staffing, organization, budget, research, and analytical work—all of which had evolved in a disjointed fashion—were now integrated in accordance with the commitment of loans and credits, the output of the Bank. The rolling five-year lending program governed the Bank's dramatic expansion. In September 1968, McNamara reported to the board of governors, "As a result of this survey, we have concluded that a very substantial increase in Bank Group activities is desirable and possible. . . . I believe that globally the Bank Group should during the next five years lend twice as much as during the past five years. This means that between now and 1973 the Bank Group would lend in total nearly as much as it has lent since it began operations twenty-two years ago."[31]

McNamara felt personally committed to achieving these goals and would make sure that they were met. He developed a system of numerical tables that provided a complete and up-to-date picture of the lending program and of all the elements related to the operational life of the organization. He designed these tables himself and was fastidious about their format and upkeep. The tables showed both history and future projections for five-year periods, with the years heading the columns of the tables. All tables had to be upright, on one page—if necessary, with a foldout section. The tables followed a carefully worked-out numbered sequence. They presented the statistical image of the organization, which McNamara carried in his head.

Much of the elaborate statistical reporting introduced by McNamara was designed to satisfy his untiring interest in the countries that the Bank was trying to help. He wanted to know more about the nature of the problems they were facing, the extent of poverty and its manifestations, and the progress being achieved. The data presented as part of the project documents progressively expanded, and the print of the tables became smaller as the number of indicators increased, often to the point that a magnifying glass was needed to read them. McNamara scrutinized these tables carefully; they became his framework as he searched for ways of solving the problem of economic backwardness. He read the small print and once complained to Hollis Chenery, his economic adviser and vice president, development policy, "I frequently notice apparent errors in the Country Data annexes to the 'President's Reports.' For example, the report on the Iraq grain storage project . . . shows in Annex 1 an infant mortality per thousand live births of 16.2. Is not this figure incorrect?"[32] McNamara wanted accurate figures and he made certain he received them. One of his peculiarities was that he insisted on getting specific estimates, a number rather than a range of values. In a note to Aldewereld and S. R. Cope, head of the European Department, he reminded them, "I have earlier asked that the summary of each appraisal report explicitly state *an overall rate of return* figure for each project rather than a range within which the rate of return is likely to fall."[33]

Much has been made of McNamara's obsessive concern with numbers, and it was surely an important aspect of the way his mind worked. He found it easy to absorb information expressed in numerical terms, and his mathematical ability allowed him to manipulate data quickly. In an interview in July 1980, Lew Simons of the *Washington Post* asked McNamara about his emphasis on quantification. McNamara replied that quantification was important "because our product is advance of people. Social and economic advance of people, and not just one person but large numbers of people. That's our job. You have to think in terms of advancing the welfare of 2 1/4 billion people. And you have to see whether you're doing it. Now, it's extraordinarily difficult . . . I don't know what the life expectancy of a Chadian is in 1980 versus 1975, but I do know that the average life expectancy of Sub-Saharan Africa is a lot more than it was 25 years ago. And it's important to know whether it's one year more, or five percent more, or whether it's 10 years more or 40 percent more, whatever it might be. . . . We are in the business of dealing in numbers—numbers of people, numbers of dollars, numbers of tons of food produced. How on earth can you run this place without thinking in those terms?"[34]

McNamara shared his system of tables freely with his managers. The programming and budgeting department, which was entrusted with the preparation and upkeep of the system, distributed copies to the members of the president's council and to budget administrators throughout the Bank. Few among the recipients had much use for the tables, and some, such as Peter Cargill, who was in charge of the Bank's operations in Asia, dismissed them openly as a reflection of McNamara's obsession with numbers. But they were a leading feature of the Bank's management by dint of McNamara's forceful leadership.

His system was not created all at once. It expanded over time, becoming more sophisticated and intrusive. The initial tables contained fairly basic information: the Bank's balance sheet, cash flow statements, the lending program, and borrowing requirements. Later the management of the Bank's administrative budget was integrated into the system. The increase taking place in the Bank's administrative budget actually did not worry McNamara unduly. He was ready to accept the judgment of his managers on the costs of their operations. He only watched to ensure that there was consistency between the budget and performance.

Initially he focused on the time required in the lending process. His list of "things to do" included early on the reminder, "Analyze the time required to process loans and credits, establish standards, and keep records of performance against the standards."[35] He kept applying pressure to speed up the process. But as late as April 1973 McNamara was still complaining to John Adler, the head of the programming and budgeting department, "I am quite concerned that we still do not have a consolidated Bank-wide five-year program of operational outputs and related inputs. We must have such a program both to make policy decisions and to make plans for staff, recruitment and financial resources."[36] In fact the relationship between inputs and outputs could never be established in a manner that satisfied McNamara. The cost of technical and analytical studies was difficult to pin down. It proved impossible to reflect factors that had a bearing on the cost and time required, such as the size or complexity of projects, the institutional environment in the borrowing country, and factors representing the quality of the work. McNamara found it hard to accept this reality.

The first four presidents of the World Bank.
Outgoing president Eugene R. Black (left) and his successor,
George D. Woods, in conversation, 1962. The portraits are those
of (left) Eugene Meyer and John J. McCloy.

John J. McCloy with Executive Director Louis Machado on a mission
to Latin America in 1948

Eugene R. Black on a visit to Germany in 1953
with Chancellor Konrad Adenauer (second from left)
and Economic Affairs Minister Ludwig Erhard (third from right).

Black with Emperor Haile Selassie of Ethiopia in Addis Ababa in 1953

Black at the annual World Bank picnic in 1954

Black with Prime Minister Jawaharlal Nehru of India in New Delhi

Black with U.S. President John F. Kennedy in 1962

George D. Woods during a Board meeting with Vice Presidents
J. Burke Knapp and Simon Aldewereld

Woods with India's Planning Minister Asoka Mehta

During the Annual Meetings in 1965: Woods with U.S. President
Lyndon B. Johnson. At left, Treasury Secretary Henry H. Fowler;
at right, George Woods and
IMF Managing Director Pierre-Paul Schweitzer.

Robert S. McNamara during a visit to the Republic of Korea in 1970

McNamara with President Jomo Kenyatta of Kenya

McNamara welcoming the leader of a German parliamentary delegation

McNamara during a review of Calcutta's slum
improvement program in 1976

A. W. Clausen in a meeting with Lieutenant Jerry Rawlings,
president of Ghana, in 1983

Clausen meeting a group of tribal leaders in Senegal

Barber B. Conable visiting a coffee farm in Kenya in 1987

Conable greeting his old friend U.S. President George W. Bush
at the Annual Meetings in 1990.
At left, IMF Managing Director Michel Camdessus.

The initial five-year lending program had been based on the staff's perceptions of the developing countries' priorities. But already at the end of May 1968, McNamara had placed the following reminder on his "list of things to do": "Replace the present procedure in which unrelated project loans, considered in isolation from another, filter up through the levels with a five-year program based on systems analysis and overall development strategy, taking account of relative priorities among countries and within sectors of each country, as directed from the top."[37] The result was the introduction in 1969 of country program papers, which brought a country and its development needs into the center of the Bank's planning. While this was (from McNamara's perspective) a move to extend his control over the activities of the Bank, it was also a response to the economists' desire to relate the Bank's project-based interventions to the recommendations arising from their macroeconomic analyses. The importance of selecting projects that truly responded to priority needs had preoccupied the Bank's leaders in the past. But it was McNamara who introduced a system that was meant to establish some consistency in this matter.

The proposed increase in the Bank's activities required a rapid expansion of the staff; the professional staff increased by 125 percent between 1968 and 1973. At the outset some staff members and executive directors were skeptical about the feasibility or wisdom of such a rapid expansion. Pieter Lieftinck, the much-respected Dutch executive director, expressed his dissent when McNamara's first budget was discussed on June 18, 1968. He thought the proposal for a large increase of project and economic staff rested on uncertain premises and was unjustified. But McNamara was not prepared to accept any compromise. Lieftinck later recalled: "He was rough. He said the board had to accept it 'because it had to follow my intentions and my policies.'"[38] In fact, the absorption of up to 25 percent additional staff in some years into a highly skill-oriented process caused considerable strain, especially because McNamara simultaneously diversified the national composition of the staff.

When McNamara joined the Bank, the Bank's organizational structure needed an overhaul. The system of checks and balances between the large centralized projects department and the complex of geographic area departments had served the Bank well when it was cautiously edging into the uncharted territory of development lending. However, with an expanding volume of business, growing experience, and an established framework of operational policies, the dualistic structure became an impediment; it required too many decisions to be made at the top. Nevertheless, McNamara took his time before embarking on a major organizational transformation. It was only toward the end of his first five-year term that he proceeded to restructure the Bank.

Early on, McNamara abolished the "country working party." This was the informal arrangement that facilitated communication and coordination among the staff representing different departments but sharing responsibilities related to a particular country or to a particular operation. It represented the collegiality that had been a hallmark of the Bank and encouraged conflict resolution at the staff level. This, however, did not correspond with McNamara's management philosophy. He believed in clearly identified responsibility and accountability and, accordingly, in a hierarchical structure.

The 1972 reorganization adhered to this management concept. The new formal structure was based on lengthy analysis and planning by McKinsey & Co., the leading management consulting firm in the United States at the time. McNamara followed the process very closely and made sure it adhered to his own views. The reorganization abandoned the dualistic structure and placed the responsibility for lending in the different regions in the hands of regional vice presidents, who now had control over the resources required to meet agreed output targets. McNamara then consolidated his control by placing people who had earned his confidence in the key positions of the new structure.

The five-year lending program, the system of statistical controls, and the reorganization resembled the innovations that had established McNamara's reputation as an effective manager at the Ford Motor Company and at the Pentagon. They were manifestations of his personal control and his top-down management of the organization. But his managerial approach also corresponded with his propensity to think of economic development as an object of directive planning and management. The role of governments was central in identifying areas of need, developing remedial plans, and channeling resources into appropriate investments. His concern about the growing disparity of incomes—which now seemed to be an unavoidable aspect of incipient development—reinforced his belief in the leading role of the public sector. Strictures against lending to public sector banking institutions or enterprises, which hitherto had been a standard feature in the Bank's outlook and policy, were relaxed. What mattered was not who owned enterprises but how efficiently they were run. The Bank, in its diagnosis of development problems and in its prescriptions, thus accepted some of the premises of socialist-type governments, such as those in India or Sri Lanka. The development strategy of Julius Nyerere, the socialist president of Tanzania, with its apparent focus on rural poverty and small farmer productivity, became a model for McNamara in Africa.

McNamara's lists of reminders regularly contained references to the importance of private investment, the role of the IFC, and the need for the IFC to support the development of private capital markets in the developing countries. But he devoted little attention to these plans. Responsibility for lending to development banks had been transferred to the IFC by Eugene Black. George Woods had transferred the Bank's entire industrial projects staff to the IFC to emphasize the key role that the private sector needed to play in industrial development. McNamara reversed these decisions soon after his arrival and brought staff and responsibility for Bank lending to industry back to the Bank. This change emphasized the universal role of the Bank and the importance of including the subject of industrial development in the dialogue with government authorities. The IFC expanded, but not as dramatically as the Bank. Measures to stimulate private investment actually received little study. The IFC's rigid policy of refusing to assist enterprises with more than 25 percent government ownership was progressively softened so that eventually even majority public sector ownership was no longer a bar to IFC participation. McNamara, in step with the prevailing views at the time, did not see private capital as a realistic option in addressing critical development needs.

The Bank thus abandoned some of its traditional economic preconceptions and became as progressive as it would ever be during the first half century of its existence. Direct government intervention would allow the Bank to support the attack on the root causes of poverty and backwardness. However, McNamara's acceptance of the leading role of governments in economic development sometimes meant turning a blind eye to coercive practices—the involuntary collectivization of tribal farmers in Tanzania, for example—which tended to undercut the Bank's poverty objectives. It also led the Bank to focus less on the inefficiency and economic cost of government policies. Concern about efficiency, the impact of economic distortions, and a suitable policy environment started to be featured in McNamara's speeches only toward the end of his tenure, when the impact of the second oil shock highlighted the growing imbalance between the need for and the availability of external resource transfers.

McNamara wanted the Bank to be actively engaged in all countries that needed help. When he came to the Bank, he compared its record of lending with a list of member countries organized by size of population. Egypt and Indonesia had received no Bank assistance in the recent past, and there were other blank spots on the map. [39] He resolved to "try to qualify Egypt, Burma, and Algeria for Bank loans or credits, [and to] list specifically what each would have to do to justify loans or credits." [40] He visited Egypt and Indonesia during his first six months in office and established a lending relationship with both. The program in Indonesia, which expanded rapidly into one of the most important country programs, received his special attention; the Bank established a large field office in Indonesia headed by Bernard Bell, who reported directly to McNamara and provided a direct link to the Indonesian authorities.

Under McNamara's leadership the Bank opened a dialogue with the People's Republic of China. In 1979 the Chinese had let it be known that they wished to take their place as an active member of the Bank. McNamara took personal charge of the negotiations. Shahid Husain, who accompanied McNamara on his first visit there in April 1980, thought that he had never seen McNamara as excited as in these discussions. [41] The prospect of extending the Bank's support to a country with a billion people was a fascinating challenge. As in Indonesia, McNamara was impressed by the sense of purpose his Chinese partners, in particular Chairman Deng Xiaoping, conveyed in talking about the assistance they expected from the Bank. McNamara used his considerable political skills to expedite the membership process, for he realized that the support of the Carter administration—then in its last year—was crucial. If there had been delays, the entry of the People's Republic of China into the Bank would have been put off for a long time (32). As it turned out, the People's Republic of China assumed its membership in the Bank on May 15, 1980, bringing the Bank a large step closer to universal representation.

The results of McNamara's effort to increase the size of the Bank and step up the volume of lending were impressive. Targets for the most important countries, for sectors singled out as critical, and for the Bank as a whole were met or exceeded. McNamara regularly reported on this progress in his annual speeches to the board of governors. The increase in Bank lending suited the industrial countries and was warmly welcomed by the developing members. McNamara's legacy in the Bank was thus closely linked to the increase in the size of the Bank and its lending. The staff of the World Bank Group grew from 1,600 at the time he took over to 5,700 when he left in mid-1981. Commitments increased in nominal terms from an annual level of around $1 billion to over $13 billion in fiscal year 1981. In his final year, commitments equaled the sum of all commitments approved before his arrival.

Funding the Global Mission

McNamara's critical assumption was that the Bank would be able to raise the funds required to support the sharply increased level of commitments. Fund-raising had always been a major preoccupation. But while earlier the concern had been to establish the creditworthiness of the Bank and to find acceptance for the Bank's paper in the traditional capital markets (principally the United States), McNamara's concern was to achieve a quantum jump in mobilizing both conventional and concessional resources. On the face of it, the situation was not encouraging. IDA negotiations were stalled, and the prospects for a successful further replenishment looked uncertain. McNamara's checklist of tasks shows that he was considering what to do "in the event the second IDA replenishment is vetoed by the United States or postponed."[42] The picture on the

Bank side was equally gloomy. The U.S. Treasury had refused permission to enter the capital market with any large issues, and the Bank's liquidity was low. The combination of these two factors had actually forced the Bank to slow its lending in 1967.[43]

McNamara's notes show that he had a clear view of what should be done: increase borrowings from central banks; break into the European pension trust market; and borrow more in Switzerland, Kuwait, and Italy.[44] He was confident that the Bank's demand on the world capital market could easily be met—if not from Wall Street, then from Germany and Japan, the two countries with growing payments surpluses, or even from the oil-rich Middle East, "and always, from all corners of the world, through the Banks in Zurich."[45] For McNamara, the diversification of financial sources was not only a necessity arising from the curtailed access to the U.S. capital market but also a desirable objective in order to achieve greater autonomy for the Bank. The traditional focus on Wall Street, and the formal requirement of government permission before a member's capital market could be accessed, hemmed in the Bank's freedom to pursue its mission.

McNamara's ambitious lending plans raised eyebrows among the leaders of the financial community. As he announced his plans, McNamara could reassure the Bank's governors that "in the past ninety days the World Bank has raised more funds by borrowing than in the whole of any single calendar year in its history."[46] But would he be able to sustain the dramatic expansion of the Bank's fund-raising effort? The Bank's treasurer, Robert Cavanaugh, who had risen through the ranks on the strength of his prudent, cautious outlook in financial matters, did not think so. He resigned. The poor response to a small Swiss bond issue immediately following the 1968 annual meeting seemed to confirm his doubts: almost half the issue remained unsold in the hands of the underwriters. Although it turned out that the failure was attributable to the underwriters' mistakes in timing and pricing the issue, McNamara was clearly stung by this experience.

Although not a banker, McNamara had gained experience in corporate finance as controller of the Ford Motor Company. Nevertheless, raising the large amounts needed for the Bank's expanding program was a difficult task in which he needed help.

McNamara devoted much thought to finding a suitable treasurer for the Bank. He was looking for someone who was neither beholden to the conventions of the world of finance nor constrained by what had been done before. Essentially, he wanted someone who would not start off by telling him that what he wanted to do could not be done. He found Eugene Rotberg.

Rotberg, a lawyer who had worked for the Securities and Exchange Commission, claimed no experience as either an investment or a commercial banker. Through his work with the commission, however, he had acquired knowledge of the securities markets. He exuded energy and optimism and was devoted to the Bank's new objectives. He described the conclusion of his first encounter with McNamara: "McNamara looked at me and said: 'So you don't know anything about finance or accounting or business or economics, and you really don't have a great sense of respect for the people who are operating in that field?' And I said: 'That's right.' He said: 'What do you think of the problems of poverty in underdeveloped countries?' I said: ' It's not a subject I know much about, but I think it's a subject worth spending one's life on.' The next thing I knew, McNamara offered me the treasurer's job."[47]

Rotberg proved to be the right man for the task. He went about the business of raising the large amounts required to fund the stepped-up lending program in an aggressive and innovative way. In his eighteen years with the Bank, he borrowed some $100 billion in fifteen different currencies all over the world. He entered new markets—such as Japan—until then closed not only to the Bank but to the outside world, and he developed new borrowing instruments, such as extensive swapping operations, that have since become standard tools of corporate finance.

McNamara made frequent visits to the financial markets in New York and Europe to gain support for the Bank's program. He recognized that maintaining the confidence of the Bank's creditors was essential. The reaction to the failed Swiss issue had confirmed the sensitivity of the media. In an address to the Bond Club in New York, McNamara announced that the Bank's net borrowings would be three times the level of the most recent five years. However, he invoked the solid reputation of the Bank he had come to lead and affirmed the principles on which the Bank had been founded by reassuring the members of the Bond Club, "I want to begin by emphasizing a point that my predecessors Eugene Black and George Woods made over and over again: the World Bank is not only a financial institution—it is a development agency. . . . But having said that, I must make equally clear that the World Bank is a development *investment* institution, not a philanthropic organization and not a social welfare agency. Our lending policy is founded on two basic principles: the project must be sound, and the borrower must be creditworthy. We simply will not make a loan unless both these criteria can be met—and met completely."[48] Indeed, these two principles were firmly enshrined in the Bank's operational policies. They embraced emphasis on careful project selection and preparation and absolute refusal to tolerate any default. Both McNamara and Rotberg were adamant about the importance of these principles to the Bank's access to the financial markets.

McNamara's ambitious program turned out to be extraordinarily successful. In search of resources, the Bank pragmatically went wherever there was money. When balance of payments surpluses created liquidity initially in Germany, then in Japan, and later in the Gulf states, the Bank was ready to borrow. When institutions such as the German savings banks—which had not been active in the international financial markets—showed interest in new avenues for investing their considerable funds, the Bank was ready to strike a deal. The Bank's net borrowings during McNamara's first five years averaged $780 million, exceeding his original plan by a substantial margin. The Bank had adequate resources to proceed with the planned doubling of lending and also to increase its liquidity.

The first oil shock put the Bank's ingenuity to a particular test. When the price of oil quadrupled, the financial needs of the developing countries increased dramatically. McNamara responded by stepping up the Bank's lending even further. The industrial countries had to worry, however, about their own balance of payments positions and limited the Bank's access to their capital markets. It was obvious to McNamara that the Bank had to tap the surpluses now being accumulated by members of the Organization of Petroleum Exporting Countries (OPEC). His senior staff traveled to the oil-producing countries to explain the problems arising from the increase in oil prices and to explore opportunities for the Bank to benefit from their growing surplus of foreign exchange resources. He accepted an invitation from the Shah of Iran in February 1974 to establish a development fund supported and controlled by OPEC but administered by the Bank. The idea failed to materialize because of the determined opposition of the United States, which rejected any move to legitimize the price action and the influence of the oil cartel. McNamara's refusal to endorse the U.S. position—that rolling back the oil price increase would be the most sensible answer to the problems of the developing countries—did not improve his relationship with the U.S. Treasury. But he was willing to pay that price if it helped the Bank achieve its goals.

The strained relationship with the U.S. Treasury became an important factor, however, in the discussions of a general capital increase. By the mid-1970s, the rapid expansion of loan commitments had brought within sight the Bank's statutory limits to further lending.[49] An internal analysis of the risks associated with the Bank's portfolio of outstanding loans concluded that the Bank's ability to absorb losses had not grown in line with the expansion of the portfolio.[50] A capital increase had become necessary. By this time, the United States was not prepared to support a general capital increase. Apart from the difficulties involved in persuading Congress to authorize further contributions to the Bank in an atmosphere of general budgetary stringency, the negotiation of the capital increase offered the U.S. secretary of the treasury an opportunity to restrain McNamara's ambitious plans. Two years of preparatory work and negotiations resulted in a selective capital increase of $8.5 billion in 1976. This increase provided some relief but was hardly sufficient to support McNamara's vision. A task force considered the "future role of the bank" and came to the conclusion that an increase of $45 billion—a doubling of the Bank's capital—was required to meet the needs of the Bank's borrowers. Although the need for a general capital increase was recognized by the Group of Seven industrial countries (G-7) at their summit meeting in 1977, the executive directors did not formally approve the capital increase of $40 billion until June 1979, when the second oil shock occurred.

The cost of funds to the Bank and the funds' maturities—matters that traditionally had been carefully considered and had often constrained the Bank in its borrowing activities—did not seem to worry McNamara unduly. In the context of the dynamic growth that he envisioned for the developing countries, the cost of their borrowing did not represent an insurmountable problem. In fact, faced with the limited availability of IDA funds, he wondered whether a higher level of hard loans could not be justified on the grounds that accelerated growth would enable even poor developing countries to carry the debt service charges.[51] The decision to make Bank loans to a number of African countries on the basis of these expectations proved problematic when, toward the end of the 1970s, the sharp deterioration of their terms of trade precipitated serious debt-servicing difficulties.

The Problem with IDA

When he arrived at the Bank, McNamara realized that the climate for a massive increase of development aid was anything but favorable. The 1960s—the United Nations Development Decade—had not generated the hoped-for concerted effort. Instead, it had brought disappointment and frustration. "The rich countries felt that they had given billions of dollars without achieving much in the way of Development; the poor countries felt that too little of the enormous increases in the wealth of the developed world had been diverted to help them rise out of the pit of poverty in which they have been engulfed for centuries past."[52] This situation emphasized for McNamara the importance of the challenge he had accepted. He was determined that the Bank would "not share in the general paralysis which is afflicting aid efforts in so many parts of the world" (4).

To arrest the sagging morale of the donor community, McNamara took up George Woods's suggestion of a "grand assize." At his request, Lester Pearson, former prime minister of Canada, agreed to head a commission of eminent personalities to take stock of the situation and develop guidelines that would govern the actions of aid donors and institutions. The commission was independent of the Bank but worked in close proximity with McNamara, whose thinking was well reflected in its recommendations.[53] The Pearson commission's recommendations gave a fresh impetus to development assistance. The commission's call for a meaningful aid target stimulated a renewed effort and, in particular, facilitated the third IDA replenishment, which doubled IDA resources for the period from 1972 to 1974. The commission supported an expanded role for the Bank in aid coordination through the creation of further consultative groups and through strengthened monitoring of the external debt incurred by developing countries. Concerning the problems faced by the developing countries and, specifically, the burden imposed by uncontrolled population growth, the commission commented, "No other phenomenon casts a darker shadow over the prospects for international development than the staggering growth of population. . . . It is clear that there can be no serious social and economic planning unless the ominous implications of uncontrolled population growth are understood and acted upon."[54]

As McNamara's plans began to unfold, his focus inevitably shifted to those countries too poor to borrow on conventional terms. The central theme of poverty alleviation was linked to the availability of concessional resources. The task of raising the necessary IDA funds thus became a particular, and very personal, challenge. The mobilization of concessional resources raised questions of aid diplomacy and burden sharing—rather different questions from those raised by the mobilization of funds in the financial markets. McNamara devoted much of his political skill to the task of mobilizing concessional resources and oversaw personally the staff work involved in preparing for the negotiations.[55] Toward the end of his presidency he recalled, "I was absolutely shocked when I came to the Bank twelve years ago on April 1, 1968 to learn the day I arrived that there were zero funds for IDA. . . . We went through an entire fiscal year, fiscal 1968, with zero IDA funds from the replenishment. . . . And I thought that would never happen again and it hasn't."[56]

The United States had always been the key to the expansion of IDA's resources. McNamara's familiarity with the U.S. government and, especially, the workings of Congress, allowed him to anticipate political obstacles. His personal relationship with many of the key actors—Henry Kissinger, George Shultz, John Connally, Edward Kennedy, and Cyrus Vance—enabled him to intervene effectively. During a press conference in May 1978, McNamara described some of his efforts: "I have been meeting informally with members of Congress . . . . I don't appear before Congressional committees, but I do meet with individual Congressmen or groups of Congressmen at the request of the Treasury when members of Congress wish to. I have been doing that. For example, I met with a group of members from the House last week, the so-called freshmen and sophomores of the 34th and 35th Congress; and the week before that I was at a breakfast meeting hosted by Senators Javits and Church with some twenty or twenty-five Senators."[57]

But McNamara later thought that his most effective strategy was to start the process of the expansion of IDA resources without the United States. He knew that if others went ahead, the United States would eventually have no choice but to follow. For this purpose he used prominent and persuasive people to lead: James Callahan and Roy Jenkins, chancellors of the U.K. exchequer; Jan Pronk, in charge of development aid in the Netherlands government; and Abdlatif Al-Hamad, head of the Kuwait Fund.[58]

McNamara was aware of the deep-seated opposition to foreign aid in the United States. In a meeting with the press he referred to a poll showing that 84 percent of the people favored cuts in federal expenditures for foreign assistance. Nevertheless, he was supremely confident that this attitude could be corrected because to him it was irrational and based on ignorance. As he said, "My experience has been that with a few exceptions, when one has a one-on-one discussion, and lays out the moral foundation for foreign assistance—particularly the national interest in development assistance, and the way in which that development assistance serves that national interest—one can persuade 90 percent of the American public. But it's very difficult to do in large groups—by television, for example, or by an article in the press—because you can't get at the level of ignorance, or the basis for misunderstanding of the mass of the people. . . . It has been my experience that when I sit down with a person who is opposed to development assistance and say, 'Tell me why you are opposed, and let's take plenty of time,'—and I spend half an hour or two talking about this—with one or two exceptions I haven't found a single individual I can't persuade."[59]

The task of helping the developing world was for McNamara both a challenge and a moral obligation. He would use carefully articulated rational arguments to persuade large audiences of the benefits of development assistance. But the punchline of his speeches was usually an appeal to the moral conscience of potential donors. All his annual addresses to the Bank's governors included powerful moral appeals. Following the first oil shock, he made this clear: "Aid is not a luxury—something affordable when times are easy, and superfluous when times become temporarily troublesome. It is precisely the opposite. Aid is a continuing social and moral responsibility, and its need now is greater than ever."[60]

McNamara kept track of the efforts donor countries were making. He would point emphatically to the declining per capita contribution of the United States, both because he hoped to shame the government and Congress into action and because he felt embarrassed by the performance of his own country. In 1970 he said, for example, "It would appear that the country is wealthy enough to support a just and reasonable foreign aid program, and at the same time deal effectively with domestic needs. And to me it is inconceivable that the American people will accept for long a situation in which they—forming 6 percent of the world's population but consuming 40 percent of the world's resources—contribute less than their fair share to the development of the emerging nations."[61] Such exhortations did not go down well with some of the Republican officials who represented the United States.

That kind of opposition had an impact on the replenishment exercises. McNamara found it necessary to resist the attachment to the appropriation of IDA funds of conditions that would restrict their use by purpose or borrower. He also resisted congressional pressure to subordinate the Bank's salary policy to the exigencies of the quest for IDA funds; he had seen in the U.S. government the deterioration of the quality of staff as a result of uncompetitive remuneration.[62]

The case of Chile was important in this regard. In 1970, following the election of Salvador Allende as president and U.S. protests over the nationalization of the copper industry, the Bank suspended lending to Chile. The Bank's decision was inevitable, since chaotic economic conditions made the implementation of sensible investment projects, and, hence Bank lending, impossible. But McNamara was still seriously considering lending to Chile, and he discussed the matter with President Allende. He failed to persuade Allende to agree to basic economic reforms that would have restored some measure of financial stability. As a result, the Bank postponed formal consideration of loan proposals. The Bank's position was that it "concurred with rather than conceded to U.S. pressures"—in retrospect, a distinction that did not make a difference. [63]

As the policy on Chile suggests, McNamara was able to make compromises if necessary. An example is the letter that he sent in November 1979 to the chairman of the House subcommittee on foreign operations promising that the Bank would make no further loans to Vietnam in the near term because of serious questions "about Viet Nam's current commitment to a rational development policy." [64] Supposedly this personal assurance was critical for getting the committee to act on the replenishment legislation. The executive directors protested that they had not been consulted and that McNamara had violated the practice of dealing only with the executive authorities of member countries. [65] Shahid Husain, the vice president responsible for the Bank's operations in East Asia, and his staff were distressed because their findings did not support McNamara's contention about Vietnam's lack of commitment. [66] Yet, when confronted by Husain, McNamara was not prepared to admit, even in private, that his decision had been based on anything but the appraisal of Vietnam's performance. [67] Presumably, McNamara's willingness to set aside principles in this instance had something to do with his own view of the merits of the particular case. Husain recalls, "There was never a frank, open discussion between McNamara and any of us on the whole affair. Whenever McNamara was confronted with the issue of Vietnam, it was an emotional affair and not a cool, rational decision" (22).

In this case and others, McNamara's tireless efforts paid off. IDA replenishment amounts in nominal terms increased from an annual rate of $400 million during the second replenishment to $4 billion during the sixth (which became effective as McNamara left the Bank). The steep increase in the amount of IDA resources reflected in part accelerating inflation, especially following the first oil shock. Within a year, the more than 50 percent increase in IDA resources achieved with the fourth replenishment was eaten up by inflation. The real value of the IDA resources contributed in three-year installments was thus declining rapidly and required ever more ambitious replenishment targets. This complicated the periodic IDA negotiations. Nonetheless, IDA resources more than doubled in real terms between the fourth and the sixth replenishments.

In his effort to cope with the critical needs of the developing countries, McNamara did not feel constrained by the established institutional framework. He was ready to reexamine the role of the Bank in the development process to ensure that the Bank was meeting the evolving needs of its members: "In such a reexamination, none of our programs or policies ought to be regarded as carved in stone. It is our mandate to promote development which is permanent, not the tools we use to implement it."[68] In this spirit he had introduced in 1975 the "third window" as an attempt to leverage limited concessional funds by using them to subsidize the interest on regular Bank loans. He was ready to explore the idea of a separately capitalized energy affiliate to assist the developing countries in the improvement of their energy position.

In light of the resistance his proposals for a capital increase had met, he was prepared to consider a radical recommendation of the Brandt commission: that the statutory one-to-one gearing ratio, the conservative relationship between the Bank's lending and its equity, be relaxed. (The independent Brandt commission on international development issues had been set up in 1978, on McNamara's suggestion, under the chairmanship of Willy Brandt, former chancellor of the Federal Republic of Germany.) This ratio had been established at Bretton Woods in the closing months of World War II and might no longer be relevant. It was now causing an unnecessary underutilization of the Bank's capital base. McNamara thought the Bank

> should continue to improve the efficiency with which it uses its immensely broad and uniquely guaranteed financial base. It must begin to use the demonstrated strength of its loan portfolio that reflects the prudent lending policies that it has followed for over thirty years. This is essential if it is to meet more fully the needs

of the developing countries without imposing additional burdens on the budgets of other governments in a period when the domestic demands of many are particularly pressing.[69]

Except for the modest experiment with the "third window" (contributing additional lending of $700 million over a two-year period), none of these attempts to mobilize more resources became reality.[70] They illustrate, however, how tireless McNamara was in his search for ways of loosening the constraints that he thought were preventing the Bank from meeting its global challenge.

Quantity or Quality?

The Bank's staff increased, the Bank's borrowing expanded, and, after some initial delays, IDA resources became more plentiful. New commitments of Bank loans and IDA credits responded only sluggishly, however, to the ambitious targets. The minutes of the senior staff meeting on October 9, 1968, note:

> The Chairman said that the planned lending activity during the current fiscal year, including work to be done in preparation for lending in the next fiscal year, had been based essentially on the recommendations of the Area and Projects Departments. . . and not imposed from above. He was disturbed to find that actual lending was beginning to deviate substantially from the program, and he had asked Mr. Aldewereld to hold monthly meetings with the departments concerned to determine how far arrears could be made up or how far the plan needed to be altered. [71]

The difficulty of stepping up lending commitments in accordance with the plans prepared in the Bank was a major theme of the McNamara years. The problem, of course, was that lending was not exclusively a function of the Bank's decisions. The Bank's willingness to lend was essential, but without suitable, well-prepared projects, it was meaningless. The difficulty of finding suitable projects had proved a constraint on the expansion of the Bank's activities virtually from the start. To improve the predictability of project development, the various steps leading up to approval by the executive directors were identified, along with the time required for each. These timetables became an integral part of life and work in the Bank. They had to be prepared, standardized, aggregated, reviewed, and discussed every month, and they normally fueled exhortations down the line of command and outward to the agencies of the borrowing countries responsible for project preparation.

McNamara took a very close interest in this process. He reviewed the aggregated reports on the state of the lending program and was not beyond intervening directly if necessary. A good example was the program in India. It had been meant to increase sharply following the second replenishment of IDA, but there were delays in the preparation of projects. The Indian executive director, S. R. Sen, blamed the delays on shortcomings in the performance of the Bank's staff; the Bank staff blamed the red tape of the Indian bureaucracy. McNamara decided to break the resulting stalemate by asking for a monthly report that would discuss each lending operation in the program and identify the reasons for delays. This report was reviewed in a meeting chaired by him and attended by the Indian executive director and the various managers down to the division chief involved in the India program. As a result, the issues affecting the processing of the Indian lending operations received priority attention both in the Bank and in India. But the effort required was large and was effective only as long as an unusual amount of energy could be devoted to it. It did not affect the underlying problems that had led to the delays.

Despite such efforts, McNamara never referred to the problem of absorptive capacity in any of his major speeches. For McNamara this was strictly a managerial problem. It was sufficient that the need for assistance in a particular area was beyond doubt; the question of project preparation and readiness then became a function of hard, dedicated work. Of course, the pressure needed to overcome the complications and frictions that threatened the smooth achievement of the lending objectives affected the product. Questions arose early about the quality of the rapidly growing number of lending operations.

McNamara was emphatic about the importance of quality. After all, he would say, how can poor-quality investments be effective means of development? He underlined from the outset that "the Bank's efforts are not merely—or even mainly—quantitative in their goal. They are, above all, qualitative."[72] But he denied the tension between lending targets and project quality. When he first announced the plan to step up lending, he expressed his belief "that [the Bank] can carry out these operations within the high standards of careful evaluation and sound financing that my predecessors have made synonymous with the name of the World Bank. Our loans will be for projects as soundly based and appraised as ever in our history."[73] Emphasis on the need to maintain project quality became a consistent part of all his pronouncements. This major concern was also reflected in his internal communications to the managers and staff of the Bank. Thus, McNamara wrote to Warren Baum, the vice president in charge of the operational policy staff, "I cannot state too strongly that there should be no 'pressures to produce projects' other than in conformity with accepted Bank standards."[74] Each division was operating according to a plan prepared by that division. "And it is the responsibility of the managers to either meet the plans or to propose changes in them. But under no circumstances will we permit achievement of the plan by violation of the quality of the standards on which the plan was premised."[75] Warren Baum said later:

> Something which struck me about McNamara was that . . .
> he had one word which was not part of his vocabulary and
> that was the word 'trade-off.' He thought you could have
> more of everything. You could have more lending . . . and
> higher quality lending. And he was right in the broad sense
> and in the long term. . . . But he generated tremendous pres-
> sure within the institution to reach lending targets and he felt
> it was a personal embarrassment to the institution if he said
> we were going to make 182 lending operations and we only
> did 176.[76]

McNamara was equally adamant about the priority of supervision. The commitment of loans could serve no good purpose if the projects they financed were not built or did not meet their objectives. The money provided by the Bank had to be disbursed. A note to Aldewereld reflects both his concern and the way he maintained pressure on the staff:

> It has been reported to me indirectly that Mr. David Knox
> believes the Transportation Projects Department cannot prop-

erly process the agreed upon project program for Fiscal 1971 and at the same time effectively supervise previously approved projects. Please inform him that I want it fully understood that the first claim on professional staff is to be given to supervision of approved projects. If he feels that following this rule he cannot process the project program on which his manpower budget was based, I should like to be informed immediately. If I recall correctly, he is authorized 104 professional staff members as of June 30, 1971, and the project program for FY71 includes 38 transportation projects. During the years 1962 through 1968, the Transportation Projects Department processed between 14 and 21 projects per year with a professional staff of from 24 to 57 members.[77]

The question of project quality became a major issue in 1976 when the Japanese executive director, in his farewell address to the board on November 16, 1976, contended that the quality of Bank projects was being sacrificed for the sake of achieving annual lending targets. His remarks were picked up by the *Wall Street Journal* and caused much concern. The issue was examined at various levels in the Bank. The operational vice presidents reaffirmed that "the quality of Bank-IDA projects was not being sacrificed but was, rather, improving year by year."[78] They also concluded that there was a widespread perception among the staff that quality was being sacrificed in order to achieve the lending targets. Operational staff felt that in the short run there was a tradeoff and that the pressure to get on with lending was overriding. This issue was never satisfactorily resolved. In 1992 it resurfaced as a prominent theme in the report of the Task Force on Portfolio Management, which focused on "the tension which has always existed between the emphasis on new commitments and the attention to effective implementation."[79]

This dilemma highlights one of the drawbacks of McNamara's management style. It was difficult to communicate up and down the line on subjects that were hard to capture statistically. There was much to support the claim that the quality of projects supported by the Bank received greater attention. The appraisal process became more rigorous and sophisticated, the amount of staff time devoted to preparation and appraisal increased, and condi-

tions designed to safeguard implementation became more extensive. But the Bank was moving into more difficult areas of lending
and was active in countries that were economically and institutionally weaker. These changes made it more difficult to maintain
the traditional standards for project success.

There was a sense in the organization that McNamara was not
interested in hearing about delays, that the staff had to resolve
problems encountered in processing a project, and that time-
consuming reservations would be regarded as obstructionist. There
was a widespread perception that rewards were linked to meeting
the lending targets rather than to the quality of loans. This also
had some effect on the quality of the staff reports. The management task force many years later found that project appraisal had
turned from a disinterested assessment to advocacy, thus under-
mining the credibility of the appraisal process.[80] This tendency and
the related deemphasis of portfolio supervision and project implementation were the result of the so-called approval culture—the
focus on commitment levels as the most visible measure of productivity.

McNamara's emphasis on quantitative lending targets appeared
grounded in his belief that the answer to the development problem
would be the transfer of resources. The emphasis on increasing the
Bank's lending at the outset would suggest that.[81] Moreover,
McNamara's propensity to think in quantitative terms may have
influenced his way of organizing the institutional response to the
development challenge. But he clearly did not believe that the nature of the development problem was one-dimensional. He was
struggling to understand its nature. His views of what was important and what worked evolved.

The War against Poverty

From the outset, McNamara tried to better grasp the causes of
economic backwardness. He wanted to provide assistance "where
it will contribute most to removing the roadblocks to development."[82] The expansion of the Bank's activities, while essential in
his view, had to involve qualitative changes in approach as well. It
could not just be "more of the same."[83] He announced that "in

looking for projects to support we shall look for those which contribute most fundamentally to the development of the total national economy, seeking to break strangleholds on development; to find those growth opportunities that stimulate further growth" (5).

As long as he headed the Bank, he was tireless in probing for and pushing new ideas and new priorities. He was a leader of restless energy and focused attention. Just to organize a major expansion of the Bank would probably have exhausted a normal executive. But McNamara's energy level was "far above normal, and through the new changes he was trying always to put together elements of a more adequate approach to development."[84] His great energy made him the undisputed leader of the Bank, always several steps ahead of a professional staff with a reputation for dedication, imagination, and experience in the analysis of developmental issues.

McNamara's initial focus was on agriculture and education, two sectors his predecessor had already singled out for special attention. These sectors were to see the largest increases in investments, with lending for agriculture increasing fourfold and lending for education, threefold. He saw that the Bank could give a push to the so-called green revolution, "where irrigation, fertilizer and peasant education can produce miracles."[85] In education, the focus was on education planning, on teacher training at all levels, and on technological innovation in teaching. Then he turned to an issue that came to characterize his presidency as few other issues did: the problem of population growth.

During his first year as World Bank president, McNamara elaborated on this theme in two major speeches before audiences particularly sensitive on this subject: Latin Americans in Buenos Aires, and Catholics at the University of Notre Dame in Indiana. For McNamara this was a particularly striking problem because it could be expressed in compelling statistical terms. "The fact must be faced that rapid population growth is the greatest barrier to the economic progress and social well-being of the citizens of our member nations."[86] For the difference in income and living conditions between the rich and the poor countries "is not a static situation. The misery of the underdeveloped world is today a dynamic misery, continuously broadened and deepened by a population growth that is totally unprecedented in history" (18). It was also a problem that demanded attention because, if left unattended, it would find its own apocalyptic solution in the form of famine and political chaos. "The threat of unmanageable population pressures is very much like the threat of nuclear war."[87]

McNamara would review progress of the Bank's program and, in particular, progress in these sectors in his annual reports to the board of governors. Initially he saw the increase in Bank lending and investments in the various sectors of the member countries' economies as a means of addressing specific problems: the gap between rich and poor countries, the lack of adequate food supplies, and limited productivity as a result of poor education. On the basis of his personal observations during well-prepared, intensive study tours of the various parts of the developing world, McNamara soon added other problems to this list: unemployment, urbanization, and ill-conceived industrial and trade policies.

It was not long before McNamara recognized that growth alone did little to change the most significant aspects of economic backwardness. McNamara noted with disappointment that the "relatively high rate of growth in GNP (in the 1960s) did not bring satisfactory progress in development."[88] Despite a 5 percent annual growth, malnutrition was common, infant mortality high, life expectancy low, illiteracy widespread, unemployment growing, income distribution within major developing countries severely skewed, and the gap between rich and poor nations widening. Although he promised that the Bank would stick to the ambitious expansion of its lending, McNamara admitted that he did not know why the fight against the most disturbing aspects of underdevelopment was so difficult. "As we enter the Seventies, in field after field, we have more questions than answers. Our urgent need is for new instruments of research and analysis with which to dispel our ignorance of the social dimensions of economic change and help us formulate a more comprehensive strategy for the decade ahead" (10).

McNamara turned for answers to Hollis Chenery, whom he had brought into the Bank in May 1970 with the mandate to build up its economic research. Chenery focused specifically on the problems related to the uneven income distribution in developing countries.

McNamara presented the conclusions to the UNCTAD conference in Santiago, Chile, in 1972. He pointed out the sharp differences in economic performance among developing countries, differences that were hidden by average growth rates. "But what is most misleading of all," he went on to say, "is to assume that once we have calculated the GNP growth rate of a particular developing country, and then expressed it in per capita terms, we have arrived at a sound picture of the level of economic development in the country. . . . For rates of growth of GNP, and of GNP per capita, tell us nothing about how income is actually distributed within a country."[89]

McNamara tried to understand the reasons for the growing inequality associated with development and concluded "that economic growth in a poor country, in its early stages is likely to penalize the poorest segment of the society relative to the more affluent sectors unless specific action is taken to prevent such an effect" (5). He thought that this applied in particular to the subsistence agrarian economies and therefore recommended measures such as land and tenancy reform, but, above all, programs to increase the productivity of small farmers.

At the annual meeting in Nairobi in 1973, McNamara presented his second five-year plan, which was 40 percent larger in real terms than the first and "the largest program of technical and financial assistance to developing countries ever undertaken by a single agency."[90] The core of the plan was a blueprint for his fight against poverty. Since the great majority of the poor were in rural areas, it was essential to direct assistance to the large number of subsistence farmers and raise their productivity and incomes. McNamara asked Baum and Montague Yudelman, director of the Bank's Agriculture Department, to give him a precise figure for the increase in agricultural production that would result from the Bank's expanded lending. They could not provide him with the number he wanted.[91] He therefore suggested as a goal that the growth rate of the production of small farms be stepped up gradually from 2.5 to 5 percent by 1985, so that their output would double by the end of the century and much of the world's poverty would be abolished.

To help the 700 million poor in the world, "the lowest 40 percent," the Bank was to increase its lending to agriculture by over 40 percent in real terms during the following five-year period and direct an increasing share of agricultural lending to small farmers. Almost three out of every four agricultural projects should include components to benefit smallholders. This condition was thought to be a helpful way of addressing hard-core poverty and, at the same time, to boost output. The strategy was backed by the finding that small farmers can be as productive as large ones and that, in fact, small farmers might potentially be more productive.[92] Because the success of the strategy depended on the availability to the smallholder of a package of complementary inputs, the prototype project for effective assistance became the integrated rural development project.

By 1975 McNamara could announce that the Bank was moving forward with an extended program of research work and with the expanded program of rural development lending. One of the models cited by McNamara was a project in the Kigoma Region of Tanzania, one of the poorest rural areas in the world.[93] McNamara was well aware of the formidable obstacles created by the lack of suitable technologies, by inappropriate pricing and subsidy policies, and, above all, by the lack of supportive institutions. "It is true," he admitted in 1974, "that the risks of failure are greater in rural development projects than in some of our more traditional investments. Complicated problems of technology, organization, land tenure, and human motivation remain to be resolved."[94] However, McNamara remained optimistic: "We have a long way to go, but the early evidence is clear: it works."[95]

The rural development strategy successfully reinforced a move toward the support of agriculture, particularly smallholder agriculture. Both in volume and coverage, the Bank became preeminent among development agencies in its focus on rural development. Millions of rural people were benefiting, especially from rural infrastructure investments. The strategy was effective in broad terms. In more specific terms the ambitious targets of enhanced smallholder productivity often proved elusive and not sustainable. The benefits for the poorest of the poor were limited. The rural development programs aimed at those with some productive assets; the rural laborers and landless benefited, at best, indirectly. Given the objective of expanding lending for rural development, the Bank could not at the same time tackle the many long-standing, politically sensitive issues affecting the prospects of the landless, such as tenurial and land reform. The most conspicuous failures among the rural development programs turned out to be the large group of area development projects, especially in Sub-Saharan Africa. The institutional weaknesses that jeopardized the implementation of these projects and the macroeconomic problems that overwhelmed Africa in the 1980s were responsible for their failure.[96]

Once the assault on poverty in the rural areas had been launched, McNamara turned his attention to the 200 million people living in urban squalor. He said of urban poverty, "it is immensely complex—even more so than the problem of poverty in the countryside."[97] Undeterred by this problem, he presented the Bank's plan of action to the governors in 1975. The approach was similar to that of the rural poverty campaign: increase the productivity of the poor. This required creation of employment opportunities and improvements in services. Unlike the rural programs, which were low-cost affairs, the urban employment and services plans raised difficult questions of affordability. "The emphasis on low capital investment per job, and low-cost standard services affordable by poor households is the key to the solution."[98] As the Bank expanded, it redirected assistance into the urban areas; guidelines called for a growing share of industrial financing to be directed toward small-scale enterprises. The program included such schemes as sites-and-services projects, squatter settlement programs, small-scale enterprise financing, and plans for basic services in transport, electricity, water supply, and education.

With the rural and urban poverty programs under way, the Bank's focus began to shift again. It was obvious that the programs to raise productivity and income levels of the poor would work, if at all, only very slowly. It would be a long time before changing economic conditions would begin to eliminate some of the most degrading manifestations of poverty; the very nature of poverty made growing out of it extremely difficult. So in 1977 McNamara concluded that "the poorest countries . . . must do everything they can to increase per capita income growth, but they must do something else as well. They must fashion ways in which basic human needs can be met earlier in the development process."[99] Under the influence of Paul Streeten and Mahbub Ul Haq, the "basic needs" approach combined the focus on the poor with an emphasis on specific needs, such as literacy, nutrition, reductions in infant mortality, and health. According to Mahbub Ul Haq, McNamara was enamored with the basic needs strategy. "He wanted short cut solutions. He was a practical man. He could identify himself with something specific. He could understand when you were talking about delivering a primary health package, a primary education package, a potable water package in the villages, or some other basic need, in a cost-effective fashion, in a short period through a delivery system which could be replicated."[100]

A preoccupation with poverty remained McNamara's central theme throughout his presidency. In his final annual address, he summed up the importance of eliminating poverty: "To reduce and eliminate massive absolute poverty lies at the very core of development itself. It is critical to the survival of any decent society. Development is clearly not simply economic progress measured in terms of GNP. It is something much more basic. It is essentially human development; that is, the individual's realization of his or her own inherent potential."[101] Poverty was a problem that represented a personal challenge to him and had to be dealt with in distinctly adversarial terms. McNamara would talk of the "war against poverty" or "the assault on poverty" when he discussed his agenda. He would report to the governors on the progress in this fight, on the number of poor to be rescued, on the nature and origin of the various aspects of poverty, and on the steps necessary for recipients, donors, and the Bank if they were to succeed in this struggle.[102]

The Oil Crisis

The most serious threat to success in the fight against poverty turned out to be the economic changes resulting from the oil shocks of the 1970s. The quadrupling of petroleum prices in 1973, within weeks of the Nairobi address, and the worldwide inflation reinforced by this development hit especially the poorest among the developing countries. These were countries with poorly diversified economies and systemic trade deficits. The instability in the international price regime accentuated the uneven distribution of incomes. The prospects of making headway against poverty suddenly became remote. The most burning question was no longer how to reduce the number of the poor but how to prevent a massive increase in their number.

McNamara responded with his proven method: assess the damage; express it in numerical terms; and then work on a solution. This was reflected in his address to the board of governors in 1974. He described in vivid terms the desperate situation of the poorest countries. "Almost every element in the current economic situation has worked to their disadvantage, and has been compounded even further for many of them by the natural disasters of flood, drought, and crop failures."[103] McNamara estimated that the poor countries needed an additional $3 billion to $4 billion in concessional assistance, and he urged the industrial countries and the oil-producing countries to provide this essential support. He was also beginning to explore the adjustments the developing countries could undertake to minimize the setback to their development. "There is much the developing countries themselves can do to create a more favorable climate for export expansion," he said in 1975. "All too often their policies of subsidized capital, overvalued exchange rates, and excessive regulation discourage entrepreneurial incentive to sell abroad."[104] Developing countries needed to change the pattern of use and production of energy, and they needed to step up the production of food grains to safeguard the survival of their growing populations.

The conditions that aggravated the problems of the developing countries also affected the availability of funds for assistance. The oil shock forced most of the Bank's major shareholders to make difficult adjustments. McNamara acknowledged these pressures but concluded that "the amounts of additional financial assistance that would mean the difference between decency and utter degradation for hundreds of millions of the absolute poor are, in relative terms, minute—perhaps 2 percent of the increase in real income the developed world can look forward to in the remaining years of the decade."[105] McNamara succeeded in raising substantial amounts in the oil-rich countries. In September 1974 he could report that the Bank had received commitments of $2 billion from OPEC. By 1975 OPEC members were contributing about 3 percent of their GNP and 10 percent of their balance of payments surplus.

The Bank's expanded lending went some way toward assisting developing countries affected by the sharp deterioration of their terms of trade. They could now strive for some growth without relying excessively on potentially volatile private capital flows. It was not a real solution, however, to the problems faced by the oil-importing countries. In the long run they needed to adjust to the new circumstances by changing the structure of their economies. From the onset of the oil crisis in 1973, McNamara emphasized the need for adjustment, the urgency of greater economy and efficiency, and the importance of increasing exports and of finding suitable substitutes for expensive imports. When the second oil shock compounded the balance of payments problems of the developing countries in 1979, McNamara urged the donor countries to support actively the developing nations' efforts to adjust.

McNamara considered the crisis at the end of the 1970s far more serious than the 1973 shock. The real cost of oil had actually come down after 1973; interest rates had been low; and the scope for the assumption of additional debt even by relatively poor countries, and for relatively easy and painless adjustment, had been great. All this changed toward the end of the 1970s. The problems of the developing countries were aggravated by a recession in the industrial world. McNamara did not expect energy prices to decline. He thought that "this new adjustment problem [was] caused by a permanent change in the world economy, not by some temporary phenomenon which will later automatically reverse itself."[106] He felt that "the sense of relief over the relatively successful adjustment in the earlier period should not be allowed to lead to a feeling of complacency now" (7).

In his address to the UNCTAD meeting in Manila in 1979 he pleaded with the international community to consider "sympathetically the possibility of additional assistance to developing countries that undertake the needed structural adjustments for export promotion in line with their long-term comparative advantage." He promised that he was "prepared to recommend to the executive directors that the World Bank consider such requests for assistance, and that it make available program lending in appropriate cases."[107] This promise took the form of a more specific proposal at the annual meeting in Belgrade in 1979, and in 1980 McNamara presented an explicit Bank program for structural adjustment.

It was obvious that the developing countries had to adjust to the changed economic environment, but McNamara was concerned that the adjustment be orderly and speedy. He warned that "if the action in a given country is delayed, or if the external financial assistance available to it is inadequate, then the adjustment process will have to take place in an internal environment of low or negative growth, of little or no social advance, and of almost certain political disorder."[108] The essence of the adjustment required by the oil-importing countries was clear: in order to pay for more expensive oil imports, these countries had to expand their exports or reduce their nonoil imports, or some combination of the two. In practice, the adjustment process called for a fundamental reorientation of economic policies to accomplish higher savings and investment rates, greater efficiency in the domestic use of capital, and a reorientation of economic activity to respond to the signals reflected by the balance of payments situation. The public sector, which had a predominant role in the economies of most developing countries, had to give way to a more vigorous, expanded private sector.

Adequate international financial support and the needed internal adjustment had to go together if the process was to succeed without crippling the development of the poor countries. As McNamara emphasized, "Adequate financing of imports is not a substitute for structural adjustment to the new external circumstances. Rather, it is a prerequisite for such adjustment: it permits the developing countries to adapt sensibly their production, trade, investment, and savings pattern to new needs" (33). McNamara felt that it was legitimate for the Bank to shoulder part of the burden of the financing required for this purpose, that it would stimulate private financing—rather than compete with it—by improving the developing countries' creditworthiness, and that it would complement the IMF's actions by dealing with the longer-term, truly structural aspects of the adjustment process.

The decision to extend structural adjustment loans triggered an internal debate with the board of executive directors. The Bank's major shareholders were not persuaded that this was a legitimate response by an institution meant to support long-term investment. They were persuaded to go along only on the assurance that program lending would remain within tightly prescribed limits. The provision of financial assistance in support of policy reform represented an expansion of the Bank's scope, as the debate indicated, but the general significance of this change became apparent only gradually. Program lending became an option now in virtually all country programs. It facilitated a degree of intrusion into the policymaking process of the Bank's borrowers that went far beyond the subtle influences traditionally associated with project lending. In fact, the involvement of the Bank in the design and administration of its borrowers' economic policies had been inevitable once the Bank started to plan its operations on a countrywide basis. Then, the link between a country's economic policies and the effectiveness of the Bank's assistance could no longer be ignored. This was a natural step as the Bank evolved into a development institution and expanded its agenda. McNamara reflected many years later, "I had become convinced by that time, and I remain even more strongly of the opinion today, that the greatest contribution the Bank can make to a developing country is in helping it formulate its macroeconomic policies and in assisting it in implementing those policies."[109]

McNamara's Bank

From the moment McNamara walked into the Bank, there had been no question who was in charge. He dominated the Bank, its staff, its board of executive directors, and almost any other audience that needed to be controlled in the pursuit of his mission. He relied on his ability to work hard and to absorb large amounts of written material on every relevant subject. He was always better prepared than anybody else and quicker on his feet than those with whom he dealt.

Toward the end of his tenure in the World Bank, McNamara reflected on his managerial orientation: "My background was a background of establishing objectives for institutions and then pursuing those objectives in effective ways. . . I always felt that business leadership had two primary responsibilities: one was to the stockholders of the firm and one was to the society they were part of. And the objectives we formulated were in those terms."[110] Earlier, he had said of his style as a manager: "The role of a public manager is very similar to the role of a private manager; in each case he has the option of following one of two major alternative courses of action. He can either act as a judge or a leader. . . . I have always believed in and endeavored to follow the active leadership role as opposed to the passive judicial role."[111]

McNamara recognized that he needed the support of the executive directors and the governors whom they represented. He was consequently determined to ensure that he obtained the backing of the executive directors with a minimum of fuss. William Clark, vice president for external relations, described the first board meeting McNamara chaired on April 9, 1968. "The meeting went extremely badly. One by one, the executive directors attacked a staff paper on the effects of devaluation on the Bank's assets." McNamara called a meeting of the president's council and expressed his dismay: "In three hours nothing had been achieved, and there had been no single mention of development. He had come to the Bank to deal with development issues, . . . not to participate in a debating society. In future, no proposal should be taken to the board unless it was already firmly established that it had the support of the majority of the voting power."[112]

McNamara took pains to avoid any outward manifestation of his dominating role. He encouraged the executive directors to speak out on issues and gave them the opportunity to discuss policy and operational matters at length. Without exception, he treated them with respect and conveyed the sense that their importance grew along with that of the Bank. His sense of accountability to the Bank's shareholders compelled him to ensure that the board was fully informed.[113] He presented the board with a growing flow of issue papers and action programs. Although this practice conveyed his view of the importance of the board as an institution, the preparation of elaborate papers on every conceivable issue was also a way of overwhelming the executive directors. He kept them busy while he was running the Bank. Of course, he read every paper that went to the board himself. In board discussions he knew the weaknesses of every project and could always answer the questions raised better than his staff. He made it a point to rephrase questions asked by the executive directors to make sure that staff in their answers addressed the real issues. If the staff gave the wrong answer, he would provide the right answer. All the while, he would be patient. He never criticized staff members who had made a mess of things, leaving that job to his vice president. You knew you had botched it if he turned to the vice president and asked him to comment further.

McNamara would usually summarize the discussion at the conclusion of a meeting. He would do that brilliantly, often condensing many hours of discussion succinctly and masterfully. But in the process, some of the directors would find that their objections had somehow been glided over and that the conclusion reflected what McNamara had wanted all along. So there was a growing sense among the executive directors that they were being manipulated.[114]

This feeling became more pronounced as the McNamara presidency advanced. The board members' resentment grew as McNamara succeeded in raising their sense of their own importance but not their sense of effective participation. They spent more time consulting with each other outside the board meetings, coordinating their positions. On critical issues they might come to a board meeting with, in effect, a board position already arrived at, even with designated speakers in some instances. To defuse the situation, McNamara began to meet informally with the board outside the board room, in his own office, to thrash out sensitive issues before they came before the board. This transferred the deliberations and the decisionmaking process from the board room to his own office.

McNamara's behavior was determined in part by his view of large meetings. To him the purpose of large meetings was to ratify decisions; consequently they had to be controlled. He did not believe in the value of debates in facilitating the exchange of views. He felt uncomfortable with large numbers of people in the room. Dissent in large meetings became a challenge to his authority, and challenges had to be put down. This earned him the reputation of being intolerant of others' views. In contrast, those who dealt closely with him, one on one, regarded him as considerate, interested, and approachable—as someone who liked to be informed and challenged in private discussions.[115]

The number of people in the Bank who dealt directly with McNamara remained limited. He relied on Burke Knapp, the senior vice president, operations, to run the Bank and execute his programs. He valued Knapp's experience and judgment. Until he retired, Knapp represented the traditions of the Bank established during the Black period, especially the strong belief in the value of the Bank's project work. He was able to reconcile those traditions with the boldness of McNamara's approach. Ernest Stern, who eventually succeeded Knapp as senior vice president, operations, was the only one who kept up with McNamara. He was able to match McNamara in the breadth and detail of the treatment of issues, and the president consulted him on a broad range of issues. Otherwise, McNamara relied on people to perform particular functions. He would turn to Chenery on economic matters, to Baum and Yudelman on rural development issues, to Cargill and Rotberg on IDA and financial matters, and to William Clark to get in touch with people, especially outside the United States.

When he needed to stimulate his thinking, McNamara seemed to give much more of his time and attention to people outside the Bank. He kept up an intensive flow of communications with people such as Barbara Ward, Maurice Strong, David Rockefeller, and a number of other public figures who gave him new ideas. He also liked to talk directly to experts on technical subjects that interested him—with Norman Borlaug on high-yielding wheat or with Daniel Benor on agricultural extension—and so add to his already formidable arsenal of information.

McNamara remained invisible to the majority of the Bank's staff. He did not walk the corridors of the Bank, never dropped into other people's offices, never ate in the Bank's executive dining room, let alone the cafeteria. As a result, the attitude of the staff toward him remained ambivalent. Everyone admired and respected his leadership. They were pleased with his thrust into rural development and urban development, the poverty focus of the institution, and the desire to be more effective as a development institution. But while they felt proud to be part of the Bank's mission, they also worried that they might not count, that they were just "data gatherers."[116]

McNamara relied on his personal assistants and his managers, resisting strenuously any suggestions to be more outgoing. Davidson Sommers, who had been the Bank's general counsel in the 1950s and worked as a consultant for the president for about ten years, recalls that he wrote a memorandum to McNamara advising him of the poor state of internal communications. McNamara called him into his office and said, "Dave, you're absolutely right. Those guys don't know how to manage." Sommers pointed out that middle-level managers needed a model and that McNamara could improve the morale of the institution if he would take some time to walk around the Bank and stick his head in a few offices. McNamara replied, "Oh, Dave, I don't want to do that. I don't want this to be known as McNamara's Bank."[117] In fact, even the practice of monthly senior staff meetings attended by departmental managers progressively fell into disuse. He rejected the suggestion that he address larger staff gatherings with the argument that he could not possibly contribute to such a meeting the equivalent in value of the time wasted by a large audience of staff members. Understandably, McNamara had "a reputation for being remote and for not getting to know people in the Bank very well."[118]

McNamara preferred written communications to oral reports. This was a matter of efficiency—he felt that he could read much faster than anyone could talk—but it was also a question of being in control. The way to gain McNamara's attention was to give him a memorandum on which he could focus. For his trips he required elaborate briefing books, which he perused thoroughly, as his marginal notations showed. Every meeting required a detailed written brief. Although there were specific instructions about the length and format of briefing papers, he never complained about the volume of briefing materials prepared for him. Of course, he preferred whenever possible to have numbers and tables.

McNamara had arrived at the Bank with a well-established reputation as a modern manager who had successfully run large organizations through the use of systems analysis. Peter Cargill was mocking his colleagues when he reported to his staff about one of the first encounters between McNamara and the senior managers of the Bank, "Everybody was trying to be cute by asking McNamara about the merits of systems analysis."[119] Although the term was apparently never used in the Bank, the spirit of systems and of control certainly pervaded the Bank in those years. Evaluations of his role as a manager—the field on which his professional reputation was based—were mixed.[120] Some thought that he was a superb manager who achieved institutional objectives with maximum efficiency. Others felt that his tendency to centralize decisionmaking and his attention to detail prevented a more effective use of the staff's potential and the necessary strengthening of institutional safeguards.

Given McNamara's success as a leader, it is fair to ask whether his transformation of the institution would be lasting. He had surely come to personify the Bank as nobody before or after him. He had so shaped the Bank to represent his views, his style, and his methods that the Bank had become "McNamara's Bank." This fateful dependence had created a management problem: it would be very difficult for a newcomer to take over and run the institution, especially a newcomer with less energy than McNamara had brought to the job.[121]

McNamara's Legacy

Although McNamara claimed that he was anxious to leave the Bank at the end of his second term, he had been in fact very eager to accept a third term. It was a sign of his dedication to the mission of the Bank, however, that he announced abruptly in June 1980 that he would leave before completing his third five-year contract. He may have had personal reasons for wanting to quit. The principal consideration, however, seems to have been his recognition that the shift to conservatism, already plainly evident in the United Kingdom, would shape the outcome of the 1980 presidential elections in the United States. The task of the Bank, the fight against poverty, had hardly begun. The challenges of the approaching decade of the 1980s would be daunting, and he thought they called for a continuity of leadership he would no longer be able to provide.

The Bank McNamara left in 1981 was completely transformed from the institution he had entered thirteen years earlier. It was a much larger organization. It was also much more complex. Its membership had continued to expand, and with the People's Republic of China's assuming full participation, it was well on its way to becoming a universal organization. Its popular name, World Bank, had become appropriately descriptive of the institution and of the global role it now played.

McNamara's leadership and bold vision had been central factors driving that transformation. Burke Knapp, who worked closely with McNamara when he came into the Bank, concluded, "in terms of bold financial planning and bold confrontation of the needs, McNamara was unique, and other more conservatively-minded or more conventionally-minded types who might have taken up the presidency of the Bank at the time he did, would not have seen the needs, or if they had, would not have been bold enough to lay claim upon resources of the magnitude that McNamara did."[122] His vision reflected his strong personal moral commitment to the objectives of the Bank. With energy and skill, he was able to bring the Bank's shareholders to support his initiatives—this at a time when the growing importance of the Bank and global economic pressures tended to sharpen the divergence of interests among the Bank's several constituencies. While the Bank under McNamara's leadership began to address problems of income disparity and poverty, it was also diversifying its sources of funds: instead of relying almost exclusively on the U.S. capital market, the Bank was drawing its resources from a growing number of international sources.

McNamara's role as a spokesman for the developing countries and their needs, and the size and financial weight of the organization he led, assured the Bank a position of authority as intermediary between the rich and poor countries. Its greatly enlarged financial resources allowed the Bank to play a critical role in many developing economies. Through cofinancing and the coordination of aid from other sources, the Bank's own assistance was further leveraged. The buildup of its research staff, and a growing flow of analytical work based on the rich data assembled in the course of its operational work, stimulated interaction with the academic community and allowed the Bank to claim a role as an intellectual leader in development matters.

There were drawbacks. The elevated profile of the Bank inevitably attracted critical scrutiny. Interest in the Bank's work was no longer confined to the *Wall Street Journal* or *Barron's*. The Bank was no longer part of the exclusive sphere of international bankers and financial statesmen. It had come to epitomize the North-South conflict and the struggle against poverty. It now attracted the attention of politicians, academicians, social activists, and the public at large. This increased attention was helpful to the work of the Bank, but it also led to controversy.

The Bank's growing size inevitably changed the character of the organization. A more complicated hierarchical structure fostered bureaucratic patterns of behavior. McNamara's personality and management style had aggravated some of these problems. The centralization of decisionmaking stifled creativity and effective communication. His overpowering leadership in terms of identifying issues and setting objectives may have numbed institutional perceptiveness and, once he was gone, may have slowed the responses to emerging situations, such as the debt crisis, the environmental issue, and the rising importance of the private sector.[123]

McNamara fervently believed that lifting people out of poverty was the purpose of economic development, and he re-created the Bank to respond to his vision. This was a vastly more complicated and risky challenge than the focus on investment and growth that had defined the Bank in its early years. It implied diversification into sectors of activity where progress was inevitably slow and unspectacular. It required much deeper involvement of the Bank in the economic and social conditions of its borrowers, and that involvement created tension. Above all, it raised the standards by which the performance of the Bank would be measured. McNamara's vision was bold and ambitious. As he left office in 1981, it was unclear whether the Bank would be able to meet the challenge he had accepted.

CHAPTER SIX

Alden W. Clausen

Navigating in Troubled Times

Alden W. Clausen had a tough act to follow. Robert S. McNamara had made the World Bank his institution. He had created and controlled its sophisticated bureaucracy. He had enlarged its lending thirteenfold and more than tripled its staff. By the force of his energy and drive, he had transformed its mission from closing the gap between industrial and developing countries to alleviating world poverty. Although he had given little indication of slowing down, he decided to retire in June 1981, when he would reach the age of 65. During the last year of McNamara's tenure, A. W. Clausen emerged as the leading candidate to succeed him.

Clausen had sound Republican credentials—an essential qualification, given that the presidential campaign of 1980 seemed to be moving toward the election of Republican Ronald Reagan. Clausen had a reputation as an experienced and able manager. BankAmerica, the largest commercial bank in the country, had expanded rapidly under his leadership in the 1970s. For several years in the difficult economic climate of the 1970s—a time of both inflation and recession—BankAmerica was the most profitable commercial bank in the United States and had substantial foreign loans, especially in the developing countries. Clausen, who had overseen the growth of foreign business, was sympathetic to the World Bank. He was familiar with the institution, having attended the joint annual meetings of the Bank and the IMF as a guest for almost a decade.[1]

McNamara visited Clausen in August 1980 to encourage him to take the World Bank presidency. In the fall of 1980 President Carter and Treasury Secretary William Miller discussed Clausen with foreign officials and congressional leaders. President Carter finally appointed Clausen in October, after clearing his choice with candidate Reagan, whose aides had checked out the prospective World Bank leader with prominent Republicans in California. Reagan indicated his approval, although Reagan's close adviser on economic policy at that time, George Shultz, later revealed that the future president admitted that had the choice been his, he might have selected someone else.[2]

An Experienced Manager

"Tom" Clausen, as he was known to friends and colleagues, was a choice unlike any of the five men who had served before him as president of the institution. Meyer and McCloy had substantial Wall Street and government experience. Black and Woods knew the IBRD intimately before their appointments. For the seven years before McNamara took the presidency, he had held the key post of secretary of defense, serving presidents Kennedy and Johnson as one of the most important advisers in their inner circle. All these men knew the ways of Washington, the Bank, or both. They had reliable contacts among officials and staff in the White House and the Department of the Treasury, as well as among the leaders of congressional committees and subcommittees.

In contrast, Clausen had spent his working life at BankAmerica, where diligence, hard work, and attention to detail had propelled him to the top post. He took pride in his mastery and knowledge of the complex, far-flung operations of BankAmerica, an 85,000-

employee, multinational business with whose growth and prosperity he identified.

When, in June 1980, acquaintances first broached the subject of the presidency of the World Bank with him, Clausen reminded them that he lacked government experience and observed that he was certain he did not have a taste for it. This had been his view of government service when, early in the Carter presidency, his name appeared among prospective candidates for secretary of the treasury. Clausen much preferred the relatively structured and familiar environment of a large corporate bureaucracy and his close working relationships with his board of directors, many of whom he had appointed. But in 1980 he had been at BankAmerica for thirty-one years—ten as its highly successful chief executive officer (CEO). McNamara's visit to Clausen in the summer of 1980 piqued his interest, and he studied carefully the financial information that McNamara left with him (2f.).

Indeed, the more he thought about it, the more interested he became in the position. At BankAmerica, Clausen had inherited a strong institution and had made his mark by expanding on that solid base. In its own way, the World Bank job seemed to present very much the same kind of opportunity. Then, too, he knew a great deal about making loans in the developing world—an area of business that he had expanded for BankAmerica. He was also on record in support of greater assistance to the developing world, and he had taken an interest in world population issues. Certainly Clausen would not alter the direction, or redefine the mission, that McNamara had set for the Bank. His goal would be to leave the Bank in as strong a financial position as it was when he took over. He understood that he would be destined to work in McNamara's shadow. But the world economy had entered a particularly difficult period at the end of the 1970s, and Clausen was confident that his experience in banking and finance could be put to good use at the Bank.[3]

His assessment of what might be needed at the time was reasonable. McNamara had centralized power, sharing it only with a trusted circle of top-level officials. He had used the Bank's organization to supply the great reams of information he always needed to make major and relatively minor decisions. Clausen—who prided himself on his managerial skills—wanted to leave an organization able to serve whoever was president. Under Clausen, the whole infrastructure of schedules and reports that McNamara had developed to control the activities of the Bank soon fell into disuse.[4] Clausen's experience had made him a believer in delegation. He had no ambitions to shape the substance of the Bank's activities.

Clausen's initial assessment of what his role might be was not wrong, but events quickly undercut what he thought he would be doing as president. He and most other public and private financial leaders had underestimated the severity of the problems that existed in the international economy even before the debt crisis of 1982 worsened the effects of a persistent global recession. Perhaps his most surprising and vexing difficulty was the hostility some members of the Reagan administration expressed toward the World Bank and the IMF. As a result, Clausen, a conservative California banker who should have felt very much at home with the new U.S. administration, found the always-difficult task of negotiating increases for IDA to be a major problem. Difficulties over the IDA replenishment spilled over into consideration of a general capital increase, which ended up having to be postponed beyond Clausen's tenure as president.

Clausen and his closest advisers in the Bank understood that the sluggish international economy increased the Bank's responsibilities to the poorest countries, especially in Sub-Saharan Africa. Within a year of taking office, Clausen—inspired by his outlook as a commercial banker— proposed new initiatives in regard to guarantees to private international lenders, interest rate mismatches, and joint financing between the IBRD and commercial banks. He also championed activities already under way; for example, to offset the effects of the doubling of crude oil prices following the second oil shock of 1979, he supported the Bank's ongoing efforts to finance energy projects in developing countries. Clausen took a particular interest in the structural and sector lending that McNamara had initiated by the time he left the presidency.[5]

Clausen's recommendations did not represent a departure from past practice. In several key policies, he followed the direction set by McNamara. During McNamara's last eighteen months in office, the Bank had begun to address the consequences for the developing world of higher petroleum prices, rising interests rates, sluggish trade, and increasing current account deficits funded by commercial borrowing. The Bank was still committed to development, but how that was to be achieved in a troubled world economy would become an important issue in the Clausen years. Indeed, when McNamara left, the full impact of what needed to be done to confront the problems of the international economy had not been fully worked out, nor was it clearly understood. This was the environment into which Clausen stepped.

The onset of a major international financial crisis in the summer of 1982 increased demands on the Bank. Some of the developing countries that had posted the most promising growth rates in the 1970s were unable to meet required payments on substantial amounts of debt held by commercial banks. The prospect of wholesale defaults on overseas loans made in the 1970s alarmed the largest commercial banks in the West, especially those in the United States. Under the circumstances, private flows of capital for the developing world dwindled. This situation forced the World Bank to act to keep capital available to the middle-income developing countries that had grown in the 1970s and to the poorest countries, which were also harmed by the sharp increase in interest payments and the drop in funds available for development purposes.

At first, many private bankers and public officials in the United States believed that the debt crisis was the result of a temporary liquidity problem that would disappear once general economic conditions improved. It was during President Reagan's second term, as the international debt problems persisted, that his administration accepted the Bank as a partner in the plan drawn up by Treasury Secretary James Baker to cope with the consequences of the debt crisis.

At the end of his term, Clausen resigned when it became clear that President Reagan would not support his reappointment. He did not have much of a retirement after leaving the Bank on June 30, 1986. Indeed, the evening of his last day at the Bank he received calls from key members of the board of directors of BankAmerica about the problems that had grown up in the years of his absence. By October BankAmerica's board had fired the top management, and Clausen was back as CEO to face up to a serious financial crisis and the threat of a hostile takeover. He threw himself into rescuing the institution in which he had invested so much of his career.[6]

A Life Focused on BankAmerica

Clausen's career was an archetypal twentieth-century American success story. As was true of many other leaders of major business and banking organizations in the decades after World War II, Clausen began his career with one institution, stuck with it for decades, and rose to the top position. Because of the prominence of his institution, he became an important figure in banking circles on the West Coast and a member of the economic and social elite in California.

Like so many other Californians, Alden Winship Clausen was an immigrant from the Midwest. He was born in Hamilton, Illinois, on February 17, 1923. His father, the successful editor and publisher of a weekly newspaper, was among the leading figures in the small town. The younger Clausen had a secure, if uneventful, youth, immune to the harsher economic realities of the depression of the 1930s. During those years, the family never wavered from a staunch Republicanism. Clausen accepted the conservative views of his parents in political matters and carried them with him into adulthood. He attended local public schools and was the valedictorian of his high school class. During his high school years he played the flute in the band, served as editor of the student newspaper, and took part in plays. In one such production, he played a character named Tom, a name that stuck long after the play was forgotten.[7]

After graduating from high school in 1940, he enrolled at Carthage College, a small institution in Kenosha, Wisconsin. He had learned the printing business from his father, and he helped pay his college expenses by working as a Linotype operator. On finishing college in 1944, he joined the Army Air Corps, where he learned meteorology and flew on missions out of the Azores. At the end of his service in 1946, he studied law at the Duluth campus of the University of Minnesota under the GI Bill. He graduated with a law degree in 1949 and quickly passed the Minnesota bar examination.

Clausen met his future wife—the sister of one of his friends—while he was in law school. During the courtship, she took a teaching job in California, and he followed her there at the end of his studies. He prepared for the California bar examination and found a part-time job at BankAmerica's main branch in Los Angeles in 1949. After passing the state bar examination, he took advantage of a new executive training program at the bank.

Despite starting his career at BankAmerica in a lowly part-time job at a cash counter, Clausen decided that he liked banking. He threw himself into the posts that opened up after the executive training program and became known among his colleagues for hard work and attention to detail. An indicator of his reputation for diligence was the easy acceptance within the institution of an apparently apocryphal story that Clausen had taken time out of his wedding day festivities to find a $10 bookkeeping mistake. His devotion to his work propelled his career along. As a lending officer, he specialized in high-tech firms, arranging loans for such successful companies as Memorex and Teledyne. By 1961 he had become a vice president, with responsibility for the electronics industry. In 1963 he moved to BankAmerica's headquarters in San Francisco to take charge of the bank's corporate finance department. Within two years, at the age of 42, he had become a senior vice president. Along the way, he took a year off at BankAmerica's expense to enroll in the advanced management program at the graduate school of business administration at Harvard University. He returned from this academic sojourn to take the post of executive vice president, which made him a member of the bank's chief policymaking management committee. In his new post, he oversaw the creation and workings of regional offices in California. This experience introduced him to what he saw as the bank's overly centralized and bureaucratic organization.[8]

In 1968 BankAmerica's chairman gave Clausen responsibility for the bank's international lending business. Clausen was clearly on the bank's managerial fast track. He oversaw the complex foreign operations and took the lead in making some of the bank's most important international loans. His penchant for detail served him well in negotiating complicated loan agreements among partners and borrowers from different countries. Putting together several notable deals burnished his image with top executives at headquarters.

After his success in heading up foreign lending, Clausen became vice chairman of the board in May 1969. Within months the CEO resigned, and the board chose Clausen as his successor. Thus, on January 1, 1970, at the age of 46, Tom Clausen became president and CEO of one of the largest banks in the United States. He was an aggressive and effective CEO. During his tenure, BankAmerica's assets quadrupled, and he reoriented the bank's business. By 1980 BankAmerica was no longer only a regional California bank. It had become a major player in the international economy, with a substantial loan portfolio that included the business of major multinational corporations and foreign governments, among them developing countries. By the time Clausen left, BankAmerica had 500 overseas branches in over 100 countries. There were years in Clausen's decade as CEO in which BankAmerica was the most profitable bank in the United States.[9]

Despite a long-term strategy of decentralizing BankAmerica's operations, Clausen remained a highly involved leader with a penchant for detailed knowledge of what was going on in his bank. He was a workaholic with an unparalleled mastery of the statistics and numbers behind the bank's operations. He was a threatening presence when he visited branches in California or abroad. On such visits, as at headquarters, he enjoyed showing up employees who did not know something about their jobs that he knew and that he clearly thought they should know. Clausen did not endear himself to his employees with such tactics, but the stockholders could not have been happier with the bank's performance.

Between 1975 and 1979 net earnings grew by an average of almost 19 percent a year. When rapid growth trailed off sharply in 1980, Clausen took personal command of a campaign to cut costs and boost returns. It was in the midst of this effort that McNamara and others approached him about the presidency of the World Bank. He had several months to accustom himself to the idea that he might be offered the job. Although he was reluctant to leave BankAmerica during his campaign to restore profits, when in October 1980 President Carter called to offer him the position, he accepted.[10]

Clausen left BankAmerica in April 1981 to prepare to start his new job on July 1. In the interim he boned up on international financial issues and traveled abroad to meet leaders in politics, finance, and business. In late May he set up shop in a BankAmerica office in Washington and began meeting with Bank officials to prepare for his new post (3).

Clausen's Agenda

When, in July 1981, Tom Clausen assumed the presidency of the Bank, the international economy was deep into one of the worst recessions of the post–World War II era. The developing countries had been particularly affected. The continuing recession in the industrial countries depressed their major export markets, and, as a result, the poorest developing countries in particular found it difficult to finance their essential import needs. Rising interest rates cut further into the available foreign exchange resources.

At the same time, a major political shift had taken place. Liberal thinking, which had focused on the need to address social inequities and had looked to governments to do so, had given way to a new conservatism in economic policies that emphasized the role of the private sector and the unobstructed functioning of the market mechanism. The conservative Reagan administration looked at official foreign aid and at the World Bank with distinct skepticism. The emphasis on poverty alleviation, which McNamara had seen as a central objective of the institution, was especially suspect and turned the Bank in the eyes of its conservative critics into a "welfare" organization relying on "giveaway" programs. The Reagan administration undertook a comprehensive review of the merits of U.S. participation in multilateral development banks, taking an especially hard look at IDA. Although the review demonstrated the merits of IDA and the support given U.S. policy objectives by the activities of the multilateral development banks, a lingering prejudice remained that affected the working relations between the Bank and its major shareholder throughout the years of the Clausen presidency.

It fell to Clausen to position the Bank in this new context and to make it respond effectively to the increasingly acute economic problems of its borrowing members despite the ambivalence of its major donor shareholders. Clausen seemed the right man to meet this challenge. As an eminent commercial banker he would be inclined to look for solutions in market-oriented development strategies; he would feel more comfortable working with the private sector than with government bureaucracies; he would shift the emphasis from concern about distribution back to economic growth; and, in general, he would once again take his cues from the financial markets rather than from the demands of the developing countries.

As a banker, Clausen took a close interest in the financial position of the Bank. He recognized the value of the Bank to the international community. He knew little about the Bank's developmental agenda and relied on his staff to tell him what he needed to know. In contrast, he saw the preservation of the Bank's financial integrity and its sound functioning as personal responsibilities.[11] When he took over the Bank, Clausen looked carefully at its financial condition. He was impressed with the established record: no losses or defaults, a healthy capital base, a conservative ratio between borrowings and lending, and high-quality liquid assets exceeding $8 billion. But he was concerned to find that the Bank was raising funds in the capital markets at rapidly escalating interest rates to meet disbursements against lending commitments that were locked in over many years at rates substantially below then-current market rates. To correct this mismatch was one of Clausen's priorities and ranked high on his initial agenda.

As a first step, the Bank doubled commitment fees on new IBRD loans, introduced commitment fees for IDA credits, and began charging supplementary front-end fees on new loans. More fundamentally, Clausen replaced the traditional practice of charging fixed interest rates for Bank loans with a system of variable interest rates to correct the mismatch between the cost of money at the time of commitment and at the time of disbursement. The board approved this change, which took effect on July 1, 1982. The new variable rates would be based on the cost of the Bank's entire pool of borrowed funds at different rates, with varying maturities, and in different currencies. The Bank's interest rates on disbursed and undisbursed portions of all loans would henceforth change every six months to reflect the cost of its borrowings.

Clausen recognized that the Bank had to find new ways to continue promoting development in a troubled international economy. "The World Bank in the 1980s," he said, "is going to have to continue to be prudent and conservative, but given the realities of the world today, great demands will be made on its creativity and inventiveness as well." The problems of the rapidly changing international economy, he said, "demand redoubled resolve, redoubled effort, and, perhaps most fundamental of all, redoubled understanding."[12]

The difficult realities of the world economy permitted the Bank "little tolerance for inefficiencies,"[13] as Clausen said in his first address to the board of governors. He did not expect quick improvement in an economic environment marked by volatile capital markets, high interest rates, rising inflation, slower growth, increasing unemployment, and shrinking trade. He went on to say that because resources for development investment would be scarce, "priorities will have to be carefully defined, investment decisions will have to be scrutinized, and available resources will have to be used as effectively as possible" (3).

To Clausen, the way to increase efficiency and achieve "pragmatic economic progress" was simple. The problems in the international economy dictated that the Bank promote free markets and private sector institutions. McNamara had focused on efficiency too but had played down the importance of ownership. In contrast, Clausen saw a clear link between efficiency and ownership and believed that improved performance demanded that preference be given to the private sector. Scarcer resources required developing countries to improve market signals and price incentives while substituting imports for expensive domestic production and increasing the efficiency of their export sectors.[14]

Clausen's entire career had convinced him of the power of vigorous private sector institutions operating in a free market for goods and capital. He stated his convictions unambiguously in remarks at a Brookings Institution conference in 1982 on the future of the Bank. "The private sector," he observed, "is what I know best, and what I called home for thirty-one years. As a commercial banker, my whole career was spent in that competitive, creative, energetic marketplace—and I have to say honestly, I loved it. And I still do"

(3ff.). But of more importance, he said: "I know [the private sec-tor] works. And what's more, most of our developing member coun-tries know it works too. The private sector, after all, currently gen-erates well over half the gross domestic product in the developing world, and there are broad sectors in many of the economies there where private enterprise can be an immensely effective agent for furthering economic development" (2). He saw that "those coun-tries have demonstrated the best economic performance that have encouraged their private sectors" (4). Consequently, he was convinced that even the poorest developing countries could accelerate their eco-nomic growth by more effectively using their private sectors.

Clausen brought one other strong conviction to the World Bank from his years in business. His overseas business experience taught him that "noisy, argumentative, complicated—but ultimately ines-capable—interdependence" characterized "our era" (30). No longer was it accurate, he believed, to think in terms of a world divided between the wealthy north and the poor south. Established indus-trial nations and newly industrializing countries were not confined to two separate geographic spheres, nor were capital markets. Al-though Sub-Saharan Africa had fallen behind in the 1970s, popu-lous countries such as China, India, and Indonesia had progressed in that decade. He believed that the Bank needed to take the new realities into account. "The multipolar world in which it operates will evolve and grow only more interdependent in the decade ahead and the Bank must evolve and grow with it."[15]

Clausen thought that the Bank was particularly well positioned to cope with the new realities of interdependence. In fact, he was optimistic that the Bank might serve as "a kind of prototype insti-tution of the world's new international era of interdependence" (54). After all, it had over thirty years of experience in working on practical issues with almost all of the world's countries. Clausen advocated that the Bank respond to the multipolar international economy by forging greater cooperation with both public and pri-vate international institutions. The Bank, as the largest interna-tional development institution, could not—and should not—try to do everything that had to be done in the development field; but cooperation would improve the prospect of using scarce resources efficiently and getting them to where they were needed.[16]

Clausen's fundamental commitment to free markets, private flows of capital, and international cooperation, together with his commercial banker's knowledge of finance, inspired innovations concerning investment guarantees and cofinancing with commercial banks. More generally, his convictions guided his choices of which among the Bank's ongoing programs to emphasize. In particular, Clausen championed increased structural and sector lending, which had the virtue of encouraging free market institutions. He also advocated expanding aid coordination—consortia, consultative groups, and close collaboration with the IMF—to improve the impact of technical and financial assistance.

Clausen's approach to Bank policy evolved slowly. Both his innovative initiatives and the increasing emphasis he placed on selective Bank programs emerged in response to the problems of the international recession and then the debt crisis. As he said in his address to the board of governors in 1984, "by no means will . . . evolutionary change dilute the essence of the Bank's role as the primary financier of long-term development investment."[17]

There had been much concern that the stringency associated with further IDA replenishments, combined with his own convictions, would lead Clausen to abandon the Bank's commitment to fight poverty. Mahbub Ul Haq remembered that Clausen announced at an early meeting that poverty alleviation "did not figure in his thinking at all."[18] The staff's critical reactions to McNamara's insistence on quantifying the effect of the Bank's activities on poverty appeared to have convinced him that the poverty focus of the Bank was just a "thin veneer" and not a central commitment.

In early 1982 an internal task force examined the continued relevance of the poverty alleviation objective and concluded that it should remain an integral part of the Bank's strategy. The task force found, however, that the "current concern with energy and structural adjustment, combined with the transition to a new chief executive, make many staff members question the Bank's commitment to this objective."[19] On the strength of this report, Clausen reaffirmed in his 1982 address to the Bank's governors that a "key and central aim of the World Bank is the alleviation of poverty."[20] The pragmatist Clausen recognized the complementarity between efficient growth and poverty reduction, the productive potential of the poor, and the link between political instability and poverty. Robert Ayres, who examined the Bank's strategy for dealing with poverty, concluded that "the ideological and programmatic differences between 'McNamara's Bank' and 'Clausen's Bank' [had] been exaggerated. . . . While McNamara's Bank had for some a 'leftist' image which obscured the real nature of its operations, Clausen's Bank [had] acquired for others a 'rightist' image which likewise obscures what the Bank [was] really doing."[21]

In his first address to the Bank's governors, Clausen announced that three established priorities—agriculture, energy, and Sub-Saharan Africa—would continue to receive special attention in both IBRD and IDA lending. During his term the thinking about how best to advance each program area changed, but these areas continued to receive the bulk of IBRD and IDA lending commitments.[22]

Throughout the five years he spent in the Bank, Clausen reiterated that agriculture and rural development would continue to receive the top priority in lending. Aside from the obvious humanitarian benefits of relieving hunger and improving living conditions in rural areas, agriculture programs had enjoyed considerable success, especially in populous South Asia. A part of the world that had suffered staggering food shortages in modern times was approaching self-sufficiency by the end of the 1970s. Those successes, Clausen thought, reflected the strength and experience of the Bank.

Since 1973, when OPEC had quadrupled oil prices, developing countries dependent on imported oil had struggled to increase domestic supplies of alternative sources of energy. The further doubling of oil prices in 1979 added urgency to Bank-supported programs to promote new supplies of energy. Clausen recognized the importance of the Bank's assistance in the energy field and announced an immediate 25 percent increase in energy lending, including substantial sums for hydroelectric power projects. The energy sector thus quickly became the single most important area for the Bank's lending in the Clausen years, regularly absorbing between one-fifth and one-quarter of the Bank's commitments.

Lending for energy was not, however, without controversy. Although the United States had at first strongly supported increased

Bank lending in the energy sector, lending for oil and gas exploration and development soon became a matter of serious dispute between the United States and the Bank, especially under the Reagan administration. In the view of the U.S. government, oil and gas lending should be left to the private sector. Accordingly, the United States strongly opposed any proposal for lending in this field, even in countries that had obvious difficulties obtaining financing on commercial terms. Clausen, in contrast, was primarily concerned with increasing "the availability of locally produced oil, gas, and coal in the developing countries" and reducing their dependence on imported oil. [23] Whether governments or private entrepreneurs dealt with the problem seemed to the pragmatist Clausen more a matter to be settled in the light of practical circumstances.

It was obvious, however, that the Bank, relying on its own resources, could not make an adequate contribution to the financing of needed energy investments. For this reason the idea of an energy affiliate had been mooted as a way of enlarging and concentrating the Bank's assistance to the energy sector. The proposal had enjoyed U.S. support until the Reagan administration turned against it as "another window for increasing the lending of the Bank, which it opposed."[24] Clausen thought the proposal had merit, but he did not like the creation of another bureaucracy. He thought there would be alternative ways of raising the necessary resources if the time was not ripe for a separate affiliate; cofinancing with other concerned donors clearly was one promising avenue to pursue. [25]

The final priority on Clausen's list was Sub-Saharan Africa. In 1979 the African governors had asked the Bank to study the barriers to economic progress for countries in their region. Concern for the plight of this part of the world had increased in the 1970s as per capita income declined there; Bank officials estimated that per capita income in Sub-Saharan Africa would not increase in the 1980s. In response to the continent's needs, the Bank proposed doubling aid to Africa to provide infrastructure, improve agriculture, and develop energy. The Bank also promised to enlist the rest of the international development community in providing assistance. The Bank's analysis of Africa's problems addressed the need for more efficient use of resources and the design of appropriate policies as essential to whatever effort would be mounted to assist the region. Clausen endorsed these ideas, especially the proposal for redesigning economic policies to promote efficiency, to encourage better market incentives for production, to reduce subsidies to uncompetitive industries, and to promote exports.

From the moment Clausen stepped into the Bank, the pressure from the borrowing countries for increased assistance, especially in quick-disbursing form, had been mounting. This reflected the financial constraints many countries were facing as a result of the recession. The situation was aggravated by the decline in net capital flows to the developing countries. Commercial banks almost halved their net lending between 1981 and 1982, from $42 billion to $24 billion. At the same time the major industrial countries were reducing their official development assistance because of budgetary constraints. Although Clausen promised to increase Bank assistance by using the additional scope for lending provided by the 1979 general capital increase, he knew that the Bank could not possibly make up for the drop in the flow of resources to the developing world.[26]

Clausen well recognized, however, the potential of the Bank to act as a catalyst and stimulate lending by others, especially during a period of flagging confidence. He thought that the flow of private investments was constrained principally by the investors' inability to manage the political risks associated with investments in developing countries. Thus, without much discussion among management and the executive directors, and guided by his experience as a commercial banker, he revived the idea of a multilateral investment insurance scheme to deal with those risks not covered by the existing framework of insurance arrangements.[27]

Clausen left the details of the proposal for others to work out. In fact, the proposal languished until 1983, when Ibrahim Shihata, who had organized a successful investment guarantee scheme in the Middle East, became the Bank's general counsel. He championed Clausen's idea, refined it—changing the language from insurance to one of guarantee—and saw the Multilateral Investment Guarantee Agency (MIGA) to fruition in 1986, after several years of arduous negotiations among the Bank's member governments.[28] MIGA, in its final version, envisioned a mission that embraced

Clausen's original ideas about encouraging private capital flows by providing guarantees against noncommercial risks. It was meant to cooperate with and complement the work of national, regional, and private investment insurance programs.[29]

Clausen also supported cofinancing as a way for the Bank to stimulate capital flows to developing countries from official sources, export credit agencies, and commercial banks. His interest in cofinancing stemmed from his experience at BankAmerica, which in 1975 first cofinanced a project with the IBRD. "I liked it then as a commercial banker," he said; "I like it now as a development banker."[30] Encouraging cofinancing, Clausen thought, would keep funds flowing to infrastructure projects, and such loans would also permit longer maturities, helping borrowers better structure their debt. Cofinancing with commercial banks, in particular, would also help reintroduce developing countries to the capital markets, following a restructuring of their debt. The Bank's credit and sound reputation for managing projects would reduce the risk to private lenders, which would help borrowers as well by encouraging lower interest rates.[31]

Cofinanced projects had declined in fiscal 1980, and Bank officials concluded that a major effort was necessary to persuade commercial banks to take part in them. Discussions of the problems in cofinanced projects with commercial banks were under way when Clausen took over the Bank. He enthusiastically endorsed the effort to improve contacts with commercial banks in the United States and abroad. The issue was one that he easily made his own, and he joined other Bank officials in meeting representatives of commercial banks to "sell" the idea.[32]

Clausen enthusiastically embraced the innovative B-loan proposal, designed to facilitate IBRD participation in commercially structured loans. The B-loan permitted the Bank to support an associated commercial loan, in addition to its own loan, without formally linking the two by cross-default provisions. The most common arrangement was direct participation of up to 25 percent of the commercial loan. The special relationship of the Bank with its borrowers gave cooperating commercial bankers the protective umbrella of the Bank's participation, with reduced risk of default and correspondingly favorable terms.[33]

The B-loan program got under way in September 1983, following a full exploration in 1982 of the Bank's increased risk in such loans, especially as it affected its customary insistence on preferred creditor status. Bank studies of the issue concluded that the B-loans would have to be carefully investigated and monitored. On balance, however, the investigations concluded that the risk was outweighed by the possibility of increasing capital flows through the enhanced leverage the loans opened to Bank capital.[34] In the years that followed, the Bank helped arrange B-loans totaling almost $5 billion for twenty-four projects. The program was eventually discontinued in 1989 because the continuing debt crisis caused concern about possible defaults.[35]

These measures, as it turned out, were only modest first steps in coping with the consequences of the international recession. In the fall of 1982, as conditions in the world economy deteriorated further, Argentina, Brazil, and Mexico announced they could not continue paying interest on their debts. A financial debacle was in the offing, as the potential losses threatened large banks in the United States and elsewhere in the industrial world. During what became known as the debt crisis, major debtor countries found it difficult to make scheduled payments on substantial loans that they had negotiated with private commercial banks in the 1970s.

The International Debt Crisis

The debt crisis of the summer of 1982 became a central concern of the Bank during the Clausen era. Along with most analysts, Clausen thought that the crisis was fundamentally a liquidity problem. The solution, he believed, would be to overcome the fall in export earnings of the developing countries, and he strongly advocated free and expanding international trade.[36] However, analysis of the circumstances that inhibited the growth of export earnings soon demonstrated the need for major restructuring of the developing economies. Clausen was prepared to use the financial strength of the Bank "as fully and as effectively as possible."[37]

Sectoral and structural adjustment operations became the centerpiece of the Bank's response to the debt crisis. They made it possible to tackle the needed economic reforms while facilitating a relatively rapid transfer of resources. Structural adjustment lending had been introduced late in the McNamara years as a way of assisting developing member countries with the adjustments necessitated by the escalation of energy prices. The loans and credits helped countries alter the structure of their economies in order to expand their export sectors, save on the use of expensive energy sources, and improve efficiency through more sensible resource allocation. This form of assistance was viewed with skepticism by the major shareholders, who insisted on strict limits on adjustment lending. The pressure to respond to the urgent demands of the Bank's embattled members, however, soon required a steady lifting of those limits. The proportion of Bank-IDA lending devoted to structural adjustment increased rapidly, from 8 percent in fiscal 1981 to 22 percent in fiscal 1986. When Clausen left, the Bank Group had committed a total of almost $12.5 billion for adjustment operations, including $2.5 billion in IDA resources for the poorest members of the Bank.

The support of structural reforms required expansion and intensification of the Bank's analytical work. The Bank became heavily involved in helping governments investigate their economic problems and identify the available options. As time went on, the Bank's economic and sector work became more rigorous and brought not only economic but, increasingly, social and institutional issues into the purview of the reform programs. The Bank, as Clausen signaled in his speeches and as Anne Krueger, his economic adviser, vigorously advocated, gave particular prominence to the issue of trade liberalization and effectively influenced the direction of the reform process, especially in Latin America. Bank studies suggested that countries which pursued outward-oriented policies generally grew faster than countries which followed inward-oriented, protectionist strategies.

The debt crisis also required closer collaboration between the Bank and the IMF. In dealing with the problems of their developing country members, the Bank and the Fund found that their concerns increasingly overlapped; structural adjustment was difficult to separate from fiscal and monetary stabilization. But the different cultures of the two institutions and the years of operating entirely apart made friction and rivalry hard to avoid.[38] Bank staff tended to see the closely controlled attitude of their Fund colleagues as doctrinaire, even arrogant. The senior Bank official at the center of the coordination effort at the time observed that collaboration was difficult because of the "nature of the Fund as a human institution which is secretive, which is arrogant, which is very patronizing in terms of what the Bank does."[39] In contrast, IMF staff tended to criticize what they perceived as the Bank's freewheeling style and relaxed attitude in dealing with confidential information.

Clausen saw clearly that the Bank and the Fund had to work together. The Fund's support of adjustment was just as vital and urgent as the Bank's support of development.[40] He developed a close working relationship with Jacques de Larosière, managing director of the IMF. The two held regular informal discussions on how to better coordinate the operations of the two institutions, and whenever there were conflicts between Bank and Fund staff, they took steps to diffuse tension and ensure effective working relations. IMF and Bank staff were instructed to keep each other fully informed of their findings and, in shaping their respective operational interventions, to take into account their counterparts' comments.

Actually, the fiscal discipline required to address the crisis, and enforced by the IMF through its programs, tended to limit the scope for the long-term investments supported by the Bank. The disbursement of project assistance provided by the Bank and other donors—never a rapid form of capital transfer—slowed perceptibly as governments struggled to allocate scarce budgetary resources for essential services.

In response, the Bank undertook a special action program to accelerate disbursements, collaborating with the other multilateral development banks and the development aid agencies of several donor governments. "Together," Clausen said, "we can give developing countries a meaningful boost in their efforts to cope with liquidity problems and stalled development." The Bank boosted disbursements of both ongoing and new projects. In fiscal 1984 and 1985, additional disbursements amounted to $4.5 billion, "almost compensating for the shortfall in regular disbursements."[41] The Bank hoped to encourage developing countries to complete projects as quickly as possible and provide the basis for a resumption of long-term growth.

Despite these initiatives, the Bank and its president were criticized for not reacting more actively to the debt crisis. The reason was that the United States, the Bank's largest shareholder, did not initially support a major role for the Bank in the debt crisis. Officials in the U.S. Treasury saw the debt crisis as a problem to be sorted out between the commercial banks and their debtors. Although the 1982 Treasury report had unambiguously confirmed the positive contribution of the Bank, there were misgivings about the Bank's venturing into the active support of policy reforms. Apart from ideological reservations, the prospect of demands for more IDA funds and for a further capital increase of the Bank may have dampened U.S. support for an enlarged role of the Bank in handling the crisis.[42]

This attitude changed when, in the fall of 1985, the new secretary of the treasury, James A. Baker, took the lead in producing a plan to cope with the consequences of the debt crisis. Up to then, U.S. officials had hoped that an improving international economy would take care of the developing world's liquidity problems. Although there were overall improvements in the international economy in 1983 and 1984, private sector lending was almost impossible to obtain for medium-income developing countries, most of which had experienced little growth and still faced problems in servicing their debts, even after rescheduling.[43]

The World Bank was meant to play an important part in the plan Baker put together in October 1985. The secretary followed a very public strategy of encouraging commercial banks, in conjunction with the multilateral development banks, to increase flows of "new monies" to the developing world by $20 billion over three years. As part of his plan, Baker commended the World Bank's cofinancing efforts. In a speech to the annual meetings of the World Bank and the IMF in 1985, he also supported the Bank's targeting up to 20 percent of its new loans for structural adjustment—a policy that the Reagan administration now applauded as a way of improving markets and private sector institutions in the developing countries.

Mobilizing Donor Support for IDA and the Bank

The more supportive attitude of the second Reagan administration was much appreciated by the Bank and its other shareholders. Clausen had been bitterly disappointed by the rejection, if not outright hostility, his proposals had encountered in the U.S. Treasury. Personally, he much preferred the pragmatic, gentlemanly Baker to the outgoing secretary, the ideological, confrontational Donald Regan. Even so, Baker, no less than Regan, wanted to limit U.S. financial commitments to IDA and to the Bank. The struggle to raise funds for IDA and to initiate a further general capital increase for the Bank, with the Bank's largest shareholder determined to limit any contributions, became the source of Clausen's major frustration. This was not a good time for foreign assistance or help to the disadvantaged countries, but Clausen's lack of familiarity with the ways of Washington probably compounded these difficulties.

Clausen struggled with the problem of raising funds for IDA from the beginning of his presidency. The periodic IDA replenishments had become a regular—and increasingly time-consuming—responsibility of the president and the Bank's top management. Difficulties arose quickly with the U.S. contribution to IDA-6 in 1981. In the last year of the Carter presidency, the administration pledged $3.24 billion to IDA-6, to be appropriated over a three-year period. Because of promises to balance the U.S. government budget, the new Reagan administration proposed sharp cuts in numerous programs, including foreign aid. When the State Department strenuously objected to draconian reductions in overseas assistance, the administration relented. But instead of the $1.08 billion per year pledged in the Carter years, the Reagan administration requested, and Congress authorized, only $500 million in the first year and $800 million in the second year of the replenishment.

The situation reached crisis proportions in September 1981. The Reagan administration's position angered other industrial nations. The United States had cut back before and had delayed pledged payments; now, enough was enough. Several industrial nations decided, in the interest of "equal burden sharing," to reduce their contributions to IDA by the same proportion as the United States had. As a result, it appeared that the total $4.1 billion planned for IDA-6 in fiscal 1982 would be cut by $1.5 billion.[44]

Clausen and his senior staff enlisted the support of ministers and heads of state, who in turn lobbied their counterparts in other countries. They also enlisted the help of leaders in Part II countries to make the case for IDA to their counterparts in Part I countries. At Clausen's request, Indira Gandhi agreed to weigh in with Margaret Thatcher. She must have done so effectively, for Prime Minister Thatcher lent her full support and persuaded other G-7 leaders not to diminish their support of IDA. As part of the effort on behalf of IDA-6, the Bank also engaged in a wide-ranging international public relations campaign. In the United States, Clausen hoped to build congressional and public support by emphasizing American self-interest in promoting growth and stability in the poorest of the world's economies.

However, Congress and the Reagan administration failed to change their views. After two years, the U.S. government had provided only about one-third of what had been pledged. Other industrial countries relented on the issue of burden sharing and agreed to pay their full IDA payments for fiscal 1983. Ultimately, the U.S. Congress authorized funds for its pledged payment under IDA-6, although the contribution was spread over four years instead of three. Because of inflation and the one-year extension of the payment, the total U.S. IDA-6 contribution represented, in real terms, an 8 percent decline from the IDA-5 contribution—the largest drop in American contributions to replenishments.[45]

Relations between the Bank and the United States had been strained before, but now both the Reagan administration and Congress proved hostile to the Bank. Factions in both parties in Congress, where foreign aid was always a hard sell, were unsympathetic to appeals for overseas assistance. Liberal politicians and commentators believed that the stringent reforms advocated by the Bank harmed developing countries or that the Bank was using public monies to bail out the commercial banks. Right-wing politicians did not want to "waste" money on foreign aid in the midst of a serious domestic economic recession.

The United States' perception of its economic role in the world had undergone a change: no longer was the American public willing to take on major international financial responsibilities. In his opening address to the 1983 annual meetings, President Reagan

agreed to support the IDA replenishment and capital increase negotiated by his predecessor; but he made clear that U.S. policy toward the Bank would be opposed to the traditional support of
government-led, public sector–oriented development. "What has
united [successful developing countries] was their belief in the magic
of the marketplace," he declared. "Millions of individuals making their own decisions in the marketplace will always allocate
resources better than any centralized government planning process."[46]

In this environment, and in the midst of the campaign to get
pledged funds for IDA-6, Clausen had to begin work on IDA-7, covering fiscal 1985–87. Funding levels for IDA-7 soon became a contentious issue between the Bank and the U.S. administration and Congress. The United States insisted on holding its contribution to less
than its contribution to IDA-6. Because of the rough experience
with collecting the funds committed to the IDA-6 replenishment,
Clausen concluded that the Bank should aim at maintaining IDA-7
at the level of IDA-6 in real terms. Clausen's strategy of supporting
a steady-state replenishment created divisions within the top ranks
of the Bank. Moeen Qureshi, senior vice president, finance, advocated the limited approach followed by Clausen, but Ernest Stern,
senior vice president, operations, believed that the Bank should
have pressed for a higher figure, more in line with the increasing
needs of the developing countries.

Clausen and his senior vice presidents, like their predecessors,
made a strong pitch to government officials from Part I countries
and to key members of the U.S. Congress. Clausen also undertook
a campaign directed outside government circles to win support for
increased IDA funding. His efforts included appeals to the pope
and to American cardinals and bishops long interested in poverty
in the developing countries. Nevertheless, the U.S. government
announced in December 1983 that on the basis of its 25 percent share, it would support a replenishment of no more than
$9 billion, a figure significantly lower than the proposed $16
billion. Administration officials maintained that Congress's
negative mood about government spending, as well as opposition to foreign aid specifically, made a larger request impossible.

Without the support of the administration, there was little hope of getting the increase that Clausen thought necessary. One of the arguments in support of an increase in IDA funding was China's need for concessional assistance. This, however, was not a persuasive argument for a government that still looked with misgivings at China's participation in the Bank and, in any event, believed that China as well as India, another large client of IDA, should rely on private sources of capital.[47] Thus, in 1984, thirty-three donor countries agreed to an IDA-7 replenishment of $9 billion, about $3 billion less than the previous one in nominal terms.

Clausen made no secret of his disappointment with this turn of events. In particular, he emphasized the consequences of the inadequate IDA replenishment for Sub-Saharan Africa. Since 1982 drought and famine had exacerbated extremely poor conditions brought about by declining per capita income, the failure of programs to increase food production, falling prices for export commodities, and increasing external debt. At the G-7 meeting in Tokyo in July 1984, a proposal initiated by Clausen, that donor countries provide supplemental funds to IDA to address the developmental needs of Africa, led nowhere. Germany and Japan refused to go along with a plan that, deliberately or not, would cause the United States embarrassment.

A subsequent "joint program of action" proposed by the Bank fared better. This program attempted to bring together donors and African governments in a cooperative multilateral approach to the continent's problems. It was based on analyses contained in the Bank's 1984 report *Toward Sustained Development in Sub-Saharan Africa.*[48] An integral part of the joint program was the creation of a three-year special assistance facility for Sub-Saharan Africa to replace the failed proposal for supplemental contributions. Clausen took a leading role in approaching governments to contribute to this effort, which ultimately collected more than $1.6 billion for African governments willing to undertake necessary policy reforms. The Reagan administration declined to participate in the facility, but Congress went ahead and authorized $225 million for the purpose. Even though the administration never requested appropriation of these funds, Congress eventually passed legislation stipulating the use of about $140 million for the facility.[49]

At the time the Sub-Saharan facility was announced, the Bank was already engaged in internal discussions about the IDA-8 replenishment. The prospects for success were, if anything, even bleaker than those for IDA-7. In a 1985 budget message President Reagan had announced that the U.S. government would not budget for future replenishments of IDA or the multilateral development banks.[50] By the time negotiations about IDA were getting more intense, James A. Baker had become secretary of the treasury, and the United States seemed to soften its approach. However, Baker proved hardly more accommodating than his predecessor. Little progress had been made toward settling the principal parameters of the replenishment by the time Clausen left the Bank and turned this problem over to his successor.

Agreement on a further capital increase for the Bank proved similarly elusive and was left for Clausen's successor to handle. The Bank had projected sharp increases in lending, which would soon approach the limits imposed by the Bank's subscribed capital. U.S. Treasury officials were concerned about the timing of the capital increase in relation to the replenishment of IDA. In the event, the Bank's lending fell short of the projected targets, and the U.S. government used this as an argument against the need for a general capital increase. The challenge persuaded Clausen to delay the increase to early 1987, with subscriptions scheduled for fiscal 1988.[51]

In his last year as president, Clausen became increasingly concerned that the U.S. position on these matters had signaled a permanent change in the U.S. government's support for the Bank. Did, as he feared, the administration believe that the Bank had reached its optimum size and that its mission could be accomplished at a static level of funding? Apart from his regular appeals to the Bank's governors to support an expansion of the Bank and its role, Clausen took the Bank's case actively to the news media, business gatherings, and bodies such as the Overseas Development Council and the Bretton Woods Committee. In meetings with Baker during the summer of 1985, Clausen made a strong personal appeal for the adoption by the administration of a constructive position on the role and the future of the Bank.[52] Thus, he may have contributed to a change in the attitude of the U.S. government—a change that became apparent, however, only after he had left the Bank.

Clausen's Style of Management

If Clausen had doubts about his effectiveness in a government setting, he was confident that he would have little difficulty in managing the Bank.[53] After a lifetime with the largest commercial bank in the country, running the World Bank did not seem to present a particular managerial challenge. To his surprise, the job of managing the Bank turned out to be more demanding than he had thought. It took him a while to understand how the Bank operated, and he was never quite confident about "pushing the buttons" to make things happen. He did not feel comfortable with the system created by McNamara, which presumed his direct involvement in the substantive work of the Bank. He saw his role as that of a manager, as someone who knew how to run a bank.[54] Instead, he found himself presiding over a sophisticated bureaucratic organization that seemed to run smoothly under the leadership of the brilliant, hardworking senior vice president of operations, Ernest Stern.

Clausen was not a chief executive who had made his career in a number of different corporations. His entire professional life had been with BankAmerica. This experience determined his approach and his style. Although it prepared him well to handle organizational problems and to address the financial difficulties that the Bank encountered in the early 1980s, it was hard for him to accept the peculiarities of the Bank, especially the presence of a full-time, resident board of directors chosen with no input from management.

Tom Clausen transferred the managerial techniques he had used at BankAmerica to the World Bank. His management style was group oriented and collegial. He had concluded quickly that McNamara's president's council, which included all the Bank's vice presidents, was too large to serve as his management team. In its place he created a managing committee made up of the Bank's top executives responsible for operations, finance, administration, economics, legal affairs, external relations, and relations with the board, who reported directly to him. He used this group to thrash out policy issues and arrive at collective decisions. It was his way of learning about major issues and about Bank operations. It allowed him to understand the complicated policy and operational issues that characterized the Bank's work as a development institution. Clausen typically adopted the role of an interested observer at the meetings of the managing committee. He allowed members to speak freely and even encouraged disagreement, but he seldom expressed an opinion outside the areas of his known competence. The conclusions of the discussions might therefore only become apparent when he issued the minutes of the meeting.

The managing committee had served Clausen well at BankAmerica. There it combined, at the top of the organization, the experience and understanding of people who had risen through its ranks and were thoroughly familiar with its business and its problems. It helped keep his top people focused on issues larger than their departmental responsibilities, and they learned to see the organization as a whole. He wanted to bring the same system to the World Bank, to create, as he said, "a feeling of brotherhood, . . . a responsibility for the totality and not just for a segment. . . . I sensed there was too much segment-thinking when I first came."[55]

The managing committee Clausen formed at the World Bank included three members who had not worked on the Bank's staff before or who, like Clausen himself, were new to the Bank: the general counsel, the secretary, and the chief economist. They had little to contribute to subjects beyond their immediate area of responsibility, and the collegiality that Clausen attempted to achieve was correspondingly limited. In practice, the committee was dominated by the senior vice presidents of finance and operations, who often disagreed.

At BankAmerica the collegial model worked well because Clausen thoroughly understood the goals of the bottom line and shareholders' values. His managing committee at BankAmerica might discuss tactics and strategy, but Clausen was in thorough command of the information necessary to make decisions, and he made them. He also understood how to evaluate whether what his committee decided was being implemented and whether it was successful. It was relatively easy to make judgments about private sector performance on the basis of profits and return on investment. Although neither of the classic private sector measures of performance was alien to the Bank, the attainment of the Bank's objectives was difficult to define quantitatively.

The difference between Clausen at BankAmerica and at the World Bank was a matter of understanding, focus, and direction. In his California career, he always knew what needed to be done. He used the members of his committee to refine his understanding of the issues from their various perspectives and to ensure that they understood his thinking. In Washington he used his committee to shape his understanding of where the Bank's mission fit into the tough, changing times of the early 1980s. The harsh new realities in the international economy, however, did not always point clearly to the direction in which Clausen should take the Bank. His cautiousness was therefore in part a reflection of his uncertainty. On many issues outside his experience as a commercial banker, he did not have an independent point of reference for making easy or quick judgments about the conflicting points of view brought to him by the members of the managing committee.

Clausen also used informal ways of gathering less official information about the Bank. He stopped by offices to talk to employees, occasionally had lunch in the Bank's cafeteria, and referred to "fellow staff members" in written communications to the staff. He had a colorful way of expressing himself, usually mixing fragments of various folksy metaphors to make his point. This did not always help to get his point across. A Romanian minister was understandably baffled when Clausen, urging liberalization, told him, "Mr. Minister, we are not going to take you to the edge of the cliff and hit you with a two by four, but we want you to open up the barn gates, and we want to see some chicken tracks."[56] His informality, gregariousness, and apparent affability benefited from the contrast with McNamara's unapproachability. Beneath the affable surface, however, he was humorless, tough, and often short-tempered and unpleasant with his immediate subordinates.

He had difficulty accepting the Bank's staff association as a representative body—there had been no trade unions at BankAmerica. Instead, he introduced, there and later at the Bank, periodic attitude surveys that gave staff an opportunity to express views on a variety of pertinent matters and that were followed by an elaborate process of evaluation and remedial response. Perhaps the most startling revelations from the surveys were the pervasive suspicion of senior management and the sense that staff views were not welcomed in shaping the business of the Bank. These feelings, which Clausen was unable to dispel, were undoubtedly a legacy of the McNamara era.

It took Clausen a while to learn how to deal with the executive directors. (He was not, it should be noted, the only Bank president to have difficulty with them.) Again, his views were shaped by his experience at BankAmerica. The outside directors of BankAmerica had been an "affinity group"—like-minded people, many of them appointed at his recommendation, to whom he could go for advice and support. The executive directors at the Bank were an entirely different kind of group.[57] Clausen at first seriously underestimated the importance of the board, and his initial lack of regard for it got the relationship off to a rough start.[58]

He learned eventually to be more solicitous of board opinions and sensitivities. His relations with the executive directors became correct but never really cordial. As time went on, he consulted with them on both formal and informal occasions—breakfasts, lunches, dinners, and receptions. But nothing in his experience prepared him for the need to work with a group responsible for second-guessing—at times quite publicly—what he was doing. Like McNamara, Clausen chafed at sitting through hours of discussions about issues that he believed could have been easily and more quickly resolved by management.

The executive directors respected Clausen's judgment and expertise in financial matters. His experience as a commercial banker had schooled him in the intricacies of international finance and the capital markets. He understood the implications of the worldwide recession and the international debt crisis for current and future flows of private capital. He proposed practical ways for the Bank to increase capital for the developing world when private capital virtually dried up. Clausen comfortably championed before the board and the investment community the innovative, if complicated, financial instruments the Bank's treasurer, Eugene Rotberg, devised to enhance the IBRD's borrowing.

Nonetheless, relations between the president and the executive directors were strained by the end of Clausen's term. These difficulties were by no means entirely of Clausen's making, although his occasional testiness with the executive directors did not help matters. Part of the problem was that the issues raised by structural adjustment lending were more controversial than those related to the traditional project loans. In particular, the always difficult questions of conditionality associated with policy-based lending increased tensions in the board and between board and management.

Clausen inherited from McNamara a more assertive, more cohesive board, prepared to take on management about major issues. The executive directors formed committees, developed positions on important issues, and came to meetings prepared to make these positions known to the president. Thus, Clausen's last weeks in office were marked by a sharp confrontation over the Bank's budget. The five major shareholders refused to support the last budget presented by Clausen because it called for a further expansion of the Bank without addressing vigorously enough the perceived inefficiency and bloated appearance of the organization. As a result, the executive directors decided to create their own budget committee to assert greater influence on the preparation of future administrative budgets.[59] The shareholders were critical of the Bank's lack of efficiency and its bureaucratic style. Their vote was less an indictment of Clausen and his leadership than an expression of their frustration over their own inability to exercise effective control over the bureaucracy.

Back to BankAmerica

Clausen presided over the Bank in difficult times, in an era of new realities. The Bank had to respond to profound changes in the international economy and in the views of the U.S. president and Congress about the institution. The Bank continued its traditional project lending and its support of educational, environmental, population, and agricultural programs. But substantial time, energy, and resources were now focused on how to help developing economies free up their own markets while positioning themselves to cope better with an increasingly competitive international marketplace.

This change in focus had begun under McNamara, but the concern about freeing up markets became a particular theme of the

Reagan administration. Clausen was very much in sympathy with the emphasis on markets. The persistent recession of the 1980s and the international debt crisis encouraged the economic restructuring of developing countries while promoting a greater commitment to private sector institutions.

These new circumstances presented Clausen with an opportunity to lead, as a free-market proponent in step with the ideology of a U.S. administration operating in a world of new economic and political realities. But he failed to cope with the tricky politics of Washington. Rather, he made his mark in areas related to his experience as one of the most successful commercial bankers of his generation. In short, he did better in adjusting Bank policies to recession and the debt crisis, and in devising ways of increasing private capital flows to the developing countries, than in persuading the U.S. Congress and the Reagan administration to perform the essential leadership role among the Bank's members.

It is not possible to say whether anybody might have navigated more skillfully through those troubled times. It is clear, though, that the president of the Bank in the early 1980s needed extraordinary political skills to overcome the reluctance of both Congress and the Reagan administration to increase support for the multilateral development institutions. Clausen simply did not possess the insiders' knowledge of Washington needed to deflect the ideologically and politically motivated attacks leveled at the Bank.

Clausen had become an ardent defender of the Bank and the multilateral concept it represented. He was an outspoken supporter of the Bank's efforts to promote population control and improvements in education. These stands, especially his outspoken support for population control, did not endear him to the Reagan administration. Nor were relations with the Bank's largest shareholder helped when Clausen dug in his heels and resisted U.S. influence in matters he regarded as the prerogative of the Bank's management. He proceeded with two senior appointments—of a general counsel for the Bank and of an executive vice president for the IFC—against the views expressed by U.S. Treasury officials. Both appointments reflected the care with which Clausen had made his choice: General Counsel Ibrahim Shihata proved critical to the successful realization of MIGA proposed by Clausen, and William Ryrie presided over the dramatic growth of the IFC.[60]

Another source of strain between the U.S. government and Clausen was his criticism of the Reagan administration's fiscal policies. His public statements were always diplomatic and circumspect, but Clausen, at heart still a conservative commercial banker, was dismayed at the Reagan administration's handling of the U.S. economy. Deficit spending and high interest rates discouraged private sector lending to developing countries. The poor performance of the U.S. economy in the early 1980s also slowed American imports of goods from developing countries. It was difficult for Clausen not to note these factors when arguing for more generous support on behalf of the poorest developing countries.

In the circumstances, it was hardly surprising that Clausen concluded in the fall of 1985 that the U.S. administration was not likely to support an extension of his contract. He announced his intention to retire at the end of his five-year term, and in July 1986 he passed the baton to his successor, an experienced congressional politician who would bring to the job those skills that Tom Clausen had lacked. It turned out that Clausen was badly needed at BankAmerica, which was facing the worst financial crisis in its history. Clausen was back at the institution that he knew best. But he later confessed that his experience at the World Bank helped him enormously when he returned to the private sector to restructure his old bank.[61]

CHAPTER SEVEN

Barber B. Conable
Dedicated to Public Service

C lausen's announcement that he would not be available to serve a second term caused a bit of a stir. The Reagan administration had failed to encourage any ambitions he might have had to stay beyond his five-year term. Yet his decision to leave found U.S. officials unprepared. There was no obvious candidate to succeed him. More important, the selection of a successor would imply the administration's support for an international development assistance organization about which some of the key figures in the same administration were, at best, ambivalent. Fortunately, a decision did not have to be made immediately because Clausen's term would not end for another nine months. So, the matter could be left to rest for a while.

In the spring of 1986, however, the identification of a successor had become somewhat more urgent. The names of several candidates had been mentioned. Some, including Federal Reserve Chairman Paul Volcker and Labor Secretary William E. Brock, turned the job down; others, such as former Treasury Secretary William Simon and former Navy Secretary J. William Middendorf, did not find support among the other major shareholders.[1] Treasury Secretary James Baker and Secretary of State George Shultz became concerned that an impasse in this matter might lead the Europeans to put up a candidate of their own.

The Accidental President

At this point, Baker called his old friend Barber Conable, a retired Republican congressman from New York, to ask permission to mention his name as a potential candidate, so as to illustrate the caliber and stature of the person who should be nominated. Conable was reluctant. He had left politics a year before and had returned to an enjoyable life, divided between some teaching and his hobbies, in upstate New York. He had no desire to return to Washington, and he knew nothing about the World Bank. As Conable recalled, Baker assured him that this was strictly a tactical move and that nothing would come of it. Two weeks later, however, Baker called him again: "Barber, I am sorry to tell you, you're the only guy we can agree on." Conable protested, but Baker pointed out that if he was not prepared to take the job, it would have to be left to the Europeans to find a candidate.[2]

Baker's appeal to Conable's sense of public duty was effective. Conable had an old-fashioned notion of public service. One had an obligation, he thought, to respond affirmatively when asked to take on a position of importance in the broader public interest. When he said he thought he was totally unqualified for the job, Baker took that as a promise that he would do a good job.[3] Conable did not know much about the World Bank, but it was one of those institutions that he had vaguely considered worthy of support. In fact, Conable later said he went back to look up his voting record and was relieved to find that he had been supportive of the Bank.[4]

Barber B. Conable was the first career politician to be appointed president of the Bank and the only one without substantial Wall Street experience. Instead, he had a distinguished twenty-year career in the U.S. House of Representatives, where he rose to be the ranking minority member of the powerful Ways and Means Committee. House colleagues in both political parties regarded him as a man of integrity and a skillful parliamentarian, and they valued him for his commitment to making the congressional process work.[5] New York's Democratic Senator Daniel Patrick Moynihan was reported to have said about Conable: "Some men meet standards; others set them. Barber Conable has been one of the others."[6] Commentators such as John M. Hennessy, chairman of Crédit Suisse First Boston, Robert D. Hormats, vice president at Goldman, Sachs & Company, and C. Fred Bergsten, director of the Institute for International Economics, noted that the World Bank presidency was a little out of line with Conable's background. But they praised his appointment because of his statesmanlike qualities, his financial knowledge, and his solid grasp of complicated trade and tax issues—he was a big-picture person well suited for the job.[7]

Conable was a Washington insider in the best sense of the term. In the course of his political career, he acquired several friends who held high office during the years he served as Bank president. These friends included Vice President and later President George Bush, whose 1980 campaign for the Republican presidential nomination Conable ran. He was also close to James Baker and George Shultz. Although quite visible as a member of the Republican leadership in Congress, he worked cooperatively with his Democratic colleagues. He was a skilled practitioner of the politician's arts of persuasion and consensus building. In a congressional career of two decades, he had mastered the political, legislative, and bureaucratic intricacies of Congress's role in putting together the large, complex budget of the U.S. government. Conable himself thought that he had been chosen to head the Bank because of his experience in resolving "difficult problems through a large collective process."[8]

Being a Washington insider meant that Conable was little known outside U.S. political circles. The Bank's executive directors reacted to the announcement of President Reagan's choice by anxiously asking, "Barber who?" He was completely unknown among the Bank's borrowers. European bankers also knew little about him and expressed surprise at the choice. Conable's political skills, his ability to listen and to communicate, would help him overcome this handicap and become as well liked among the Bank's members as he had been on Capitol Hill. As developed as his political skills were, however, they did not prepare him to be a manager and leader of a major bureaucratic organization. Indeed, Conable himself joked that the largest organization he had ever headed was the small staff in his personal congressional office. His lack of experience became evident early in his tenure, when he undertook a major reorganization of the Bank that proved disruptive and traumatic.

Despite the bitter controversy over that reorganization, Conable warmed to his job. He enjoyed having a platform from which to speak about major developmental issues. He took a keen interest in, and often spoke about, reviving the Bank's focus on alleviating poverty. He thought that during the Clausen years the Bank, in its emphasis on structural adjustment, had lost sight of the importance of fighting poverty. He was personally committed to this fight and to other issues that became important to the Bank in the 1980s. Publicly, he advocated increasing the Bank's attention to environmental problems, promoting programs to curtail population growth, and advancing the role of women in development. These positions won him admirers among the executive directors, within management and the staff, and in the leadership of the nongovernmental organizations (NGOs) that were pressing the Bank on environmental and social issues in the 1980s.

From Warsaw to Washington

Conable's acceptance of the presidency as a matter of duty reflected the values of small-town, rural America. Born in Warsaw, New York, he had maintained his principal residence while in Congress in nearby Alexander, New York, a town of 500 inhabitants. He returned there as often as he could during his two decades in Congress. Daily life in such communities consists of interactions among people well acquainted with each other. The regard in which one is held is important, especially to members of the town's leadership of physicians, attorneys, judges, newspaper publishers, and elected officials. Such people expect those with whom they associate to be responsible, reliable, trustworthy, and modest.

Conable exemplified the qualities prized in his community. Because he was a lawyer, he was naturally in the local elite. He had graduated from Cornell University and its law school. During both World War II and the Korean War he served in the U.S. Marines, rising to the rank of colonel. Following military service, he returned to upstate New York and began practicing law in Buffalo and Batavia. He served one term in the New York State legislature and then, in 1964, won election to the U.S. House of Representatives, in which he was to serve ten terms. During his long legislative career, he became a leader of the Republican Party in Congress, serving as the chairman of its Policy and Research committees. While not well known nationally, he was a figure of consequence within his party and Congress. He served on the Budget, Ways and Means, and Ethics committees. As a member of the Ethics Committee, he set a standard in campaign financing by refusing to accept contributions of more than $50.

After two decades in Congress, he announced his retirement in 1984. He left partly out of frustration over the administration's aloof attitude toward House Republicans, but principally because he felt it was time "to move on."⁹ He joked that "when I came to [Washington], I swore to my friends that I would not become a professional politician. . . . I must confess that after twenty years my amateur status is in some doubt."¹⁰ To make clear the break with Washington, he moved back to his home in Alexander. He rejected offers to join Washington law practices and lobbying organizations. He did not want to become part of the permanent political class that has long been resident in the capital.

After leaving Congress, Conable began a stint as a distinguished visiting professor at the University of Rochester. He also accepted posts on corporate boards of directors and the New York Stock Exchange. Beyond these responsibilities, he had ample time to indulge his eclectic interests. He had a long-standing interest in the history of the native Americans indigenous to the Finger Lakes region of New York State and was an avid collector of American Indian relics. He loved to study history and politics. He was a prolific reciter of poetry ranging from Omar Khayyam to Henry Wadsworth Longfellow. His literary interest was evident in his speeches as World Bank president, on which he worked using his own typewriter. No conversation with him was without colorful quotations from Shakespeare to illustrate his point. Indeed, he thought poetry and literature much more interesting and exciting than the goings on in political Washington. On one of his visits to his constituents he startled his assembled listeners by asking whether they would not rather hear him recite poetry than give a report on what happened in the capital. To his disappointment, his audience preferred by a narrow margin to hear him talk about Washington.[11]

After July 1, 1986, the pleasures of his short-lived retirement were quickly replaced by the duties of World Bank president. Like his predecessors, he became a prisoner of a calendar filled with meetings, travel, and personal appearances. His first eighteen months on the job were very trying.

The 1987 Reorganization

Conable returned to Washington about a month before assuming his new job and moved into an office in the vicinity of the Bank. Since he did not know much about the Bank, he thought it would be important to learn as much as he could before taking over. He was disappointed by the briefing process, though. Copious briefing material and numerous encounters with individuals who were available to answer his questions failed to give him a palpable sense of the institution. It was only when he became president that he began to see what he had taken on.[12]

One of the events he had followed as an observer from across the street was the discussion of the Bank's administrative budget for 1986–87, the initial year of his presidency. He was shocked to learn that the five major shareholders refused to endorse the budget proposed by Tom Clausen. Conable turned to his friend Treasury Secretary Baker and asked why he would first twist his arm to take the job and, once he had taken it, pull the rug out from under him by voting against the budget he needed to run the organization. Baker suggested that there was a "lot of fat" in the Bank, a reaction that quickly led Conable to think of a major reorganization (5).

Critics of the budget proposal had focused on the Bank's growing administrative costs. Important U.S. officials, especially in the Treasury Department, routinely criticized what they saw as a bloated, overpaid Bank bureaucracy. There was nothing new in American complaints about Bank employees' salaries. The United

States had been criticizing the salaries since the 1960s and continued to do so even after the introduction in 1979 of a compensation scheme the United States had actively promoted.[13] Concern about the growth of the Bank's total administrative budget remained muted as long as the Bank's lending and services grew. By 1986, however, lending had slowed down, and the proposal of a further increase in the size of the Bank's staff met stiff resistance from the executive directors. Early indications of unwillingness to support the proposed expansion seemed to go unheeded. The lack of response increased the sense among executive directors and officials in the capitals of member countries that the Bank was somehow an organization out of control.

The united opposition of the major member countries to the budget troubled Conable. As a seasoned politician, he reacted to what he thought were the wishes of a key Bank constituency—its owners. Looming largest among them was the U.S. government, which had nominated him and persuaded him to accept the job. Conable concluded that the shareholders' concerns had to be addressed—and not with piecemeal moves—and that it was his mandate to cut costs and restore the efficiency he was told had been lost. He discussed the matter not only with Secretary Baker and other U.S. Treasury officials—such as Assistant Secretary David Mulford, one of the Bank's most vocal critics—but with those of his friends and acquaintances he thought knowledgeable on the subject. A conversation with Robert McNamara, in particular, convinced him that a reorganization was overdue and that there was room to increase the Bank's flexibility and efficiency. Indeed, McNamara told him: "I wish I'd done this before I left."[14] Conable also turned for advice to New York banker David Rockefeller, an old friend. Soon after that conversation, he approached the management consultants Rockefeller recommended.

In early fall Conable hired the firm of Cresap, McCormick and Paget to assess the Bank's current operations and recommend changes in its organizational structure and business processes. In the months following, the consultants carried on intensive discussions with the executive directors and senior managers. They also spent time with younger members of the staff, who had many suggestions for change in the Bank's operations. The consultants recorded complaints about cumbersome, time-consuming procedures that took little account of the needs and wishes of borrowers. They concluded that only a thorough restructuring would allow the Bank to be more flexible and responsive to the needs of its member countries.

The consultants realized that apart from the broad outlines of the organization, detailed changes should be worked out by the staff of the Bank itself. They knew they lacked the necessary detailed knowledge of how the Bank worked; they also wanted to ensure acceptance of the reforms by the Bank's staff. Accordingly, the consultants identified about a dozen staff members in the course of their interviews who would bring fresh and innovative ideas to the table. At the consultants' recommendation, Conable decided to ground the exercise in the Bank itself, and he appointed a task force. Kim Jaycox, the recently appointed vice president for Eastern and Southern Africa, who had impressed the consultants with his perceptive observations about what was wrong in the Bank, was chosen to head the task force. He also became the chairman of a steering committee, with members from both inside and outside the Bank, which had been set up to oversee the whole reorganization. McNamara was a member of the steering committee and became an aggressive advocate of radical change. The existing senior management establishment—in particular the powerful and influential Ernest Stern, senior vice president, operations—was kept out of the process and was not even consulted. Stern's absence reflected Conable's belief, supported by the consultants' diagnosis, that the bureaucratic establishment was part of the problem, which had to be dealt with by a thorough revision of the Bank's structure.

Although new to the Bank and without management experience, Conable had arrived at his own views about what was wrong with the institution. He found that the compartmentalized structure of the organization, the staff support available to him, and the way decisions were made in the Bank did not allow him to take charge. Specifically, he thought that a disproportionate amount of resources and decisionmaking authority was concentrated in the office of the senior vice president, operations. Conable also felt that his office did not receive the information and analytical resources he needed to provide leadership and monitor performance.[15]

Conable felt strongly about the role he should play as president. Within two months of coming to the Bank, he abolished the managing committee, which he felt led to compromise rather than to clear decisions and created confusion about who was ultimately responsible for the Bank's decisions.[16] He made it clear to the consultants and to Jaycox that he wanted to be a "hands-on" executive, not an aloof arbiter who relied on a chief operating officer to run the business for him.[17] This decision reflected the way he interpreted his responsibilities; there should be no doubt that accountability rested with him. Unfortunately, he was not well prepared for the role of an active chief executive, as the process of reorganization itself would soon reveal.

Decisions about the basic structure of the Bank were made relatively early. They called for the creation of three—later, four—senior vice presidencies responsible, respectively, for operations, planning and policymaking, finance, and administration. The separation of operations from the formation of operational policy represented the only significant change from the previous organization in this basic design. In January 1987 the task forces began to work out the details of the new structure. They defined the role of the new senior vice presidencies and examined ways of decentralizing decisionmaking and making the Bank more responsive to its clients' needs.

The reorganized Bank shaped the operations complex around four instead of six regions. The four regions, each the responsibility of a vice president, were Africa; Asia; Europe, the Middle East, and North Africa; and Latin America. Within each regional group, country departments took on functions formerly divided between program and project departments.

The task force worked hurriedly. Tight deadlines left no room for prolonged, general discussion once the task force had made its recommendations. The steering committee submitted its final report to the president in early April 1987.[18] At the end of April Conable presented to the executive directors formal proposals on the reorganization.[19] On May 19 the board considered and approved the reorganization plan. The management had also submitted a supplementary budget request for $150 million to cover the costs of the reorganization—essentially, the cost of "separating" the almost 400 people who would have to leave to bring down the size of the Bank.[20]

Dismay among the executive directors over the cost of the reorganization and its impact on the nationality representation in the management structure of the Bank convinced Conable that the implementation should move expeditiously so as to limit the agony of the process and show the Bank's critics that the organization could be responsive. Perhaps the reorganization would also demonstrate that Conable—with no experience as an administrator—had prowess as a top executive. He felt strongly that the reorganization should be essentially completed before the annual meetings in September 1987; the aim was also to demonstrate in the administrative budget for the following year the savings resulting from improved efficiency. For this purpose an implementation monitoring committee chaired by Conable was set up and followed the process closely.

The four new senior vice presidents—those at the top of the new administrative structure—were selected by Conable as soon as the reorganization plan was approved, and they took office on May 31. Conable decided that the two former senior vice presidents—Ernest Stern, operations, and Moeen Qureshi, finance—should switch places. "Nobody would have believed I had reorganized the Bank if I left Ernie [Stern] in charge of operations," Conable said later.[21] He was concerned that because Stern was so firmly in control of the operations side of the Bank, he would have prevented effective decentralization of decisionmaking, one of Conable's principal objectives. Once the senior vice presidents were in charge, the selection of the next layers in the management followed quickly. Managerial appointments were completed during June 1987. Not until October, however, had all staff been reassigned, with a significant number of "unresolved" cases requiring attention well into the following year.

The rapid and substantial change caused personal stress, which translated into a high level of organizational tension. A large, complex bureaucracy was uprooted. Not surprisingly, the reorganization caused major disruptions in the work process. Staff members were preoccupied with finding out how the reorganization was going to affect their lives. It became difficult to persuade staff to travel because they felt they might miss important opportunities. The personnel cuts mandated by the reorganization put an end to the expectations of the many staff members who saw themselves as international civil servants in a career dedicated to public service. To assist those forced to leave the Bank and to assuage their feelings, the Bank offered a generous separation package, which, Conable later thought, caused the loss of U.S. government support for the reorganization (5). The separation package also proved a powerful incentive for many valuable and qualified staff members to leave the Bank. Among those who remained, there were reassignments and, for some, demotions.

Particularly stressful was the process by which employees were reassigned. Instead of grafting the reorganized structure into the existing organization, the new Bank was created from the top down. In effect, everyone had to consider himself without a job, unless and until chosen for reassignment. The reorganization process suspended the established personnel and career management planning system, which was blamed for ineffective performance evaluation. Managers were now given responsibility for choosing their staffs, relying entirely on their own assessment of the qualifications of those they picked. Old friendships were thrown into the balance as mentors selected their protégés and leaders their followers. In theory, merit and previous performance were important, but personal ties played a strong role in the selection process. Jockeying for position became the name of the game.

The reorganization became the subject of much criticism and adverse publicity. Commentators focused on the disruption it caused, the costs associated with it, and the demoralization of the Bank's staff.[22] A report on the reorganization in December 1987, prepared for the executive directors, tried to be optimistic in its conclusions: "The process has been a difficult and painful one so far. While much of the media and public attention to the reorganization has been negative, there has also been some balancing reinforcement of the image of the Bank as an institution willing and able to confront the need for improvement and change, and an institution seeking to be fair and generous to those most affected by the change process."[23]

Nobody was more aware of the distress caused by the reorganization than Conable himself. "We had a very tough time," he later recalled, "and for two years my name was Barber B. Mud."[24] Although he accepted the responsibility for having initiated the reorganization at the urging of the Bank's membership and recognized the severe disruption caused by the reorganization, he felt that he was unfairly blamed for the way the reorganization was carried out. This was something the Bank had somehow done unto itself.

From the outset, there were doubts about the effectiveness of the reorganization. Robert Picciotto, the new budget director, reported in July 1987 that "the new (reorganized) Bank is as top heavy as the 'old' Bank."[25] There were sixty more senior positions than provided for in the reorganization plan. Conable himself complained that the number of front office staff in the regions and in the office of the senior vice president, operations, was "considerably higher" than envisaged in the plan.[26] If Conable had found the Bank compartmentalized and "cylindrical" in its structure, the new Bank was, if anything, more compartmentalized. Coordination among the senior vice presidencies, especially among the operations and the policy, planning, and research complexes, became difficult. Kim Jaycox later thought that the initial enthusiasm and innovation associated with the reorganization were soon lost: "The system became complex again very quickly. We gravitated back to the layering and the second-guessing and the second-checking and the centralization very rapidly."[27] Jaycox attributed the tendency to return to the traditional bureaucratic attitude to the unchanging culture of the Bank, which only powerful leadership can affect in a lasting way (28).

The process of change continued much longer than originally planned. In late 1989 a campaign under the heading "fine tuning" was trying to iron out remaining wrinkles in the structure and the process. Two years later, Lewis T. Preston, Conable's successor, replaced the senior vice presidents with managing directors to reduce the layers in the organization. He also reasserted centralized control in the personnel and accounting areas and undid some features of the decentralization.

Conable thought that the Bank had become a more effective and responsive institution as a result of the reorganization. Even though he believed that the reorganization had been "long overdue," he did not cherish the exercise and was eager to put the experience behind him.[28] After all, the criticism of the Bank's administrative budget was not the only challenge that awaited him when he became president.

Fund-Raising

While the reorganization put Conable into unfamiliar territory, the negotiations over the replenishment of IDA and the general capital increase (GCI) of the Bank made him feel more at home. He took a keen interest in the give and take in and outside the Bank on these issues. He was familiar with many of the key players, understood their concerns, and was able to give the institution the kind of leadership it needed.

When Conable took office, the Reagan administration became more sympathetic to the Bank and the Fund than it had been throughout most of the Clausen years. As a result, Conable experienced less foot-dragging by the U.S. administration than had Clausen. Discussions of the IDA-8 replenishment and the GCI had been under way for some time when Conable took over. Nervousness about congressional critics of foreign aid generally—to say nothing of critics of the Bank and its "bloated" bureaucracy, in particular—dictated that the U.S. administration propose the GCI only after congressional approval of IDA-8.[29]

Conable was able to facilitate the IDA replenishment. Negotiations moved more quickly and smoothly than those for the previous replenishment, and, in fact, some of the ground lost earlier was regained in the agreement reached in 1987. In planning for IDA-9 three years later, in 1990, the United States agreed to sustain in real terms the amount it contributed in 1987 but insisted on bringing down its share of the total.[30]

Conable took an active part in accommodating the interests of the major donor countries in the IDA replenishment. The United States, as it had earlier, demanded alterations in Bank policy as the price of its cooperation in IDA-8. It insisted on raising the share of IDA lending for Sub-Saharan Africa while limiting credits going to China and India and shortening the terms of IDA credits. Other donors had little difficulty with the provision of greater support for Sub-Saharan Africa, but the other U.S. demands proved more controversial and were accepted only reluctantly.

The United States, however, had to make some concessions as well. Japan had long insisted on increasing its influence in line with its enhanced contributions to the Bank. Its support of IDA-8 hinged on the board's agreeing to give Japan a larger share in the control of the institution. To increase the Japanese share, the United States would have to slip below 20 percent of total shares—the minimum required to veto statutory changes. Eventually, the United States agreed to drop its shareholding below 20 percent to accommodate the Japanese, when the Articles of Agreement had been amended and the qualified majority required to pass statutory changes had been increased from 80 to 85 percent of the shareholding (98).

Once Congress approved IDA-8 in 1987, the administration took up the GCI with Congress. Conable again took an active role in pressing for the increase. He was careful not to give the appearance of overtly lobbying his former colleagues in Congress—it was not the role of the president of the World Bank to buttonhole parliamentarians—but his reputation and friendship with members of Congress helped smooth the process. Conable made clear on the GCI, as well as on IDA, that he was willing to intervene with James Baker and George Bush if necessary to get what he thought the Bank needed.[31] After much wrangling with liberal congressmen (who objected to what was called the Bank's bailing out of commercial banks) and with conservative congressmen (who thought the Bank was supporting socialist countries hostile to the United States), the U.S. administration won solid support for the capital increase. "The outcome was in part a vote of confidence for Conable," Catherine Gwin concluded, "and in greater part the result of a renewed executive branch effort to gain support for the Bank."[32] The United States committed itself to a paid-in contribution of about $70.1 million a year for six years, for a total paid-in contribution of almost $421 million.

Congress was not the only place where the GCI raised questions. Indeed, there had been extensive discussions in the board before agreement was reached on the amount of the GCI and, more significantly, on how the new capital should be used. It was nothing new for donor countries to attach strings to an IDA replenishment and a GCI. Nevertheless, some executive directors complained that the lending objectives of the GCI gave disproportionate weight to issues of importance to the United States, such as Latin America and the promotion of private sector institutions. The GCI also provoked discussion about the distribution of shares and voting within the Bank's board. Several executive directors worried about the erosion of the voting strength of developing countries, most of which were small.[33]

Despite these rumblings, the GCI was a success, and Conable received well-deserved credit. There was no gainsaying the importance of his political skills and contacts. The successful authorization for increased capital relieved anxiety within the Bank about headroom. The GCI enhanced Conable's standing, mitigating somewhat the discontent brought about by the reorganization.

From Baker to Brady

Conable's appointment as the Bank's president was widely assumed to be linked to the role the Bank was expected to play under the Baker Plan.[34] Conable accepted the continuing debt crisis as one of the challenges of his new job and the implementation of the Baker Plan as an appropriate blueprint for addressing the crisis. The plan called for new monies (up to $20 billion) to be lent by official financial institutions and commercial lenders to countries engaged in acceptable structural reforms. The banking community, short of any other alternative, endorsed the plan but argued for shifting the burden of new financing to the multilateral official institutions.[35]

Although Conable argued vigorously for the implementation of necessary adjustments in the developing countries and for active Bank support, it was already becoming clear in 1986 that the approach Baker envisaged was not working. In practice, the various participants were not performing as Baker had hoped. In particular, the commercial banks did little to meet the U.S. government's expectations. The international financial community had been skeptical about the plan from the beginning. Few professional financiers thought that it would regenerate private capital flows, and the experience between 1986 and 1988 bore out their skepticism. Private sector capital flows to the middle-income developing countries continued to decline. The troubled state of these economies became worse as local capital fled to more secure investments abroad.[36] In his first address to the Bank's governors, Conable proclaimed that it was not enough to endorse the Baker Plan; "the private financial community must move forward from approval in principle to action in practice."[37]

As criticism of the Baker Plan mounted, the most constructive line of commentary proposed some form of debt relief or forgiveness. Increasingly, this was the view of academics, journalists, and key members of Congress specializing in the debt crisis.[38] But the Reagan administration did not buy into these ideas. Conable accepted U.S. opposition to proposals for debt relief and maintained that the answer to the problems of the developing countries was continued adjustment, which would ultimately bring about a renewed flow of private capital.

Nonetheless, in an interview in August 1986 he did not categorically rule out the need for debt relief, advocated by Senator Bill Bradley.[39] Conable was in touch with Senator Bradley and took a close interest in his proposals.[40] At the annual meetings in 1987, Conable conceded that the adjustment process and the resumption of growth were proving more difficult than expected. He announced that the Bank, together with the Fund, would help in assembling specially designed debt-restructuring packages, "including the development of a broader range of instruments to facilitate the reduction of debt and to supplement direct new lending."[41]

At that point the provision of some debt relief had also become an important prerequisite for the Bank's own continued new lending. Bank officials were concerned about the impact on developing countries of increased debt service to the IBRD. Since 1982 IBRD's large, fast-disbursing loans to highly indebted countries had helped ensure continued interest payments to the Bank, as well as to other creditors. By early 1987, however, it was becoming clear that "net transfers from the Bank to many of these countries will soon turn negative: that is, they will owe more in debt service payments to the Bank than they receive in new disbursements."[42]

Conditions in the developing countries did not improve in 1987 and 1988, and several countries were having difficulties making payments on their debt. Some form of debt reduction became an acute issue in late 1988, especially after Argentina stopped servicing its private bank debt in November. Brazil was also having increasing problems in meeting its obligations.[43] A consensus was in the making that debt relief was necessary. Among those espousing this idea were executives at Citibank and Morgan Bank, prominent members of Congress, foreign finance ministers, and officials of the new Bush administration.

The large banks were doing more than talking. The debt most of them carried on their books already traded at considerable discounts. By the end of the 1980s they had virtually stopped making new loans to developing countries, had sold off what they could of outstanding debt, and had increased reserves against default on what they still held (238).

In the first months of the Bush administration, the new treasury secretary, Nicholas F. Brady, announced an initiative that reversed the position of the U.S. government. The March 1989 statement recognized the obvious: the debt crisis was structural and not simply a liquidity problem. The Brady Plan proposed a mechanism by which selected countries could work out programs for debt relief.[44]

Conable's close ties to the Bush administration had brought him early into the discussions of what became the Brady Plan. Like the Baker Plan, Brady's expected both the Bank and the IMF to take central roles. Selected debtor countries had to agree with the Bank and the Fund on an economic adjustment program before debt reduction could be discussed or implemented. The Bank's role in the new debt strategy was to provide loans to reduce outstanding debt principal and so enhance the credit of heavily indebted middle-income countries. Debtor countries that received such loans could then repurchase, at a discount, some of their outstanding debt from commercial banks or have it converted into long-term bonds at reduced rates of interest. The Bank was in a position to undertake this activity because of the recently approved GCI. In 1989–90 the GCI would allow the Bank to increase its lending commitments from $15 billion to $20 billion.[45]

When Conable left the presidency, debt and debt-service reduction plans were in effect for five of the twenty countries that had been identified as eligible. Mexico and Venezuela had achieved modest success in improving their creditworthiness, repatriating capital, and attracting new foreign direct investment. Although the Bank had devoted much less to the program than it had originally expected, the approach proved effective in eventually bringing the crisis under control, and Conable could take some credit for setting things in motion. He had successfully aligned the Bank's role with the perspective of the U.S. government on the debt crisis. It proved more difficult to maintain simultaneously the essential close coordination with the IMF.

World Bank and IMF collaboration was a key aspect of the Brady Plan. Conable easily entered into the spirit of collaboration. He met regularly with the Fund's managing director and, like Clausen before him, exhorted Bank staff to work closely with their IMF counterparts. Conable's readiness to accommodate the Bank to the position of its major shareholder, however, severely strained his relationship with the IMF and led to an embarrassing public controversy in the fall of 1988.

At that time, the Bank and the IMF were regularly cooperating to meet the substantial debt-related financing and adjustment requirements of their members. The policy changes initiated by the Bank also affected fiscal and monetary stabilization and so impinged on areas traditionally dealt with by the Fund. In turn, the Fund could no longer ignore a longer-term and supply-oriented perspective. To accommodate members with concessional and long-term needs, the Fund introduced a structural adjustment facility and later an enhanced structural adjustment facility. Thus the Fund, traditionally focused on correcting short-term imbalances and balance of payments disequilibria, began inevitably to concern itself with growth.[46]

The United States had for some time pressed the Bank and the Fund to formalize their collaborative arrangements. In March 1986 the two institutions had agreed to prepare jointly with donor countries policy framework papers as a prerequisite of the Fund's structural lending. The papers outlined the country's major problems, specified a three-year program that included macroeconomic and structural policies, and stipulated the necessary financial resources (28ff.).

Although friction between the Bank and the Fund was inevitable because of their converging concerns with policy and conditions for loans, there was progress toward collaboration. It was Conable himself who inadvertently precipitated a blowup over lending to Argentina.

In the summer of 1988 Baker encouraged Conable to extend further support to the democratically elected government of Argentina and thus prevent a crisis for large American banks heavily exposed there. Argentina had received assistance from both the Bank and the Fund during the 1980s. Indeed, the country had taken on something of the aura of a special case, and hopes for a major improvement in the Argentine economy were high. But even in the Bank, there was skepticism about Argentina's prospects, and the Fund was much less optimistic about the country. Its experience with Argentina throughout the 1980s had been far from satisfactory. Of twenty calendar quarters covered by various programs, Argentina had needed waivers in all but three. In 1988 the Fund and the Bank continued discussions about how to cope with Argentina's problems. When Argentina showed no sign of meeting the Fund's conditions, the Fund decided to pull out. This left Secretary Baker very much concerned, especially as Argentina was moving toward an election.[47]

It is in this context that Conable, in the midst of the annual meetings in Berlin, announced a $1.25 billion set of adjustment loans to Argentina. He immediately found himself at the center of a nasty public dispute with his counterpart at the IMF. Michel Camdessus, who had taken over from Jacques de Larosière in May 1987, was outraged. So, too, were some representatives of donor countries, who insisted that the Bank not make loans without an IMF plan in place. In the meantime, Conable's friend and patron James Baker had left the U.S. Treasury to manage George Bush's presidential campaign, and U.S. Treasury officials were among the first to criticize the Bank's action. Conable was unhappy about the controversy, but he felt particularly betrayed by the U.S. criticism of his behavior. Relations between the Bank and the IMF remained strained for months. Conable's embarrassment was heightened when, in early 1989, the Bank also gave up on Argentina, as the Fund had done the year before. After disbursing only one of the loans, the Bank canceled the rest when Argentina failed to meet fiscal targets set in the agreement. Nonetheless, the Bank's action may well have conveyed a sense of confidence in Argentina during the period leading up to the elections. It certainly enhanced the Bank's standing in Argentina and allowed the Bank to play an effective role following the establishment of the Meném government and to contribute to the spectacular recovery of the Argentine economy.[48]

The conflict with the IMF forced the two institutions to reexamine their working relationship. A strict code of collaboration between the Bank and the Fund could no longer be avoided, and a formal understanding clarifying the respective roles of the two institutions was negotiated.[49] This concordat allocated primary responsibilities between the two institutions, in addition to reaffirming once again the need for close collaboration. Since the document gave the Fund primary responsibility in the macroeconomic arena, it was widely seen as a defeat for the Bank. In practice, however, the new code changed little, apart from epitomizing that constructive collaboration was essential to maintain the credibility of both institutions.

Environmental and Social Issues

The Bank's leadership in development matters had been readily accepted when McNamara staked out a larger role for it. Economic development and the alleviation of poverty were goals that seemed beyond controversy. In any case, the Bank enjoyed respect and encountered little questioning, let alone hostile criticism. By the mid-1980s, the situation had begun to change. The Bank's push for painful economic reforms was meeting opposition in developing countries, which were worried about the political fallout and the impact of economic adjustment measures on the poorer segments of their societies. Questions were also raised about the effect of adjustment on activities essential to the Bank's goal of long-term, sustainable growth. Most important, however, the Bank had become the target of activist groups critical of its environmental record. They singled out the Bank's role in the Polonoroeste settlement program in Brazil's Amazon Forest and in the construction of the Sardar Sarovar Dam on the Narmada River in India as particular examples of environmental irresponsibility. The Bank, which by virtue of its objectives had seemed beyond reproach, suddenly found itself under attack.

As an experienced politician, Conable was sensitive to public perceptions of the Bank. Certainly, the Bank's new critics could not be ignored. The Polonoroeste and Sardar Sarovar projects became rallying points for a strong international coalition opposing the Bank on a wide range of issues. Representatives of environmental groups became particularly active in the United States and in Europe. Before U.S. congressional committees they denounced the Bank's environmental record and opposed requests for IDA replenishments and for the GCI. They organized letter-writing campaigns and picketed international meetings. Environmental activists noisily picketed the Bank's annual meeting in 1986, the first one attended by Conable as president.[50] Conable believed that analysis and reason—the Bank's language—would not in themselves be sufficient to convince or even to quiet the critics of the Bank's activities. He recognized that the Bank had made mistakes and concluded that it must be responsive in both substance and perception.

"Even though there were a lot of individual environmentalists here," Conable said, "institutionally [the Bank] . . . resisted" environmental commitments. That was a mistake, he thought, in view of the evidence of and the growing international concern about environmental degradation.[51] The Bank had to do better on environmental issues. In a May 1987 speech to the World Resources Institute, a highly regarded think tank devoted to studying the environment, Conable quoted Mark Twain's dictum that "nothing so needs reforming as other people's habits" and added, "the Bank will begin by reforming its own."[52] The Bank needed to acknowledge the looming environmental problems and anticipate the environmental implications of its decisions. This, in his view, was part of the Bank's mission and the appropriate response to the environmentalists and to representatives of NGOs interested in other issues.

Conable admitted that in Polonoroeste, as in other places, the Bank had "stumbled." The lessons of Polonoroeste were "not that we should avoid projects with environmental implications" but rather that "the Bank must be a positive force to strengthen" environmental safeguards. The Bank had to remain an active force in support of economic development and in finding solutions for the future. But it also had to take responsibility for the environmental consequences of what was happening as a result of its lending (22f.).

At the time he gave this speech, the Bank's reorganization had already embedded a stronger environmental presence in the institution. Additions to the Bank's structure included a thirty-person department designed to review and direct research and policy on the environment. The department was also to encourage regular discussion with borrowers over the environmental implications of proposed projects and programs. The technical departments in each of the four regions were to review projects for environmental soundness and were also charged with helping to implement specific environmental measures included in projects.

Conable involved the Bank actively in a number of highly visible international environmental efforts. For example, the Bank increased its support of a global program to conserve tropical forests. Similar programs to prevent deforestation, especially in Africa, received more official attention, and the Bank assumed the funding of a U.N. program to protect the Mediterranean Sea. In November 1990 the Bank took a prominent role in a joint effort with two U.N. agencies in the establishment of a Global Environment Facility (GEF), a three-year program with resources of almost $1.5 billion, contributed by twenty-one countries, for concessional financing of environmental programs and projects in developing countries. The GEF focused on reducing hazards to the ozone layer, ensuring biodiversity, limiting greenhouse gases, and protecting international waters. After three years of operation, the pilot program's activities were to be transferred to the Bank and the regional development banks.[53]

Conable understood that these cooperative actions were only first steps. He also appreciated that his efforts to put a positive face on the Bank's new-found commitment to the environment would not quickly, if ever, change environmental groups' skepticism about the Bank. "There is no doubt in my mind," he said, "that we will be under continuing and growing pressure from shareholders and

NGOs [on environmental issues]. We must anticipate the demands that will be made of us, and channel our energies in relevant ways."[54]

By 1991 in-depth consideration of environmental issues had become a routine part of the Bank's activities. Within the Bank, of course, Conable had never been alone in his concern for the environment. Nevertheless, his forceful public identification with environmental protection had changed the Bank's policies and image. He had strengthened the hand of those in management and staff who wanted to make the institution more environmentally relevant. Now, there was progress. An increasing number of projects had substantial environmental objectives and important environmental aspects.[55]

While the Bank was thus beginning to internalize environmental concerns, it had difficulty in resolving specific controversies. The Sardar Sarovar project in India proved especially troublesome. The Bank's efforts to respond to its environmental effects were deemed inadequate by critics both in India and abroad. Neither the Bank's staff nor the Indian government—nor, for that matter, the executive directors—seemed able to suggest a way out of the predicament. Conable therefore asked an independent commission to review the project and recommend appropriate steps to be taken. The commission, headed by Bradford Morse, a former head of the United Nations Development Programme and, like Conable, a former congressman from upstate New York, found much to criticize in the way the Bank had handled the project, but it failed to come up with a solution. The matter was eventually resolved when the government of India asked the Bank to cancel its loan for the project. The commission, however, inspired the creation of the Bank's permanent inspection panel to investigate complaints about the Bank.

Conable's dedication to public service and his sense of social responsibility led him from the start to focus on the social dimensions of the development phenomenon. He reaffirmed emphatically the Bank's commitment to poverty alleviation. In his first address to the board of governors in September 1986, he emphasized the link between development and poverty. "Genuine economic growth," he said, should be "the healing antidote wherever poverty is poisoning people's lives." In talking about the long-term

issues of development, he referred to "the need to stress population concerns, the need to protect the environment as we promote
economic advance, and the need to ensure that women are fully
integrated in, contribute to, and benefit from development programs."[56]

For Conable this was more than public relations rhetoric. In
December 1986 he appointed a task force of senior staff, chaired
by Shahid Husain, to review Bank poverty programs and do the
groundwork for collective action by governments, multilateral institutions, the private sector, and NGOs.[57] Conable accepted that
deliberate measures were needed to deal with the social consequences of economic adjustment. Adjustment programs needed to
be better designed to reduce their impact on income and consump-
tion of the poor.[58] With Conable's active involvement, the Bank's
World Development Report 1990 later amplified the poverty message.[59] It accepted that over the long run, economic growth was
essential to alleviate mass poverty. Yet severe consequences of poverty (starvation, poor health, illiteracy, overpopulation) required
immediate attention and directed spending.

Conable spoke out with equal force in defense of women in development and population control. His wife Charlotte had been
identified with these issues before Conable joined the Bank, having written about women's education and actively participated in
major conferences on women in development. Presumably, her interest helped shape his thinking. Early in his tenure, in February
1987, Conable spoke out on safe motherhood at a conference devoted to the subject in Nairobi. He saw a clear connection between
women's health and development; he also saw that the women of
the developing countries were the poorest of the poor and that the
struggle against poverty would turn on women's effective participation in development.[60]

Conable used managerial tools to move the organization to respond to the needs he perceived. Promoting poverty alleviation,
human resource development, and women in development were
declared activities of "special operational emphasis." These activities were budgeted and monitored separately, and measurable
progress in them became indicators of performance. As a result,
the Bank moved forward in the areas of emphasis. Its annual re-

port for 1991, for instance, indicated that almost 40 percent of the projects approved during the year contained specific plans for enhancing women's role in development, compared with only 11 percent in 1988.[61]

Supporting the Private Sector

The special operational emphasis was not limited to the social dimensions of economic development or to the protection of the environment; it covered all matters that, in the eyes of the Bank's critics, had been neglected. This included the Bank's contribution to the development of the private sector in the developing countries.

Conable's firm belief in the central role of private initiative and entrepreneurship had always been an important element in his conservative outlook. He recognized the role private initiative and enterprise had played in the history of the United States. There was no doubt in his mind that developing countries would likewise benefit from policies that allowed the undistorted functioning of markets and the free flow of private investment. His leadership of the Bank was thus an important opportunity to advance the necessary reforms in the developing world. In supporting the focus on the private sector, as in the environmental and social development initiatives, Conable recognized the changing perceptions of development priorities. He was able to catalyze and strengthen the Bank's resources and move the institution to respond to these priorities.

The idea that the role of governments in the economy needed to be restrained in favor of a more vigorous private sector was generally accepted when Conable came to the Bank, as a result of the disappointing experience with centralized decisionmaking and control in economic management. The Bank itself had played a role in establishing the consensus in favor of furthering economic growth by promoting market economies and the private sector. Through its adjustment lending operations, the Bank had given support to private sector institutions and policies supporting the free expression of market forces. Under Conable's leadership these operations expanded further and became a standard element in the Bank's assistance strategy in practically all active countries.

The Bank Group also became very active in supporting private investment directly. The IFC had expanded its operations slowly through the 1970s but had remained a limited force. Its operations were concentrated in Latin America and East Asia and were focused on manufacturing investments. Now, under the management of its executive vice president, Sir William Ryrie, the IFC's operations grew substantially in both amounts invested and number of operations. It moved vigorously into Africa and South Asia and into new areas of activity and started a special financial advisory service to promote the flow of private investment into the developing countries. Much greater emphasis was being placed on capital market development, corporate restructuring, privatization, and assistance to small and medium-size enterprises through financial intermediaries. In addition, in 1988 the Bank launched the Multilateral Investment Guarantee Agency (MIGA), which had been initiated by Conable's predecessor to insure private investors against political risks and meet one of the more intractable obstacles to the flow of private investments.

Conable was not alone in thinking that these new approaches had come so quickly that they lacked coherence. Executive directors expressed concern about the need for effective coordination among the different parts of the Bank Group and, especially, for a proper delineation of private sector activities between the Bank, the IFC, and MIGA. Although the principles of coordination were clearly spelled out, there was a perception that the different perspectives of the Bank and the IFC caused contradictions in the response to clients.[62] To deal with this problem and to recommend policies and changes that could enhance the effectiveness of the Bank Group in supporting the private sector, Conable appointed a private sector review group composed of well-known international experts, as well as Bank and IFC staff, and chaired by Burke Knapp, a former senior vice president of the Bank.[63] In May 1988 the group presented many sensitive suggestions but no definitive answers. Discussions on how to promote the private sector as an aspect of development assistance continued beyond Conable's tenure as president. Nor was the difference in the outlook of the different parts of the Bank Group resolved; Bank staff continued to complain about the "micro" orientation of the IFC and its narrow focus on profitability, and IFC staff believed that the Bank's methods as a development institution had not adapted themselves as fully as necessary to the new thinking about the private sector.[64]

These issues were raised again in the context of the IFC's capital increase in 1991. The emphasis on the need to support the development of the private sector in the developing countries had given the IFC a tremendous boost. Conable presided over a period during which IFC commitments increased by 20 to 25 percent a year. From a relatively small organization, dependent on the Bank for its financial resources, the IFC had grown into a powerful AAA-rated financial institution with a significant net income and direct access to the world's capital markets. The IFC's expansion in the second half of the 1980s had been supported by a doubling of its authorized capital, from $650 million to $1.3 billion. By the end of the decade, however, it was clear that a further expansion of the IFC's activities, especially in response to the demands of the countries in Eastern Europe, required another capital increase. To his surprise, Conable discovered that the U.S. Treasury opposed his proposal for a further doubling of the IFC's capital.

Despite his political skills and contacts, it took Conable a year and a half to achieve agreement on the IFC's capital increase by a somewhat smaller amount. With the departure of Baker from the Treasury in August 1988, Conable lost a key contact. The new secretary, Nicholas Brady, while friendly, was not as interested and engaged in Bank issues as Baker had been. Treasury officials sought to tie reforms in the Bank to the IFC negotiations. They proposed internal reforms to strengthen the Bank's capacity to aid private sector development. They also proposed that a study be undertaken to explore removing the prohibition in the Bank's Articles of Agreement against direct lending to the private sector without government guarantees. Finally, they insisted that the Bank should commit itself to providing 50 percent of its lending directly to the private sector. Although the IFC's exclusive focus on the private sector should have made it an attractive institution for the U.S. government, Treasury argued that the capital increase was premature, that the IFC was growing too quickly, and that its portfolio was too risky.

Other donor countries no doubt agreed that helping develop the private sector in developing countries was a central challenge, but they resented the manner and the revolutionary content of the U.S. demands. Conable became heavily involved in the political infighting engendered by the challenge to the IFC's capital request. He was frustrated by the episode and spoke out publicly on the issue. His frustration seemed to resonate with his former colleagues in Congress. The foreign operations subcommittee of the House Appropriations Committee criticized Treasury because it had not consulted Congress on its agenda of change for the World Bank, and it recommended that the United States fund its share of the IFC capital increase even though Treasury had not requested any funds for that purpose.[65]

Conable was puzzled by the obstinate resistance of the Treasury officials. He understood that Treasury was not prepared to agree to the capital increase without tough conditions; the trouble was that Treasury officials did not have a very clear idea of what they wanted to achieve.[66] This was reflected in the final phase of the board discussions, when the U.S. director first agreed to support the capital increase, then withdrew his support, only to reverse his position again, "leaving a bitter taste in the mouths of all involved."[67] Conable's skill as an experienced Washington insider, especially his direct access to the White House, once again led to the successful conclusion of this campaign. But the tension between the Bank and its major shareholder tested his firm belief in working out differences and avoiding confrontation. It was especially galling that this should happen with a government he knew so well and over an issue everybody agreed deserved full support: providing the resources to assist the organization dedicated to assisting the development of the private sector.

New Challenges

Among the developments that had important consequences for the Bank was the breakdown of the Soviet bloc. Hungary, Poland, Bulgaria, and Czechoslovakia successively joined the Bank between 1985 and 1990. Support for the systemic transformation of the economies of these countries represented a new and fascinating challenge for the Bank.

The end of the cold war brought the long-awaited prospect of peace and prosperity. It was important, though, to seize the opportunity of the collapse of the Soviet regime to put in place the political and economic safeguards that would protect the rights and the welfare of the people in Eastern Europe and prevent a reversal of the process of liberalization. The G-7, and the United States in particular, looked to the Bank and the Fund to play a central role in supporting the economic transition. Conable understood the need to act quickly. He was happy to dedicate the Bank to the support of the economic transformation that would extend the new opportunity for political choice and competition into the economic sphere.

Conable was getting ahead of actual events when he speculated about Soviet membership in the Bank as early as 1986, but he recognized that the dissolution of the communist system would soon engulf the U.S.S.R. itself. At his request, the Bank's general counsel briefed him on the issues a membership application by the U.S.S.R. would raise.[68] In an interview, Conable referred to the possibility that the U.S.S.R. could become a member of the Bank just like the other Eastern European countries which were then beginning to join. No doubt he was carried away by his enthusiasm about welcoming the former Soviet satellites into the Bank. His remarks caused a bit of a stir. The shareholders of the Bank, especially the United States, were evidently not prepared as yet to address this possibility.

Events in Eastern Europe continued to unfold rapidly, and in 1990 the Bank, along with other international organizations, was heavily involved in a comprehensive assessment of the needs of the Soviet economy. Now the shoe was on the other foot. The U.S. administration was anxious to get the Bank and the Fund actively involved in the U.S.S.R., and in December 1990 the president of the United States asked the U.S. governor to explore the possibility of special associate membership for the Soviet Union "that will give Moscow access to the economic and financial expertise in those institutions."[69]

Conable traveled to Eastern Europe to offer advice and assistance. In Poland he delivered a major address when he signed the Bank's first loan agreements in early 1990. "We are proud to join you in the historic effort you have launched," he proclaimed. He assured his Eastern European audience that the Bank would be swift and flexible in providing assistance. He recognized the need to be pragmatic: "We do not come here with a crisp, simplistic or ideological reform recipe."[70]

He also emphasized that the Bank had pressing obligations elsewhere and that assistance to Eastern Europe should not come at the expense of other borrowers, especially the poorer countries. This was in response to the concerns expressed by the Bank's traditional borrowers, who were worried that the Bank's attention and limited resources would now be diverted to the service of new political priorities. Conable did not think that there was any conflict because the countries in Eastern Europe were not expected to compete for IDA's concessional funds.

In a more general sense, the end of the cold war would have important consequences for development assistance and for the Bank. The tensions resulting from the confrontation between the Eastern European countries and the Western alliance had provided a powerful argument for the activities of the Bank throughout its entire history as a development institution. This argument was now fading away, making the mobilization of resources more difficult and, in fact, raising questions about the need for the Bank.

Conable did not have to deal with these questions, which would preoccupy his successor, but he seized important opportunities for enlarging the agenda of issues addressed by the Bank. The easing of East-West tensions allowed him to speak up on issues that had long troubled those concerned with the alleviation of poverty: the level of military expenditures and the quality of governance.[71] In the past, the Bank's borrowers had turned away any suggestion that these could be legitimate concerns of the Bank, citing the apolitical nature of the Bank and their own sovereignty. Their objections were generally accepted because nobody wanted to disturb the precarious military and political balance between East and West. The end of the cold war removed these reservations, and both Conable and Camdessus, the managing director of the Fund, started to speak out on these issues. "As we think about the tasks of development in the coming years," Conable told the Bank's governors in 1989, "we can no longer neglect a sensitive component of the fiscal problem: military spending. All countries have the sovereign right and responsibility to defend themselves. But let us hope that resources are increasingly allocated to more productive purposes, in industrial countries as well as developing countries."[72]

The failure of the communist regimes and the emphasis on more participatory ways of managing public affairs stimulated a lively debate about transparency and accountability, particularly in Africa, where the needed reforms failed to succeed because of the weaknesses of the political and administrative institutions. The Bank had to recognize that massive investments in physical assets and human resources and accurate analyses of policy and institutional deficiencies were of little avail unless the quality of the political process allowed sensible decisionmaking and implementation. Conable sensed that governments in Africa were ready to confront this issue. He chose the forum of the Organization of African Unity, the region's political organization, to address "those aspects of governance that impede development and impair the quality of life for your people."[73] Reflecting the cautious attitude of the executive directors on this issue, he was careful to assure his audience that as a development institution the Bank would confine its attention to those aspects of governance "that directly affect development—accountability, transparency, predictability, adherence to the rule of law" (170).

The call for transparency, accountability, and participation by the people affected by economic and financial decisions was ultimately also addressed to the Bank itself. Nobody understood this more clearly than Conable. The environmental criticism of the Bank, spearheaded by NGOs, called for direct response and interaction. Conable was not bothered by the seeming contradiction that a government-owned and controlled organization should be directly responsive to the people affected by the Bank's interventions. He interacted freely with outside critics, not just to seek their views and support but because he accepted their legitimate role. He led the Bank into a new era of greater openness and more complicated relations of responsibility.

Reaffirming the Bank's Purpose

Conable came to the Bank knowing little about the institution and the real work of development. He accepted the presidency of the

Bank in the spirit of his dedication to public service and, given his perspective as a retired U.S. congressman, as an extension of the public service that he had given to his country over much of his life. It was natural that he should look to his friends and patrons in the U.S. government as he set out on his unfamiliar assignment.

It did not take long to discover contradictions between the positions held by the U.S. administration and the Bank. Conable's sense of public service led him to embrace the poverty mission of the Bank with enthusiasm. His instincts related his responsibilities and the work of the Bank naturally to the needs of the people in the developing world. "When we read statistics, we must see real people," is the way he put it in his first address to the board of governors.[74] This was not an empty phrase; it reflected his involvement with the reality of economic problems as distinct from preoccupation with economic or financial abstractions. He was confident when he could follow his instincts and social conscience, although he soon found that he was following an agenda that the United States supported only with strong qualifications. He was particularly frustrated by the indifference toward development issues in his own country. "Here we are in the United States," he told the Bretton Woods committee at the end of his tenure, "the nation that created the Marshall Plan, that provided key leadership in creating the Bretton Woods institutions, including the World Bank. Yet even otherwise knowledgeable Americans don't know what the World Bank is."[75]

Conable had a knack for dealing with people. He understood politicians, their concerns, and their way of looking at problems. He therefore became an effective spokesman for the Bank and persuasively advanced the Bank's sensitive reform agenda. He developed a particular affinity for the problems of Africa. His several visits there exposed him to the difficulties the continent was facing in the aftermath of the oil shock and the debt crisis.

Conable was approachable, friendly, and warm in his contacts with the members of the board and with the Bank's staff. Notwithstanding the resentment created by the 1987 reorganization, he enjoyed much respect among the members of the board and a certain popularity toward the end of his five-year term, so that he was confident he would be elected for a second term if he wished and if he was not satisfied with the choice of his successor.[76]

Conable's principal handicap was his lack of managerial and administrative experience. Despite the upheaval caused by the reorganization, the attempt to change the bureaucratic culture of the Bank was unsuccessful. Conable felt that the Bank's president needed to be directly involved in the operational work and decisionmaking. He tried to become the hands-on executive who could maintain tight control over the organization, but he lacked the requisite organizational skill, and his attempts to assert himself were often deflected by rivalry and bickering among his senior vice presidents.

Conable's political background served the Bank well in resolving the troublesome funding issues he inherited from his predecessor. Here he was very much in his element, and his experience and contacts helped bring these issues to a relatively quick resolution. Most important, his political experience and sensitivity allowed him to sense the changes in the environment of the Bank. He recognized the significance of ecological and social demands, and he moved the Bank toward meeting them. From the outset he made the issues relating to the Bank's central mission—the fight against poverty—the focus of his presidency. This is where he exerted real and effective leadership, guided by a firm conservative orientation in economic matters, but inspired by a liberal social conscience.

Reflections

The presidents of the World Bank, as chairmen of the board of executive directors and chief executive officers of the organization, exert a powerful influence on the Bank's policies and the conduct of its business. By exercising their power, they shape the way this important organization adapts to the needs of a changing environment. This record of adaptation in turn defines a central aspect of the Bank's history.

The role of the president has itself undergone change—starting from the moment the Bank opened for business. The Articles of Agreement provided that the executive directors would select the president, that the president would be the chairman of the board of executive directors, and that he would be the chief of the Bank's staff and conduct the business of the Bank "under the direction" of the executive directors.[1] But what this meant in practice, and, in particular, how the president and the executive directors would work together, remained to be sorted out. Throughout the past fifty years, the relative roles of the management, as it came to be known, and of the board have varied, reflecting principally the style and assertiveness of the individual presidents and of the members of the board. But there was never any doubt that it was up to the president of the Bank to energize the institution and to set its course.

It is the prerogative of the United States to nominate the Bank's president. In practice, this put the presidency of the Bank in the gift of the White House. The president of the United States decides whom the executive directors will consider for the job. This arrangement has never been openly challenged, but with the declining role of the United States in development assistance and of New York among the world's capital markets, the atmosphere of appointment has changed. The concurrence of the other members in the suitability of the candidates presented by the U.S. executive director has become more than a routine matter.

Nonetheless, the established tradition of leaving the choice of the candidates to the U.S. president, as well as the location of the Bank in the capital of the United States, has had its impact on the attitude of the Bank's membership. Unless there were strong reasons to take a particular position on certain issues, the other shareholders have generally looked to the United States for leadership. For the donor countries U.S. leadership was significant in matters relating to the contribution of IBRD capital or IDA resources, and for the borrowing members U.S. support was important for the approval of their projects. As a result, the Bank's president always had to pay particular attention to the perspectives of its largest shareholder. The president's ability to reconcile the views of the powers-that-be in Washington with the interests of other shareholders, to protect the integrity of the Bank's professional approach, and to advance the interests of the institution has been a critical test of his success.

Unlike the managing director of the IMF, whose job has called for extensive technical expertise in fiscal and monetary affairs, a candidate for the presidency of the World Bank does not have to have specific professional qualifications. The variety of problems of concern to the Bank and the diverse responsibilities of its president have made it impossible to define rigid criteria. Nonetheless, the process of selecting candidates for the Bank's presidency has remained remarkably free of the political wrangling normally associated with White House appointments. The rest of the membership has always praised the professional accomplishments of the candidates in areas relevant to the Bank's needs and has unanimously endorsed the candidates chosen by the United States.

The U.S. administrations' perception of the current needs of the Bank has influenced the selection of candidates. Naturally, the prevailing view has been to think of the Bank as needing firm financial direction. To the present day, all but two of the Bank's presidents have been bankers or have had close links to Wall Street. Such a choice was clearly advantageous in the early years, when the Bank had to establish itself as a creditworthy, financially sound institution and the confidence of Wall Street in the candidate was of paramount importance. It remained a tradition even when the Bank had achieved the highest credit ratings and when other challenges seemed to put a premium on such qualifications as international stature, political skill, or experience in large-scale management. Surprisingly, first-hand knowledge of the primary business of the Bank—economic development—was never a determining consideration in the choice of the Bank's leaders; none of the Bank's presidents had more than limited exposure to the problems of the developing countries before coming to the organization.

The Bank's presidents did not usually come into office with a particular mandate—indeed, several of them actually knew little about the institution when they were selected to lead it. They all had to learn on the job. It took time to gain a full understanding of the needs of the Bank's membership and to visualize how the Bank could respond effectively. Not surprisingly, the two presidents who most profoundly shaped the character and evolution of the Bank headed the institution for thirteen years each—significantly beyond the normal five-year term. This has led many to conclude that effective leadership of the Bank requires a commitment extending at least across a decade. According to reports in the press, the selection of the present incumbent, James D. Wolfensohn, involved this consideration explicitly.[2]

Whatever the length of their service, the presidents have had to reshape the role the institution was to play, changing its operational objectives, priorities, and policies. They had to innovate because the institution was working in largely unexplored territory. The Bank's growth in part reflected their ability to discern changing needs early and to adjust to those requirements. They also had to manage the organization—a relatively easy task in the early years, when the Bank was small and its structure simple. George Woods, who prepared a list of desired qualifications for the presidency, thought that the president should "occupy himself more with the Bank's external relations and broad policy problems than with the routine of internal management and organization."[3] Day-to-day management became a challenge, however, as the Bank expanded and its interventions became more diversified. The presidents had to attend to management while at the same time preserving the Bank's financial integrity and remaining sensitive to the concerns of the Bank's creditors.

Above all, the Bank's leaders had to have the diplomatic skills needed for dealing with the Bank's shareholders and their diverse interests. They had to be "internationally and impartially minded, above any bias or prejudice (racial, political or cultural); and not be too identified (even involuntarily) with the policies of [their] own country."[4] It was up to the organization's presidents to bring about consensus among the Bank's members that would allow the organization to move forward effectively. They could rely to some extent on the executive directors, who represent the diverse interests of the Bank's membership. As in any large corporate structure, however, there was always a natural tension between the board and the Bank's presidents—a tension that made close collaboration difficult. As a result, the presidents used their personal contacts in member states in pursuing their most important objectives or in resolving difficult issues.

The emergence of vocal nongovernmental constituencies has added a new dimension to the president's responsibilities. The Bank's responsiveness to the demands of these constituencies has become a test of its credibility, and this, in turn, has required the president to play a more visible and assertive public role. The new demands were not a problem for the Bank's presidents, who were accustomed to a prominent public role, but were more difficult to accept for the institution—which has traditionally relied primarily on the interaction with officials in member governments—and for the professional staff oriented to the appraisal of technical or economic factors rather than to the social and political concerns of borrowers and beneficiaries.

The professional character of the organization has shaped the posture of the Bank's presidents in important ways. It deeply affected the general direction the Bank followed in approaching its mission. The Articles of Agreement stipulate that "only economic considerations" shall be relevant to the Bank's decisions and that they shall be "weighed impartially."[5] The Bank is not supposed to interfere in the political affairs of its members or be influenced in its decisions by their political character. This provision, included in the Articles to assuage Soviet concerns that the Bank could be "systemically" prejudiced, helped shape the character of the institution and the attitude of its staff. The Bank was, of course, inspired by capitalist principles. Its membership became defined by the cold war. Although among its active early members were countries with socialist and even communist governments, its analysis and approach betrayed a distinctly pro-business orientation. The Bank tended to look for solutions to economic problems in neoclassical terms, to believe in the vitality of the private sector and to assume that a market-based price system would normally function effectively.

Although the Bank's decisionmaking was never immune to political pressure, especially after the creation of IDA, the institution's professional character leaned against such intrusions. Political considerations sometimes played a role in decisions not to support projects that might otherwise have met the Bank's criteria. Yet the professional character of the institution generally prevailed and dominated its work. This was in large part the result of the cooperative nature of an organization that involved the entire membership in policymaking and made lending decisions in a transparent manner. Both lending and borrowing members, industrial and developing countries, rich and poor nations, were represented on the Bank's board of executive directors. Although the dominant position of the United States as the largest shareholder and host was recognized and the influence of members differed, depending on the number of shares they held, the economic objectives of the Bank and the openness of the decisionmaking process worked against the application of political pressure.

The Bank's presidents all used the institution's professional character to protect their ability to stand up to political pressure. The early presidents emphasized banking principles and technical criteria, which guided the decisionmaking process. Thus, they helped establish the Bank's credit on Wall Street, which, after all, was where the Bank had to raise its resources. Creditors were understandably concerned lest an organization owned and controlled by governments be guided by motives inimical to the profitability and security of its investments. That would have endangered the Bank's capacity to service the debts to its bondholders. More recently, while continuing to point to the Bank's financial strength and profitability, presidents have defended the impartiality of the institution, emphasizing the need to maintain the credibility and effectiveness of its technical advice. As the Bank's influence pushed beyond concerns directly linked to the projects it financed and affected sensitive aspects of economic policymaking and management, it became both more difficult and more essential to preserve the institution's integrity.

Throughout, the performance of the Bank's presidents was dependent on the staff they recruited and on their ability to motivate the Bank's personnel. The presidents were able to rely on a succession of exceptional lieutenants—effectively, chief operating officers—who served them and the institution loyally and who provided the necessary continuity in the Bank's operations. As the presidents recognized, it was important to attract talented and devoted people to serve the institution at all levels. From the outset, the Bank drew to its service people outstanding for their technical abilities and their dedication to the Bank's goals. They were drawn from the public and private sectors, from academic pursuits, and from government work in economic and financial affairs. Over time, they came from a large number of the Bank's member countries. As the organization grew in size and complexity, day-to-day administration became a major challenge in itself. More elaborate procedures for planning and budgeting and increasingly frequent reorganizations reflected the struggle to keep the institution vibrant and efficient. For its presidents, the task of managing the Bank became a more time-consuming and critical aspect of their job.

As the experience of the several presidents illustrates, there can be no simple, unchanging list of responsibilities that defines the job of the Bank's president. Each president faced particular challenges. Each had to interpret the job, set priorities, and decide how to perform his tasks in the light of his personal experience. Eugene Meyer opened the Bank for business and recruited its core staff. John McCloy defined the relationship between the Bank's management and its board of executive directors and initiated the Bank's lending and borrowing activities. Eugene Black established the Bank's reputation as a prudent financial intermediary that effectively achieved the goals originally visualized at Bretton Woods. George Woods accelerated the transformation of the Bank from a conventional financing institution into a development institution defined by the needs of its developing members. Robert McNamara positioned the Bank to respond to the global development challenge and moved the struggle against poverty to the top of the agenda. Tom Clausen held the Bank on course during a period of severe financial turmoil and declining support for the goal of economic development. And Barber Conable renewed the Bank's commitment to the fight against poverty while giving greater emphasis to the preservation of the environment, to the role of the private sector, and to the interests of the people affected by Bank-supported investments.

The Bank's presidents provided leadership and a sense of mission—an essential determinant of all organizational performance. Their contributions were especially critical for an international organization operating in a complex, rapidly changing environment. The word "vision" has been overused, but it connotes well one of the essential contributions of the Bank's presidents. They worked hard to understand the needs and opportunities of their time, to establish appropriate long-term goals, and to inspire the Bank's members and its staff to pursue its mission with enthusiasm. The innovations they introduced were tested by the great events that continually reshaped the institution. Humility and a realistic appraisal of the limits to their authority thus became among the most important prerequisites for their success.

Some of the Bank's presidents stand out prominently as innovators, as agents of change, inspired by a vision of great opportunities. But wise leadership did not always involve dramatic change. At times, it also involved incremental adaptation to strong pressures in the institutional environment or the consolidation of achievements following a period of rapid change. The men who led the Bank during the past fifty years thus had diverse styles and very different accomplishments. In their different ways, they all helped build the institution, they kept it relevant to the demands of its members, and they guided it in the effective fulfillment of its vital mission.

Notes

IBRD, International Bank for Reconstruction and Development; IDA, International Development Association; IMF, International Monetary Fund; MIT, Massachusetts Institute of Technology; *NYT, New York Times;* WBGA, World Bank Group Archives. The World Bank Group comprises the IBRD, and IDA, the International Finance Corporation, the Multilateral Investment Guarantee Agency, and the International Centre for Settlement of Investment Disputes.

Introduction

1. The United Nations Monetary and Financial Conference, held at Bretton Woods, New Hampshire, in 1944, was convened to formulate proposals for an international monetary fund and, possibly, a bank for postwar reconstruction and development. Forty-four countries, including the U.S.S.R., were represented at the conference, which was chaired by the United States.

2. *Articles of Agreement of the International Bank for Reconstruction and Development,* Art. I. World Bank, Washington, D.C.

3. Report of Commission II (IBRD) to the Executive Plenary Session, July 21, 1944, *Proceedings and Documents of the United Nations Monetary and Financial Conference.* Bretton Woods, N.H., July 1–22, 1944 (Washington, D.C.: Government Printing Office, 1948), vol. 1, p. 1101.

4. J. Keith Horsefield, *The International Monetary Fund 1945–1965*. Vol. 1. *Chronicle* (Washington, D.C.: IMF, 1969), p. 135; see also Ansel F. Luxford, interview with Robert W. Oliver, July 1961, Columbia University Oral History Office, p. 22.

Chapter One. Eugene Meyer: The Bank's First Steps

1. Edward S. Mason and Robert E. Asher, *The World Bank since Bretton Woods* (Washington, D.C.: Brookings Institution, 1973): 39f.; *NYT* (June 5, 1946), p. 3.

2. Mason and Asher, pp. 37–40.

3. Merlo J. Pusey, *Eugene Meyer* (New York: Alfred A. Knopf, 1974), pp. 136–44.

4. Alfred E. Eckes Jr., *A Search for Solvency: Bretton Woods and the International Monetary System 1941–1971* (Austin, Tex.: University of Texas Press, 1975), pp. 1–33.

5. Ibid., 39f.; Robert A. Pollard, *Economic Security and the Origins of the Cold War, 1945–1950* (New York: Columbia University Press, 1985), pp. 10f.

6. Eckes, pp. 42–57.

7. Mason and Asher, p. 14.

8. Eckes, pp. 116–18.

9. Mason and Asher, p. 14f.

10. Eckes, pp. 155f.

11. Mason and Asher, pp. 21f.; Eckes, pp. 138f.

12. One billion is equal to 1,000 million.

13. Mason and Asher, pp. 11f., 17f., 23f.; J. Burke Knapp, remarks at meeting of the Investment Committee of the National Association of State Insurance Commissions, Portland, Oregon, June 11, 1946, Library of Congress, Eugene Meyer Papers.

14. Mason and Asher, pp. 17f., 24–27.

15. Eckes, pp. 194–202.

16. "Eugene Meyer," *NYT* (June 6, 1946), p. 20.

17. Pusey, pp. 242–48.

18. Knapp, p. 4.

19. Ansel F. Luxford, transcript of interview by Robert W. Oliver, July 1961, World Bank Oral History Project of Columbia University, WBGA, p. 36.

20. Donald C. Stone to Harold Smith, memorandum, June 20, 1946, Series 4234 (General files—Organization), WBGA; Ansel F. Luxford to Harold Smith, memorandum, July 10, 1946, Series 4155 (General files—Organization), WBGA; Harold Smith to Frank Coe, memorandum, August 29, 1946, Series 4155 (General files—Administration), WBGA; Harold Smith to Eugene Meyer, memorandum, October 16, 1946, Series 4155 (General files—Administration), WBGA.

21. Mason and Asher, 42f.; Richard H. Demuth, transcript of interview by Robert W. Oliver, August 1961, World Bank Oral History Project of Columbia University, WBGA, pp. 6f. For the executive directors' thinking about the issues of administration and staffing see Report of the Committee on Administration (R-2 Second draft), June 21, 1945, Series 4234 (General files—Administration), WBGA.

22. John J. McCloy to Eugene Meyer, letter, June 13, 1946; Eugene Meyer to John J. McCloy, letter, June 17, 1946; John J. McCloy to Eugene Meyer, letter, June 21, 1946; John J. McCloy to Eugene Meyer, letter, June 25, 1946, Library of Congress, Eugene Meyer Papers.

23. Luxford, interview, pp. 42f.

24. "High Posts Filled by the World Bank," *NYT,* November 1, 1946, p. 33.

25. Mason and Asher, pp. 42f., 51; John H. Crider, "World Bank Is Ready for Lending Program," *NYT,* October 13, 1946, E9.

26. Luxford, interview, pp. 11f.

27. Mason and Asher, p. 42; Eckes, pp. 211–21.

28. Leonard B. Rist to Eugene Meyer, memorandum, Functions of the Research Department, July 23, 1946, Series 3974 (Staff and Executive Directors papers—Leonard B. Rist papers), WBGA; minutes of the President's staff meeting, October 17, 1946, Series 3991 (Senior staff meeting minutes), WBGA.

29. Draft Ad Hoc Committee on Organization Reports, November–December 1946, Series 4234 (General files—Organization), WBGA.

30. Ibid.

31. Meeting at Federal Reserve Bank of New York, Monday August 19, memorandum for the files, August 20, 1946, Library of Congress, Eugene Meyer Papers; Mason and Asher, pp. 105–07.

32. Meeting at Federal Reserve Bank, memorandum.

33. Mason and Asher, p. 127.

34. George A. Mooney, "Savings Bankers Here Await New World Bank's Securities," *NYT,* November 17, 1946, F1.

35. Mason and Asher, pp. 55f.

36. Eugene Meyer to Maj. Gen. L. W. Rooks, letter, July 19, 1946; Eugene Meyer to Trygve Lie, letter, July 24, 1946; Eugene Meyer to Trygve Lie, letter, August 27, 1946; Eugene Meyer to Gen. Frank E. Stoner, letter, October 25, 1946, Library of Congress, Eugene Meyer Papers.

37. See, for example, memorandum of staff meeting, November 7, 1946, Series 3991 (Senior staff meeting minutes), WBGA.

38. IBRD, *First Annual Report by the Executive Directors* (Washington, D.C., September 27, 1946); Report of the Ad Hoc Committee on Organization, November 25, 1946; Draft Partial Report, Ad Hoc Committee on Organization, December 6, 1946, Series 4234 (General files—Organization), WBGA.

39. Mason and Asher, p. 128.

40. Luxford, interview, pp. 41f., 49–51.

41. Demuth, interview, p. 59.

42. Pusey, 34–36; "High Posts Filled," *NYT,* November 1, 1946, p. 33.

43. Emilio G. Collado, interview by Theodore A. Wilson and Richard D. McKinzie, July 7, 1971, Harry S Truman Library, p. 63f.

44. Luxford interview, p. 37; Chester A. McLain to Daniel Crena de Jongh, memorandum, October 1, 1946, Series 4223 (General files—Operations policy files—Policy and procedures), WBGA; Mason and Asher, p. 47.

45. Luxford, p. 50.

46. Luxford, p. 51; Demuth, interview, pp. 8f.

47. Pusey, p. 353.

48. Robert H. Fertridge, "Stock Market's Faith in Early End of Coal Tie-up Proves Justified," *NYT,* December 8, 1946, p. F1.

49. Demuth, interview, pp. 56–58.

Chapter Two. John McCloy: Starting up the Business

1. As remembered by Robert Garner, *This Is the Way It Was* (Chevy Chase, Md.: Chevy Chase Printing, 1972), p. 207.

2. Mason and Asher, p. 1.

3. Kai Bird, *The Chairman: John J. McCloy, The Making of the American Establishment* (New York: Simon & Schuster, 1992); Michael R. Beschloss, "Serving neither Too Wisely nor Too Well" (review of Bird, *The Chairman*) *Washington Post Book World,* April 12, 1992; Joseph Finder, "Ultimate Insider, Ultimate Outsider" (review of Bird, *The Chairman*), *New York Times Book Review,* April 12, 1992.

4. Bird, p. 23.

5. Bird, p. 19.

7. Walter Isaacson and Evan Thomas, *The Wise Men: Six Friends and the World They Made* (New York: Simon & Schuster, 1988), p. 71.

8. Quoted by Bird, p. 57.

9. Isaacson and Thomas, p. 336.

10. Bird, p. 662.

11. Cited in Isaacson and Thomas, p. 68.

12. Bird, p. 661.

13. Richard H. Demuth, "A Look Backward," in Fifteenth Anniversary Edition, *International Bank Notes,* vol. 15, June 1961.

14. Isaacson and Thomas, p. 428.

15. Addresses by John J. McCloy and Eugene R. Black, *The Role of the American Investor in the World Bank* (Investment Bankers Association of America, French Lick, Ind., May 21, 1947), p. 3.

16. In June 1946, Meyer had asked McCloy to be the Bank's general

counsel. McCloy, unwilling to leave the law firm he had just joined as a name-partner, turned down the offer. Instead he strongly recommended McLain for the post.

17. Bird, pp. 284f.

18. Eugene R. Black, transcript of interview by Robert W. Oliver, August 6, 1961, World Bank Oral History Project of Columbia University, WBGA, pp. 1f.

19. Thomas Basyn, Series 3973 (Staff and Executive Directors papers—Thomas Basyn papers), WBGA.

20. James Grigg to Bridges, cable, January 9, 1947, Treasury Series, Public Record Office, Kew Gardens, London.

21. Memorandum of the Informal Special Session, January 15, 1947, World Bank, Secretary's Office.

22. Bridges to Grigg, personal, January 17, 1947, Treasury Series, Public Record Office, Kew Gardens, London.

23. James Grigg to Bridges, cable, January 30, 1947, Treasury Series, Public Record Office, Kew Gardens, London.

24. Bridges to James Grigg, cable, January 31, 1947, Treasury Series, Public Record Office, Kew Gardens, London.

25. Hugh Dalton to John Snyder, letter, January 28, 1947, Harry S Truman Library, Independence, Mo.

26. Pusey, p. 354.

27. James Grigg to Bridges, cable, February 18, 1947, Treasury Series, Public Record Office, Kew Gardens, London.

28. Robert L. Garner, diary entry, February 28, 1947, Harry S Truman Library, Independence, Mo.

29. Ibid.

30. Black, interview, pp. 3f.

31. Garner, diary entry, February 24, 1947, Harry S Truman Library.

32. Report of the Committee on Organization, R-106 (final) , approved June 4, 1947, Series 4234 (General files—Organization files), WBGA.

33. Report of the Ad Hoc Committee on Organization, R-17 (revised), approved July 18, 1946, Series 4234 (General files—Organization files), WBGA.

34. IBRD, *First Annual Report,* p. 5.

35. IBRD, *Second Annual Report, 1946–1947,* Washington, D.C., p. 21.

36. Hugh Dalton to John Snyder, letter, March 3, 1947, Harry S Truman Library, Independence, Mo.

37. John J. McCloy to President Truman, letter, March 25, 1947; President Truman to John J. McCloy, letter, April 2, 1947, Amherst Archives.

38. Robert L. Garner, transcript of interview by Robert w. Oliver, July 19, 1961, World Bank Oral History Project of Columbia University, WBGA, pp. 5f.

39. Black, interview, p. 4.

40. Davidson Sommers, transcript of interview by Robert W. Oliver, August 2, 1961, World Bank Oral History Project of Columbia University, WBGA.

41. Black, interview, p. 4.

42. Daniel Crena de Jongh, transcript of interview by Robert W. Oliver, August 1, 1961, World Bank Oral History Project of Columbia University, WBGA, p. 15.

43. Memorandum on meeting at the Ministry of Finance, Paris, May 25, 1954; see also Crena de Jongh, interview, p. 16.

44. Articles of Agreement, Art. I (i).

45. Garner, interview, p. 10.

46. "Bretton Woods in Practice," *Economist,* March 8, 1947, p. 339.

47. Mason and Asher, p. 153.

48. President to the Executive Directors, recommendation on the Netherlands Loan Application, August 6, 1947, Series 4335 (Operational correspondence—The Netherlands, Ln 2 NE), WBGA.

49. Claude G. Bowers to President Truman, letter, July 21, 1947, Series 4477 (Presidents' papers—John J. McCloy—President J. McCloy correspondence), WBGA.

50. President of the United States to the Secretary of the Treasury, memorandum, August 5, 1947, Series 4477 (Presidents' papers—John J. McCloy—President J. McCloy correspondence), WBGA.

51. Mason and Asher, p. 131.

52. Bird, p. 291.

53. *Newsweek,* July 28, 1947, cited in Bird, p. 291.

54. Paul Heffernan in *NYT,* May 24, 1948, as quoted by Mason and Asher, p. 131.

55. Articles of Agreement, Art. III, Section 1 (a).

56. *Presentation Address, Second Annual Report, by John J. McCloy at the Second Annual Meeting of the Board of Governors,* London, September 12, 1947, Series 4479 (Information and Public Affairs—President John J. McCloy speeches), WBGA.

57. John J. McCloy, address before the Economic Commission of the Ninth International Conference of American States, Bogotá, Colombia, April 5, 1948, Series 4479 (Information and Public Affairs—President John. J. McCloy speeches), WBGA, p. 2.

58. John J. McCloy, address before the Foreign Policy Association, Cincinnati, Ohio, June 1, 1948, Series 4480 (Information and Public Affairs—President John J. McCloy speeches), WBGA, p. 7.

59. Mason and Asher, p. 131.

60. John J. McCloy, address to Governors, September 12, 1947.

61. *Financial Times,* February 24, 1947, quoted by Bird, p. 287.

62. Bird, p. 288.

63. Davidson Sommers, interview by Jochen Kraske, 1993.

64. Bird, p. 293.

65. John J. McCloy, "Europe's Hope for Recovery," address before the Chamber of Commerce, Philadelphia, January 15, 1948, Series 4479 (Information and Public Affairs—President John J. McCloy speeches), WBGA, p. 14.

66. John J. McCloy to the President, memorandum, United States Foreign Lending and the International Bank, January 7, 1949, Series 4219 (General files—Operations policy files: US government and foreign aid), WBGA.

67. John J. McCloy, "The Lesson of the World Bank," *Foreign Affairs,* July 1949, p. 558.

68. McCloy, memorandum on foreign lending, p. 14.

69. McCloy, "Lesson of the Bank," p. 554.

70. Articles of Agreement, Art. V, Section 8.

71. Demuth, interview, p. 19.

72. Text of the Agreement between the United Nations and the Bank, in IBRD, *Proceedings of the Second Annual Meeting of the Board of Governors,* September 11–17, 1947, p. 25.

73. John J. McCloy, speech before the Bond Club of New York, May 26, 1947, Series 4479 (Information and Public Affairs—President John J. McCloy speeches), WBGA.

74. John J. McCloy, "International Investment of Capital," address to the New York Chapter, American Society of Charter Life Underwriters, April 18, 1947.

75. Bird, p. 290f.

76. Russell C. Leffingwell to McCloy, letter, May 29, 1947, Series 4477 (Presidents' papers—John J. McCloy—President John J. McCloy correspondence), WBGA.

77. Garner, *The Way It Was,* p. 211.

78. John J. McCloy, personal notes on conversation with Leon Baranski [1948], Amherst Archives.

79. George Barrett, "McCloy Denies Aim to Bar East Loans," *NYT,* March 3, 1949.

80. R. B. Stevens, Foreign Office to Gordon Munro, cable, October 28, 1947, Public Record Office, Kew Gardens, London.

81. IBRD, *Third Annual Report 1947–1948,* Washington, D.C., p. 14.

82. Alan Brinkley, "Minister without Portfolio," *Harper's Magazine,* February 1983, p. 32.

83. Sommers, interview by Oliver, p. 27.

84. See, for instance, Brinkley, p. 32.

85. Garner, *The Way It Was,* p. 220.

86. Morton M. Mendels, transcript of interview by Robert W. Oliver, July 17, 1961, World Bank Oral History Project of Columbia University, WBGA, p. 45.

87. Quotation is from Mason and Asher, p. 96; Davidson Sommers,

"The Early Days of the Bank," address to Professional Staff Meeting, May 5, 1960 (Staff and Executive Directors papers—Davidson Sommers papers), WBGA.

88. John J. McCloy, Statement before the United States Senate, Committee on Foreign Relations, January 16, 1948, Series 4479 (Information and Public Affairs—President John J. McCloy speeches), WBGA.

89. Bird, p. 302.

90. John J. McCloy, meeting with President Truman on Saturday morning, April 30, 1949, personal note, n.d.

91. Black, interview, p. 51.

Chapter 3. Eugene Black: Bringing the Developing World to Wall Street

1. Isaacson and Thomas, p. 428.

2. Black, interview, p. 2.

3. James Morris, *The Road to Huddersfield: A Journey to Five Continents* (New York: Pantheon, 1963), pp. 57f.

4. Eugene R. Black, "Nationalism Today," in *The Diplomacy of Economic Development and Other Papers* (New York: Harvard University Press, 1963), p. 59 (address delivered on the occasion of Founders Day at the University of Virginia, Charlottesville, April 13, 1962).

5. "Profile of a President," *International Bank Notes,* vol. 13 (7–8, July–August 1959), pp. 4f.

6. Sommers, interview by Kraske.

7. Morris, p. 55.

8. See, for instance, Eugene R. Black, "Some Considerations Affecting Foreign Aid," address to the Economic Club of New York, January 14, 1953, Series 4480 (Information and Public Affairs—President Eugene Black speeches), WBGA; Eugene R. Black, address to the Board of Governors, Paris, September 8, 1950, p. 2.

9. "Bretton Woods in Practice," *Economist,* vol. 152 (March 8, 1947), p. 339, quoted in Mason and Asher, p. 125.

10. Only 2 percent of members' subscriptions had been paid in gold or U.S. dollars; 18 percent was paid in the members' currency but was usable only with the permission of the respective members; 80 percent of the subscription was available only in case the Bank was unable to meet its financial obligations.

11. Mendels, interview, p. 37.

12. Demuth, interview, p. 10.

13. In the United States, institutional investors needed legislative authorization to invest in particular financial instruments. The Bank was a new organization that did not fit into any of the established categories of investments.

14. Mason and Asher, p. 110.

15. Black, interview, p. 20.

16. Mason and Asher, p. 147.

17. Eugene R. Black, address before the Annual Convention of the Savings Banks Association of the State of New York aboard the *Nieuw Amsterdam*, October 23, 1949, IBRD Press Release No. 153, October 24, 1949, Series 4480 (Information and Public Affairs—President Eugene Black speeches), WBGA, p. 1.

18. Mason and Asher, pp. 24f.

19. Articles of Agreement, Art. III, Section 4 (vii).

20. IBRD, *Fifth Annual Report 1949–1950,* Washington, D.C., September 6, 1950, p. 8.

21. Sommers, interview by Oliver, p. 38; IBRD, *Fifth Annual Report,* p. 7.

22. Mason and Asher, p. 258.

23. Eugene R. Black, address to Governors, September 8, 1950, p. 5.

24. Eugene R. Black, "The World Bank at Work," *Foreign Affairs,* April 1952, pp. 407f.

25. Demuth, interview, p. 64.

26. Sommers, interview by Oliver , p. 34.

27. Articles of Agreement, Art. IV, Section 3 (c).

28. IBRD, *Fifth Annual Report,* p. 11.

29. Sommers, interview by Oliver, p. 34.

30. Comments of President Eugene Black on discussion of Annual Report, IBRD, *Summary Proceedings, Eleventh Annual Meeting of the Board of Governors, Washington, D.C., September 24–28, 1956,* Washington, D.C., November 15, 1956, p. 13, quoted by Mason and Asher, p. 233.

31. Mendels, interview, p. 45.

32. Sommers, interview by Kraske.

33. Garner, *The Way It Was,* p. 224.

34. Morris, p. 61.

35. Harold Graves, "Looking Back at Mr. Black: Glimpses in Retrospect," *1818 Society Newsletter* 45 (August–September 1992), p. 16.

36. Eugene R. Black to John McCloy, letter, n.d., received July 23, 1948, p. 4.

37. Davidson Sommers, "Eugene Black," *Bank's World,* 11 (March 1992), p. 8.

38. Black, interview, p. 6.

39. Eugene R. Black, "The Indus, A Moral for Nations," *New York Times Magazine,* December 11, 1960, p. 51.

40. Black, interview, p. 47.

41. Eugene R. Black, *The Diplomacy of Economic Development and Other Papers* (New York: Atheneum, 1963), pp. 24, 36.

42. Anthony Sampson, *The Money Lenders* (London: Hodder and Stoughton, 1981), p. 89.

43. Eugene R. Black, address to the Board of Governors, September 25, 1954, IBRD Press Release, Series 4480 (Information and Public Affairs—President Eugene Black speeches), WBGA, p. 8.

44. Eugene R. Black, address to the Board of Governors, September 13, 1949, Washington, D.C., IBRD Press Release, Series 4480 (Information and Public Affairs—President Eugene Black speeches), WBGA, p. 2.

45. Black, "The World Bank at Work," p. 410.

46. Eugene R. Black, address to the Economic Club of New York, January 14, 1953, Series 4480 (Information and Public Affairs—President Eugene Black speeches), WBGA, p. 4.

47. Eugene R. Black, address to the University of Chattanooga, Tenn., June 11, 1951, Series 4480 (Information and Public Affairs—President Eugene Black speeches), WBGA, p. 2.

48. Black, *Diplomacy,* p. 8.

49. Eugene R. Black, The Cyril Foster Lecture, Oxford University, U.K., March 3, 1960, IBRD Press Release, Series 4480 (Information and Public Affairs—President Eugene Black speeches), WBGA, p. 5.

50. Black, address to Governors, September 8, 1950, p. 2.

51. Eugene R. Black, address to the U.N. Economic and Social Council, Santiago, Chile, March 6, 1951, IBRD Press Release No. 237, Series 4480 (Information and Public Affairs—President Eugene Black speeches), WBGA, p. 4.

52. Black, "The World Bank at Work," p. 402.

53. Black, interview, p. 37.

54. Black, Cyril Foster Lecture, p. 13.

55. Black, "The World Bank at Work," p. 404.

56. Black, address to Governors, September 8, 1950, p. 6.

57. Eugene R. Black, address before the Banker's Club of Chicago, January 10, 1951, Series 4480 (Information and Public Affairs—President Eugene Black speeches), WBGA, p. 2.

58. Eugene R. Black, address to the Board of Governors, Washington, D.C., September 10, 1951, Series 4480 (Information and Public Affairs—President Eugene Black speeches), WBGA, pp. 10f.

59. Black, "The World Bank at Work," p. 411.

60. Black, address to Governors, September 8, 1950, p. 7; Black, address to the Economic Club of New York, p. 6.

61. Eugene R. Black, address to the Board of Governors, September 18, 1962, IBRD Press Release, Series 4480 (Information and Public Affairs—President Eugene Black speeches), WBGA, p. 19.

62. Articles of Agreement, Art. I (ii).

63. Garner, interview, p. 49.

64. See, for example, Sommers, interview by Oliver, pp. 30ff.

65. Eugene R. Black, address before the 19th Session of the U.N. Economic and Social Council, New York, April 7, 1955.

66. Eugene R. Black, address to the Board of Governors, Washington, D.C., September 25, 1956, IBRD Press Release No. 2, Series 4480 (Information and Public Affairs—President Eugene Black speeches), WBGA, p. 13.

67. Richard H. Demuth, Representing the Views of the Management before the United Nations Economic, Employment and Development Commission, New York, May 17, 1951. In *Economic Development Statements by Officials of the IBRD* (Washington, D.C.: IBRD, 1951), p. 30.

68. Black, address to the U.N. Economic and Social Council, March 6, 1951, IBRD Press Release No. 237, Series 4480 (Information and Public Affairs—President Eugene Black speeches), WBGA, p. 7.

69. Eugene R. Black, Statement before the Second Committee of the General Assembly, Paris, December 10, 1951, Series 4480 (Information and Public Affairs—President Eugene Black speeches), WBGA, p. 5.

70. Black, address to the Economic Club of New York, p. 7.

71. Eugene R. Black, address to the Board of Governors, New Delhi, October 7, 1958, IBRD Press Release, Series 4480 (Information and Public Affairs—President Eugene Black speeches), WBGA, p. 9.

72. J. Burke Knapp, transcript of interview by Robert W. Oliver, July 1961, World Bank Oral History Project of Columbia University, WBGA, pp. 34f.

73. IDA provides interest-free credits to the poorest countries. It is funded entirely by government credits, which are replenished periodically. For example, IDA-7 refers to the seventh replenishment of IDA, covering fiscal years 1985–87.

74. Sommers, interview by Kraske.

Chapter Four. George D. Woods: Transforming the Bank

1. Black, interview, p. 51.

2. Robert W. Oliver, *George Woods and the World Bank* (Boulder, Colo.: Lynne Rienner, 1995), p. 24.

3. Black, interview, p. 14.

4. Harold R. Bunce, "Woods Helps Blaze Trails for India, United Europe," *New York World-Telegram and Sun,* March 29, 1957, p. 29, quoted by Oliver, p. 48.

5. Sir William Iliff, transcript of interview by Robert W. Oliver, August 12, 1961, World Bank, Oral History Project of Columbia University, WBGA, p. 40.

6. George D. Woods, address before the Society for International Development, Washington, D.C., March 11, 1965, Series 4530 (Information and Public Affairs—President George D. Woods speeches), WBGA, p. 2f.

7. John F. Kennedy to George Woods, telegram, April 28, 1961. G. D. Woods's Papers (Foreign Economic Assistance Task Force/AID), Columbia University.

8. Arthur M. Schlesinger Jr., *A Thousand Days: John F. Kennedy in the White House* (Cambridge: Houghton Mifflin, 1965), p. 594.

9. George D. Woods to Harry Addinsell, cable, August 24, 1961.

10. George D. Woods to Harry Addinsell, cable, August 31, 1961.

11. Mrs. Grace Woods Johnson, notes of Robert W. Oliver, New York, March 16, 1986, G. D. Woods Papers (Louise Woods), Columbia University. Quoted by Oliver, *George Woods*, p. 3.

12. Edward Townsend, transcript of interview by John T. Mason, Jr., February 14, 1984, George D. Woods Oral History Project of Columbia University, pp. 10f.; Mrs. George David Woods, interview by John T. Mason Jr., New York, January 14, 1983, George D. Woods Oral History Project of Columbia University, pp. 25f, quoted by Oliver, *George Woods*, pp. 10f and 25f.

13. Robert Sheehan, "First Man at First Boston," *Fortune Magazine*, June 1959, p. 146.

14. "Conciliation Experts, They Help to Close a Suez Chapter," *NYT*, April 30, 1958, p. 9.

15. Quoted in "A Most Peculiar Institution," *Forbes Magazine*, December 15, 1963, p. 23.

16. Sheehan, p. 245.

17. Quoted by Sheehan, p. 246.

18. "Conciliation Experts," *NYT*, April 30, 1958, p. 9.

19. "U.S. Studies Pay for Dixon-Yates Outside Contract," *NYT*, July 19, 1955, p. 1.

20. Quoted in "Wenzell Reveals a Secret Meeting over Dixon-Yates," *NYT*, July 9, 1955, p. 1.

21. "U.S. Studies," *NYT*, July 19, 1955, p. 55.

22. Townsend, interview, p. 53.

23. The first quotation is from Oliver, *George Woods*, p. 24, the second from Sheehan, p. 245.

24. Richard H. Demuth, transcript of interview by Robert Asher, March 19, 1984, World Bank Oral History Program, WBGA, pp. 2f.

25. George D. Woods, address to the Board of Governors, annual meeting, September 30, 1963, Series 4530 (Information and Public Affairs—President George D. Woods speeches), WBGA, p. 3.

26. George D. Woods, address to the U.N. Economic and Social Council, April 5, 1963, Series 4530 (Information and Public Affairs—President George D. Woods speeches), WBGA, p. 14.

27. At the time, the World Bank Group comprised the International Bank for Reconstruction and Development (IBRD), the International Development Association (IDA), and the International Finance Corporation (IFC).

28. Woods, address to Governors, September 30, 1963, p. 7.

29. Mason and Asher, p. 407.

30. The Bank's Policy concerning Reserves, Loan Charges, and Dividends: B. Loan Charges, FPC 63-5, January 31, 1963, Series 4219 (General files—Operational policy), WBGA.

31. Mason and Asher, p. 100.

32. George D. Woods, Off the record talk at the Council on Foreign Relations, New York City, May 27, 1964, Series 4530 (Information and Public Affairs—President George D. Woods speeches), WBGA.

33. *NYT,* March 12, 1964.

34. Aaron Broches, transcript of interview by Robert W. Oliver, Conversations about George Woods and the World Bank (CalTech), November 7, 1985, WBGA, p. 1.

35. Mason and Asher, p. 100.

36. Woods, address to Governors, September 30, 1963, p. 5.

37. George D. Woods, address to UNCTAD, Geneva, March 25, 1964, Series 4530 (Information and Public Affairs—President George D. Woods speeches), WBGA, p. 7.

38. Demuth, interview by Asher, p. 4.

39. Woods, address to UNCTAD, p. 3.

40. George D. Woods, address to the Board of Governors, annual meeting, Tokyo, September 7, 1964, Series 4530 (Information and Public Affairs—President George D. Woods speeches), WBGA, p. 4.

41. Woods, address to Governors, September 30, 1963, p. 6.

42. Woods, address to Economic and Social Council, April 5, 1963, p. 11.

43. Woods, address to Governors, September 30, 1963, p. 10.

44. Mason and Asher, p. 570.

45. Demuth, interview by Asher, p. 6; Mason and Asher, p. 571.

46. Broches, interview, p. 1.

47. Rainer Steckhan, transcript of interview by Robert W. Oliver, November 13, 1985, Conversations about George Woods and the World Bank (CalTech), WBGA, pp. 10f.

48. George D. Woods to Aaron Broches, memorandum on the subject of the Economic Committee, March 10, 1965, Series 4527 (Presidents' papers—George D. Woods—President George D. Woods chronological files), WBGA.

49. Irving S. Friedman, transcript of interview by Robert W. Oliver, March 1974, Conversations about George Woods and the World Bank (CalTech), WBGA, p. 15.

50. Andrew Kamarck, transcript of interview by Robert W. Oliver, November 2, 1985, Conversations about George Woods and the World Bank (CalTech), WBGA.

51. Friedman, interview, pp. 15ff.

52. Demuth, interview by Asher, p. 12.

53. Benjamin B. King, transcript of interview by Robert W. Oliver, July 24–25, 1986, World Bank Oral History Program, WBGA, p. 32.

54. Friedman, interview, p. 19.

55. Woods, Off the record talk, pp. 12f.

56. George D. Woods, address to the Canadian Club, Toronto, November 9, 1964, Series 4530 (Information and Public Affairs—President George D. Woods speeches), WBGA, p. 7.

57. Woods, address to Governors, September 30, 1968, p. 4.

58. Woods, address to UNCTAD, p. 4.

59. Woods, address to Economic and Social Council, April 5, 1963, p. 14.

60. Woods, address to Canadian Club, p. 6.

61. Oliver, *George Woods,* pp. 107ff.

62. Woods, address to UNCTAD, p. 5.

63. George D. Woods, address to the Development Assistance Committee of the Organization for Economic Cooperation and Development, Paris, July 22, 1965, Series 4530 (Information and Public affairs—President George D. Woods speeches), WBGA, p. 3.

64. Quoted by Mason and Asher, p. 408.

65. Demuth, interview by Asher, p. 9.

66. "Lean Years for Aid," *The Economist,* September 30, 1967, p. 1210.

67. George D. Woods to John D. Miller, memorandum on the subject of IDA replenishment, November 7, 1967.

68. Demuth, interview by Asher, p. 9.

69. Ibid., p. 10; Mason and Asher, pp. 408ff.

70. George D. Woods, address to the Board of Governors and concluding remarks, annual meeting, Rio de Janeiro, September 25 and 29, 1967, Series 4530 (Information and Public Affairs—President George D. Woods speeches), WBGA, p. 2.

71. Mason and Asher, p. 136.

72. Broches, interview, p. 24; William Bennett, transcript of interview by Robert W. Oliver, Conversations about George Woods and the World Bank (CalTech), January 20, 1988, WBGA, p. 15.

73. George D. Woods, address to the Board of Governors and concluding remarks, annual meeting, Washington, D.C., September 26 and 30, 1966, Series 4530 (Information and Public Affairs—President George D. Woods speeches), WBGA, p. 2.

74. George D. Woods, address to the Board of Governors and concluding remarks, annual meeting, Rio de Janeiro, September 25 and 29, 1967, Series 4530 (Information and Public Affairs—President George D. Woods speeches), WBGA, p. 2.

75. Broches, interview, p. 24.

76. Demuth, interview by Asher, p. 3.

77. Mason and Asher, p. 675.

78. David B. H. Denoon, *Devaluation under Pressure: India, Indonesia and Ghana* (Cambridge, Mass.: MIT Press, 1986), p. 59, quoted by Oliver, *George Woods,* p. 127.

79. President's memorandum on Bank financial policy, FPC 63-8, July 18, 1963, Series 4219 (General files—Operational policy: Committee on Financial Policy), WBGA.

80. Meeting of Executive Directors, Statement by Chairman on India's Debt Servicing Problem, Sec. M-67-163, July 11, 1967, and R-67-115, July 20, 1967, Executive Directors' Library.

81. Minutes of the meeting of the Executive Directors on March 19, 1968, March 26, 1968, Executive Directors' Library.

82. Mason and Asher, pp. 682f.

83. King, interview, p. 25.

84. S. Boothalingam, *Reflections of an Era* (Delhi: East West Press, 1993), p. 144.

85. William Gilmartin, transcript of interview by Robert W. Oliver, Conversations about George Woods and the World Bank (CalTech), November 14, 1985, WBGA, p. 16.

86. George D. Woods, address before the Second UNCTAD Meeting, New Delhi, India, February 9, 1968, Series 4530 (Information and Public Affairs—President George D. Woods speeches), WBGA, p. 2.

87. Demuth, interview by Asher, p. 3.

88. Mason and Asher, p. 99.

89. Broches, interview, p. 20.

90. See, for instance, Nathaniel M. McKitterick, interview by Robert W. Oliver, July 24, 1985, pp. 8ff.

91. Oliver, *George Woods,* p. 49.

92. Bernard Bell, transcript of interview by Robert W. Oliver, November 13, 1985, Conversations about George Woods and the World Bank (CalTech), WBGA, p. 24.

93. George D. Woods to Davidson Sommers, letter, December 17, 1963, Series 4527 (Presidents' papers—George D. Woods—President George D. Woods Chronological files), WBGA.

94. Friedman, interview, p. 16.

95. Bell, interview, p. 19.

96. Edwin L. Dale Jr., "Happy Fund, Troubled Bank," *NYT,* September 24, 1967, Section 3, p. 1.

97. William Diamond, transcript of interview by William Becker and David Milobsky, April 12, 1993, World Bank Oral History Program, WBGA, p. 28.

98. J. Burke Knapp, transcript of interview by Robert W. Oliver, September 5, 1986, Conversations about George Woods and the World Bank (CalTech), WBGA, p. 10.

99. Demuth, interview by Asher, p. 9.

100. Diamond, interview, pp. 32f.

101. Broches, interview, p. 19.

102. Pieter Lieftinck, transcript of interview by Robert W. Oliver, November 19, 1985, Conversations about George Woods and the World Bank (CalTech), WBGA, p. 9.

103. Knapp, interview, p. 12.

104. President Lyndon B. Johnson to George D. Woods, letter, April 18, 1966. G. D. Woods Papers (White House), Columbia University.

105. Lieftinck, interview, p. 13.

106. Bennett, interview, p. 15.

107. Demuth, interview by Asher, p. 8.

108. Steckhan, interview, p. 5.

109. Knapp, interview, p. 10.

110. King, interview p. 56.

111. Roger Chaufournier, interview by Robert W. Oliver, July 22, 1986, World Bank Oral History Program, WBGA, p. 46.

112. King, interview, p. 25; Steckhan, interview, p. 15.

113. Woods, address to the Board of Governors, September 26, 1966, p. 7.

114. William Clark, *From Three Worlds* (London: Sidgwick and Jackson, 1986), pp. 231f.

115. George D. Woods, "Development—The Need for New Directions," address to the Swedish Bankers Association, Stockholm, October 27, 1967, Series 4530 (Information and Public Affairs—President George D. Woods speeches), WBGA, p. 9.

Chapter Five. Robert S. McNamara: Champion of the Developing World

1. Transcript of press conference held by George D. Woods on November 30, 1967, Washington, D.C., Series 4530 (Information and Public Affairs—President George D. Woods speeches), WBGA, pp. 3f.

2. Robert S. McNamara, *In Retrospect: The Tragedy and Lessons of Vietnam* (New York: Random House, 1995), p. 312.

3. Broches, interview, November 7, 1985, p. 20.

4. David Halberstam, *The Best and the Brightest* (New York: Random House, 1973), p. 645.

5. "Texts of Statements on the New Post for McNamara," *NYT,* November 30, 1967, p. 16.

6. McNamara, p. 311.

7. See also, Halberstam, p. 645. "Without checking with McNamara, Johnson announced in November 1967 that his Secretary of Defense was going to the World Bank. The move came as a surprise to the Secretary and he did not know whether or not he had been fired. The answer was that he had been."

8. Halberstam, p. 215.

9. McNamara, p. 4.

10. See Henry L. Trewhitt, *McNamara* (New York: Harper and Row, 1971), p. 26; Deborah Shapley, *Promise and Power. The Life and Times of Robert McNamara* (Boston: Little, Brown & Co., 1993), pp. 8f.

11. Trewhitt, p. 27.

12. McNamara, p. 15.

13. Shapley, p. 21.

14. McNamara, p. 13.

15. Trewhitt, pp. 50f.

16. McNamara, p. 23.

17. Roger R. Trask, *The Secretaries of Defense: A Brief History 1947–1985* (Washington, D.C.: Historical Office, Office of the Secretary of Defense, 1985), p. 31.

18. McNamara, p. 22.

19. Joseph Kraft, "McNamara's Departure Means Failure in Managerial Faith," *Washington Post,* February 27, 1968, p. A7.

20. Saul Pett in *Washington Star,* February 4, 1968, quoted by Shapley, p. 459.

21. McNamara, p. 323.

22. Robert S. McNamara, North American press seminar, edited transcript of meeting with the press on June 15, 1980, Wye Plantation, Md., Series 4547 (Presidents' papers—Robert S. McNamara—Statements), WBGA, p. 15.

23. McNamara, p. 313.

24. Clark, *Three Worlds,* p. 243.

25. Robert S. McNamara, *The Essence of Security* (New York: Harper and Row, 1968), p. 149.

26. Robert S. McNamara, address to the Board of Governors, Washington, D.C., September 29, 1969, p. 26.

27. Robert S. McNamara, address to the Board of Governors, Washington, D.C., September 30, 1968, p. 6.

28. William Clark, "Robert McNamara at the World Bank," *Foreign Affairs,* vol. 60, no. 1 (October 1981), p. 169.

29. Robert S. McNamara, address to Governors, September 30, 1968, p. 4.

30. Clark, "McNamara," p. 168.

31. McNamara, address to Governors, September 30, 1968, pp. 4f.

32. Robert S. McNamara to Mr. Chenery, memorandum, June 7, 1973, Series 4541 (Presidents' papers—Robert S. McNamara—Chronological files [o.]), WBGA.

33. Robert S. McNamara to Mr. Aldewereld and Mr. Cope, memorandum, July 27, 1971, Series 4541 (Presidents' papers—Robert S. McNamara—Chronological files [o.]), WBGA.

34. Robert S. McNamara, transcript of interview by Lew Simons of the *Washington Post* for *Smithsonian* magazine, July 29, 1980, attachment to memorandum, H. Martin Koelle to Robert S. McNamara, August 13, 1980, Series [A95263] (Information and Public Affairs—President's press relations), WBGA, p. 5.

35. Robert S. McNamara, personal notes, item 16, May 25, 1968, Series 4541 (Presidents' papers—Robert S. McNamara—Chronological files [o.]), WBGA.

36. Robert S. McNamara to John H. Adler, memorandum, April 10, 1973, Series 4541 (Presidents' papers—Robert S. McNamara—Chronological files [o])), WBGA.

37. Robert S. McNamara, personal notes, item 84, May 25, 1968, Series 4545 (Presidents' papers—Robert S. McNamara—Personal chronological file), WBGA.

38. Lieftinck, interview, p. 17.

39. Robert S. McNamara, interview by John Lewis, Richard Webb, and Devesh Kapur, October 3, 1991, World Bank History Project of the Brookings Institution.

40. Robert S. McNamara, personal notes, item 94, May 25, 1968, Series 4545 (Presidents' papers—Robert S. McNamara—Personal chronological file), WBGA.

41. S. Shahid Husain, interview by Louis Galambos, William Becker, and David Milobsky, April 20, 1994, World Bank Oral History Program, WBGA, p. 31.

42. Robert S. McNamara, personal notes, items 34, 35, 49, 50, May 25, 1968, Series 4545 (Presidents' papers—Robert S. McNamara—Personal chronological file), WBGA.

43. R. W. Cavanaugh, notes from interviews by Harold Graves, November–December 1968, Series 4100 (Bank Oral History Project interviews), WBGA.

44. Robert S. McNamara, personal notes, item 69, May 25, 1968, Series 4545 (Presidents' papers—Robert S. McNamara— Personal chronological file), WBGA.

45. Clark, "McNamara," p. 169.

46. McNamara, address to Governors, September 30, 1968, p. 6.

47. Eugene H. Rotberg, interview by William Becker and David Milobsky, April 22, 1994, World Bank Oral History Program, WBGA, p. 9.

48. Robert S. McNamara, address to the Bond Club of New York, May 14, 1969, p. 1.

49. Articles of Agreement, Art. III, Section 3, limits the total amount of outstanding loans and guarantees to the amount of the subscribed capital and reserves.

50. I. P. M. Cargill to Robert S. McNamara, memorandum, Loan Portfolio Analysis Unit—Second Progress Report, September 17, 1975, cited

in John P. Lewis, Richard C. Webb, and Devesh Kapur, *The World Bank as a Development Promoting Institution* (Washington, D.C.: Brookings Institution, forthcoming), ch. 18.

51. Robert S. McNamara, personal notes, item 48, May 25, 1968, Series 4545 (Presidents' papers—Robert S. McNamara—Personal chronological file), WBGA, p. 4.

52. McNamara, address to Governors, September 30, 1968, p. 1.

53. See Ernest Stern, interview by Patricia Blair on the Pearson and Brandt Commissions, March 2, 1983.

54. *Partners in Development: Report of the Commission on International Development,* Lester B. Pearson, chairman (New York: Praeger Publishers, 1969), p. 55.

55. See, for example, memorandum for the record, January 13, 1976, which describes how McNamara strategically assigned the task of briefing major IDA donors to the staff working with Senior Vice President Peter Cargill on the replenishment.

56. North American Press Seminar, p. 5.

57. Robert S. McNamara, transcript of a speech to a press seminar at the World Bank, May 10, 1978, Series 4550 (Staff and Executive Directors papers—J. Burke Knapp papers [McNamara file]), WBGA, p. 5.

58. Robert S. McNamara, interview by John Lewis, May 10, 1991, World Bank History Project of the Brookings Institution.

59. McNamara, North American press seminar, pp. 3f.

60. Robert S. McNamara, address to the Board of Governors, Washington, D.C., September 30, 1974, p. 25.

61. Robert S. McNamara, address to the Board of Governors, Copenhagen, September 21, 1970, p. 10.

62. McNamara, transcript of press seminar at the World Bank, May 10, 1978, pp. 9f.

63. Catherine Gwin, *U.S. Relations with the World Bank 1945–92,* Brookings Occasional Papers (Washington, D.C.: Brookings Institution, 1994), p. 65.

64. Robert S. McNamara to Clarence Long, letter, November 1, 1979.

65. Clark, "McNamara," p. 181.

66. S. Shahid Husain to Robert S. McNamara, memorandum, August 31, 1979.

67. S. Shahid Husain, interview, p. 21.

68. Robert S. McNamara, address to the Board of Governors, Belgrade, October 2, 1979, p. 33.

69. McNamara, address to Governors, September 30, 1980, p. 38.

70. Summary of Third Window Operations, Sec. M-77-573, July 12, 1977, Executive Directors' Library.

71. Senior Staff Meeting, minutes, October 9, 1968, Series 3991 (Secretary's Department—Senior staff meeting minutes), WBGA.

72. Robert S. McNamara, address to the Board of Governors, Washington, D.C., September 29, 1969, p. 4.

73. McNamara, address to Governors, September 30, 1968, p. 5.

74. Robert S. McNamara to Warren Baum, memorandum, December 1, 1976, Series 4541 (Presidents' papers—Robert S. McNamara— Chronological files [o]), WBGA.

75. Ibid.

76. Warren C. Baum, interview by Robert W. Oliver, July 23, 1986, World Bank Oral History Program, WBGA, p. 13.

77. Robert S. McNamara to S. Aldewereld, memorandum, July 14, 1970, Series 4545 (Presidents' papers—Robert S. McNamara—Personal chronological file), WBGA.

78. Minutes of Operational Vice Presidents' meeting, November 22, 1976, November 30, 1976, Series 4000 (Operational Vice Presidents' meeting minutes), WBGA.

79. Lewis T. Preston to Chairman of the Joint Audit Committee Jean-Pierre Landau, memorandum, October 2, 1992, accompanying "Report of the World Bank's Portfolio Management Task Force. Effective Implementation: Key to Development Impact," September 22, 1992.

80. "Report of the World Bank's Portfolio Management Task Force," p. 14.

81. Andrew Kamarck to William B. Bundy (editor of *Foreign Affairs* magazine), letter, December 11, 1981; Kamarck, the former head of the Bank's Economics Department, distinguished between "those people who emphasize the dependence of development in the poor countries on the volume of the transfer of resources from rich to poor and those who instead emphasize that development depends, first and foremost, on the improvement in the allocation and management of the resources (in the widest sense) at command of the poor country." He felt that McNamara belonged in the first group.

82. McNamara, address to Governors, September 29, 1969, p. 4.

83. McNamara, address to Governors, September 30, 1968, p. 6.

84. Clark, "McNamara," p. 171.

85. McNamara, address to Governors, September 30, 1968, p. 10.

86. Robert S. McNamara, address to the Inter-American Press Association, Buenos Aires, Argentina, October 18, 1968, p. 8.

87. Robert S. McNamara, address to the University of Notre Dame, Notre Dame, Indiana, May 1, 1969, p. 3.

88. Robert S. McNamara, address to the Columbia University Conference on International Economic Development, New York, February 20, 1970, p. 7. This conference had been organized by Columbia University to discuss the findings and recommendations of the Pearson Commission Report.

89. Robert S. McNamara, address to UNCTAD, Santiago, Chile, April 14, 1972, p. 4.

90. Robert S. McNamara, address to the Board of Governors, Nairobi, Kenya, September 24, 1973, p. 9.

91. Baum, interview.

92. McNamara, address to Governors, Nairobi, p. 15; address to Governors, Belgrade, p. 13.

93. McNamara, address to Governors, September 30, 1974, p. 5; address to the Board of Governors, Washington, D.C., September 1, 1975, p. 16.

94. McNamara, address to Governors, September 30, 1974, p. 7.

95. McNamara, address to Governors, September 1, 1975, p. 19.

96. For an evaluation of the Bank's lending in support of rural development see, for instance, "World Bank Experience with Rural Development 1965–1986. Operations Evaluation Department, Document of the World Bank," October 16, 1987.

97. McNamara, address to Governors, September 1, 1975, p. 19.

98. McNamara, address to Governors, Belgrade, p. 15.

99. Robert S. McNamara, address to the Board of Governors, Washington, D.C., September 26, 1977, p. 22.

100. Mahbub Ul Haq, interview by Robert E. Asher, December 3, 1982, World Bank Oral History Program, WBGA, p. 13.

101. Robert S. McNamara, address to the Board of Governors, Washington, D.C., September 30, 1980, p. 19.

102. For this purpose, McNamara wanted estimates of the "poverty content" and the numbers of poor benefiting from the Bank's agricultural and urban lending, which the staff resisted.

103. Robert S. McNamara, address to Governors, September 30, 1974, p. 24.

104. McNamara, address to Governors, September 1, 1975, p. 5.

105. McNamara, address to Governors, September 30, 1974, p. 26.

106. McNamara, address to Governors, September 30, 1980, p. 8.

107. Robert S. McNamara, address to UNCTAD, Manila, the Philippines, May 10, 1979, p. 29.

108. McNamara, address to Governors, September 30, 1980, p. 6.

109. McNamara, interview, October 3, 1991.

110. McNamara, interview by Simons, p. 8, attachment to memorandum, Koelle to McNamara, p. 6.

111. McNamara, *In Retrospect*, p. 23.

112. Clark, *Three Worlds*, pp. 240f.

113. Ernest Stern, interview by Louis Galambos and Jochen Kraske, December 29, 1994, Oral History, p. 13.

114. Baum, interview, p. 21.

115. Stern, interview, p. 12; Ul Haq, interview, p. 9; Rotberg, interview, p. 21.

116. Baum, interview, p. 30.

117. Davidson Sommers, transcript of interview by Robert W. Oliver, 1985, Conversations about George Woods and the World Bank (CalTech), WBGA.

118. William Clark, interview by Robert Asher, October 5, 1983, World Bank Oral History Program, WBGA, p. 4.

119. Cargill claimed that he had entered the discussion by asking, "Systems analysis? Isn't that the new husband of Jacqueline Kennedy?"

120. Rotberg, interview, p. 20; Baum, interview, p. 17; Ul Haq, interview, p. 9; Stern, interview, p. 13.

121. William S. Ryrie, interview by William Becker and Louis Galambos, August 10, 1993, World Bank Oral History Program, WBGA, p. 12.

122. J. Burke Knapp, transcript of interview by Robert E. Asher, October 6 and 29, 1981, WBGA, p. 13.

123. David Milobsky and Louis Galambos, "The McNamara Bank and Its Legacy, 1968–1987," *Business and Economic History,* vol. 24, no. 1 (Winter 1995).

Chapter Six. Alden W. Clausen, Navigating in Troubled Times

1. A. W. Clausen, address to the Board of Governors, Washington, D.C., September 29, 1981, p. 1.

2. A. W. Clausen, interview by John Lewis, Richard Webb, and Devesh Kapur, June 8, 1992, World Bank History Project of the Brookings Institution, p. 2.

3. Gary Hector, *Breaking the Bank, The Decline of BankAmerica* (Boston: Little, Brown, 1988), p. 127; Scott W. Fisher, "Tom Clausen," in Larry Schweikert, ed., "Banking and Finance, 1913–1989," in William H. Becker, ed., *Encyclopedia of American Business History and Biography* (New York: Facts on File, Inc., 1990), pp. 56f.

4. Rotberg, interview, p. 33.

5. McNamara, address to Governors, September 30, 1980; Managing Committee meeting, minutes, October 11, 1984, Series 3963 (Presidents' papers—A. W. Clausen—Managing Committee files), WBGA.

6. Hector, pp. 306f., 315f., 319ff.

7. Ibid., pp. 74ff.; Fisher, pp. 54ff.

8. Fisher, p. 54.

9. Hector, pp. 96ff.

10. Clausen, interview, pp. 1f.

11. Rotberg, interview, p. 35.

12. A. W. Clausen, "Global Interdependence in the 1980s," address to the Yomiuri Economic Society, Tokyo, January 13, 1982, in *The Development Challenge of the Eighties: A. W. Clausen at the World Bank.*

Major Policy Addresses 1981–1986 (Washington, D.C.: World Bank, 1986), p. 53.

13. A. W. Clausen, address to the Board of Governors, Washington, D.C., September 29, 1981, in *The Development Challenge of the Eighties,* p. 8.

14. A. W. Clausen, remarks before the Brookings Institution Seminar on the Future Role of the World Bank, January 7, 1982, Series 3962 (Presidents' papers—A. W. Clausen—Speeches), WBGA, pp. 3ff.

15. A. W. Clausen, "Global Interdependence," p. 54.

16. A. W. Clausen, address to Governors, September 29, 1981, p. 7.

17. A. W. Clausen, address to the Board of Governors, Washington, D.C., September 24, 1984, in *The Development Challenge of the Eighties,* p. 337.

18. Ul Haq, interview, 16.

19. Quoted by Robert L. Ayres, *Banking on the Poor: The World Bank and World Poverty* (Cambridge, Mass.: MIT Press, 1983), p. 230.

20. A. W. Clausen, address to the Board of Governors, Toronto, Canada, September 6, 1982, in *The Development Challenge of the Eighties,* p. 107.

21. Ayres, p. 238.

22 Clausen, address to Governors, September 29, 1981, pp. 9ff.

23 A. W. Clausen, remarks before the Brookings Institution Seminar, p. 11.

24. Catherine Gwin, *U.S. Relations with the World Bank 1945–92* (Washington, D.C.: Brookings Institution, 1994), p. 75.

25. A. W. Clausen, remarks before the Brookings Institution Seminar, pp. 11ff.

26. "Clausen's Investment Framework," *Pakistan & Gulf Economist,* January 1–7, 1983, pp. 10ff.

27. Heribert Golsong to A. W. Clausen, memorandum, Multilateral Investment Insurance Agency, July 12, 1982; Ernest Stern to A. W. Clausen, memorandum, Multilateral Investment Insurance Scheme, August 5, 1982, Series 3957 (Presidents' papers—A. W. Clausen—Alphabetical files: MIGA), WBGA.

28. Ibrahim F. I. Shihata, interview by William Becker and David Milobsky, May 11, 1994, World Bank Oral History Program, WBGA, pp. 20ff.

29. Draft report of the Executive Directors on the Convention Establishing the Multilateral Investment Guarantee Agency, August 8, 1985, Series 3957 (Presidents' papers—A. W. Clausen—Alphabetical files: MIGA), WBGA, pp. 4ff.

30. A. W. Clausen, remarks, "Briefing Session with Non-U.S. Commercial Banks," May 19, 1982, Series 3957 (Presidents' papers—A. W. Clausen—Alphabetical files: Co-financing), WBGA.

31. Frank Vibert to Ernest Stern, memorandum, Measures to Increase

Cofinancing with Commercial Banks, July 15, 1981, Series 3957 (Presidents' papers—A. W. Clausen—Alphabetical files: Co-financing), WBGA.

32. "Clausen's Investment Framework," pp. 11–13.

33. "Cofinancing with Commercial Banks," paper for the Managing Committee, April 1, 1982, Series 3957 (Presidents' papers—A. W. Clausen—Alphabetical files: Co-financing), WBGA; see also report of World Bank Task Force on Cofinancing, Review of Cofinancing at the World Bank, February 25, 1994, WBGA, pp. 15f.

34. Office of the President to the Executive Directors, memorandum, Cofinancing with Commercial Banks, July 2, 1982, pp. 15ff.

35. Report of Task Force on Cofinancing, pp. 15f.

36. A. W. Clausen, statement before the GATT Ministerial Meeting, Geneva, Switzerland, November 24, 1982, in *The Development Challenge of the Eighties,* p. 128.

37. A. W. Clausen, address to Governors, September 6, 1982, in *The Development Challenge of the Eighties,* p. 112.

38. Jacques J. Polak, *The World Bank and the IMF: A Changing Relationship* (Washington, D.C.: Brookings Institution, 1994), pp. 21ff.

39. Stanley Please, transcript of interview by Charles Ziegler, August 26, 1986, World Bank, Oral History Program, p. 10.

40. A. W. Clausen, statement before the Commission on Security and Economic Assistance, Washington, D.C., June 27, 1983, pp. 14–15.

41. A. W. Clausen, address to the Board of Governors, Seoul, Republic of Korea, October 8, 1985, in *The Development Challenge of the Eighties,* p. 400.

42. Gwin, pp. 41ff., 62f.

43. "Washington's Gambit to Head Off a Debtor Revolt," *Business Week,* September 23, 1985, p. 35.

44. A. W. Clausen, remarks to the Business Council, May 7, 1982, pp. 13f.; Gwin, pp. 37ff.

45. Clausen, remarks to Business Council, pp. 10ff.

46. Opening remarks by President Ronald Reagan, *Summary Proceedings of 1983 Annual Meetings of the Boards of Governors* (Washington, D.C.: World Bank, 1983), p. 2.

47. Gwin, p. 41.

48. Proposed Special Assistance Facility for Sub-Saharan Africa, January 8, 1985 (paper prepared for special meeting of donors on Sub-Saharan Africa, Paris, January 31–February 1, 1985), Series 3957 (Presidents' papers—A. W. Clausen—Alphabetical files: Sub-Saharan Africa Special Fund), WBGA; World Bank, *Toward Sustained Development in Sub-Saharan Africa* (Washington, D.C.: 1984).

49. Gwin, p. 41.

50. Hobart Rowen, "U.S. May End Support of IDA Programs," *Washington Post,* February 5, 1985, p. C1.

51. Managing Committee meeting minutes, February 13, 1984; July 24, 1985; August 5, 1985, Series 3963 (Presidents' papers—A. W. Clausen—Managing committee files), WBGA.

52. David R. Bock to A. W. Clausen, memorandum, Talking Points for Meeting with Secretary Baker, July 29, 1985.

53. Clausen, interview, p. 1.

54. Rotberg, interview, p. 34.

55. Clausen, interview, p. 16.

56. Attila Karaosmanoglu, interview by William Becker, Jochen Kraske, and David Milobsky, January 18, 1995, World Bank Oral History Program, WBGA.

57. Clausen, interview, p. 5.

58. Managing Committee meeting minutes, July 30, 1981, Series 3963 (Presidents' papers—A. W. Clausen—Managing committee files), WBGA, pp. 2ff.

59. Managing Committee meeting, minutes, July 1, 1986, Series 3963 (Presidents' papers—A. W. Clausen—Managing committee files), WBGA, pp. 2f.

60. Clausen, interview, pp. 49, 52.

61. James M. Boughton and K. Sarwar Lateef, eds., *Fifty Years After Bretton Woods: The Future of the IMF and the World Bank. Proceedings of a Conference Held in Madrid, Spain, September 29–30, 1994* (Washington, D.C.: International Monetary Fund and World Bank Group, 1995), p. 70.

Chapter Seven. Barber B. Conable: Dedicated to Public Service

1. Hobart Rowen, "Conable to Head World Bank," *Washington Post,* March 14, 1986, p. A1.

2. Barber B. Conable, interview by John Lewis, Richard Webb, and Devesh Kapur, May 8, 1991, World Bank History Project of the Brookings Institution, p. 1.

3. Alan Drattell, "Meet Barber Conable," *Bank's World* 5 (7 July 1986), p. 5.

4. Conable, interview, p. 3

5. Peter Behr, "Conable Widely Respected for Intelligence, Ability," *Washington Post,* March 14, 1986, p. C11.

6. Robert Pear, "A Fiscal Conservative Headed for the World Bank," *NYT,* March 14, 1986, p. D1.

7. James Sterngold, "Reaction Warm to Conable Selection," *NYT,* March 14, 1986.

8. Drattell, p. 4.

9. Stephen E. Nordlinger, "Reagan Picks Conable to Head the World Bank," *Baltimore Sun,* March 14, 1986.

10. Michael Clements, "Scramble for Conable's Job," *Democrat and Chronicle,* Rochester, New York, February 7, 1984, pp. 1A, 5A.

11. Albert R. Hunt, "Former Rep. Conable Brings Mastery of Trade, Politics to World Bank Post," *Wall Street Journal,* March 19, 1986, p. 62.

12. Conable, interview, p. 4.

13. Gwin, pp. 77f.

14. Conable, interview, p. 5.

15. Rodman L. Drake, Managing Director, Cresap, McCormick and Paget. Letter to Barber B. Conable, September 8, 1986, p. 2 [R-92-104] (Presidents' papers—Barber B. Conable—Stanton reorganization files), WBGA.

16. Stewart Fleming, "A Banker's Balancing Act," *Financial Times,* September 10, 1986, p. 19.

17. Edward V. K. Jaycox, interview by Jochen Kraske, Louis Galambos, and David Milobsky, May 9, 1995, p. 10.

18. Steering Committee on the Reorganization of the World Bank to the President, report, Reorganizing the Bank, An Opportunity for Renewal, April 6, 1987, Series 41 (Presidents' papers—Barber B. Conable—Haug reorganization files), WBGA.

19. Barber B. Conable to the Executive Directors, memorandum, Reorganization of the Bank, April 29, 1987, R-87-84, Series 4453 (Office of the Senior Vice President of Operations—Qureshi files—Reorganization), WBGA.

20. Ibid., p. 3. The emphasis of the reorganization, according to the formal proposal submitted to the executive directors, was, however, "to create a more responsive and more efficient World Bank, not to 'downsize' the institution or to achieve administrative budget reductions per se."

21. Conable, interview, p. 7.

22. See, for instance, "The Fallout Following the Shake-Up," *Far Eastern Economic Review,* October 1, 1987, pp. 54f.; Franz M. Oppenheimer, "Don't Bank on the World Bank," *American Spectator,* October 1987.

23. Vice President and Secretary to the Executive Directors, memorandum, Report on the Reorganization, December 16, 1987, Sec M87-1257, p. 19 [R-92-104] (Presidents' papers—Barber B. Conable—Stanton reorganization files), WBGA.

24. Conable, interview, p. 6.

25. Robert Picciotto to W. David Hopper, memorandum, July 8, 1987.

26. Barber B. Conable to M. A. Qureshi, memorandum, July 6, 1987.

27. Jaycox, interview, p. 26.

28. Barber B. Conable, address to the Board of Governors, Washington, D.C., September 29, 1987, in *The Conable Years at the World Bank: Major Policy Addresses of Barber B. Conable* (Washington, D.C.: World Bank, 1991), p. 31.

29. "Request for Affiliate May Spoil World Bank Capital Increase," *Journal of Commerce,* July 28, 1987, pp. 1A, 12A; Gwin, p. 48.

30. Gwin, p. 49.

31. Conable, interview, p. 10.

32. Gwin, p. 49.

33. The upshot of this discussion was the creation of an ad hoc committee for allocation of shares of bank capital, which met for years and ultimately deferred the issue when agreement could not be reached. Vice President and Secretary to Executive Directors and Alternates, memorandum, "Summary of Discussion at the Board Seminar on the General Capital Increase," February 10, 1988, February 17, 1988, pp. 5f.; *World Bank Annual Report 1991,* Washington, D.C., pp. 22f.

34. See "Lender in Chief," *Time,* March 24, 1986, p. 51; "Guess Who's Banking on the World Bank," *U.S. News and World Report,* March 24, 1986, p. 56; "Mr. Conable's Important Job," *Philadelphia Inquirer,* March 16, 1986.

35. Morgan Guaranty and Trust Company, *World Financial Markets* (New York: Morgan Guaranty International Economics Department, 1987), p. 2.

36. Karin Lissakers, *Banks, Borrowers and the Establishment* (New York: Basic Books, 1991), p. 230.

37. Barber B. Conable, address to the Board of Governors, Washington, D.C., September 30, 1986, in *The Conable Years,* p. 5.

38. Statement by U.S. Senator Bill Bradley, Brazilian Moratorium, Crisis Management, and the Inter-American Partnership, March 3, 1987, Subcommittee on International Development Institutions and Finance, U.S. House of Representatives Banking Committee, Washington, D.C.

39. Timothy B. Clark, "Conable Charts New Course for Bank," *National Journal,* August 30, 1986, p. 2072.

40. Percy Mistry to Moeen Qureshi, memorandum, Conable-Bradley meeting, March 10, 1987; Percy Mistry to Barber Conable, memorandum, Senator Bradley on Debt, March 10, 1987.

41. Barber B. Conable, address to the Board of Governors, Washington, D.C., September 29, 1987, in *The Conable Years,* p. 34.

42. Jean Baneth to the Members of the Policy Committee, memorandum, Interim Report on Debt Problems of Middle-Income Countries, July 31, 1987 [R-92-107] (Presidents' papers—Barber B. Conable—Haug subject files: Debt), WBGA.

43. Lissakers, p. 232.

44. Memorandum to President, Implications of Debt Reduction Proposals, April 28, 1989, Sec M89-521 [R-92-107] (Presidents' papers—Barber B. Conable—Haug subject files: Debt), WBGA.

45. David Bock and others to Barber Conable, memorandum, The Brady Plan: Issues for the Bank, March 23, 1989 [R-92-107] (Presidents' pa-

pers—Barber B. Conable—Haug subject files: Debt), WBGA; Ernest Stern to Executive Directors, memorandum, Moody's Special Comment on International Debt Strategy, April 3, 1989, Series 51 (Presidents' papers—Barber B. Conable—Liaison with US Government: Bradley initiative), WBGA; Peter Truell, "World Bank Sets Rules for Role in Debt Strategy," *Wall Street Journal*, June 2, 1989, p. A12.

46. Polak, *The World Bank and the IMF,* pp. 10f.

47. Conable, interview, p. 3; Polak, pp. 30ff.; S. Shahid Husain, interview, pp. 18ff.

48. S. Shahid Husain, interview, pp. 19f.

49. Managing Director, IMF, and President, IBRD, to the Executive Board of the International Monetary Fund and the Board of Executive Directors of the World Bank, memorandum, Bank-Fund Collaboration in Assisting Member Countries, March 30, 1989, Series 4456 (Office of the Senior Vice President of Operations, Qureshi subject files: IMF), WBGA.

50. Philippe Le Prestre, *The World Bank and the Environmental Challenge* (Selinsgrove, Pa.: Susquehanna University Press, 1989), pp. 177ff.

51. Conable, interview, p. 13.

52. Barber B. Conable, address to the World Resources Institute, Washington, D.C., May 5, 1987, in *The Conable Years,* p. 23.

53. Ernest Stern to Barber Conable, memorandum, Funding for the Environment, February 28, 1989[R-92-107] (Presidents' papers—Barber B. Conable—Haug subject files: Environment) WBGA; *World Bank Annual Report 1991,* pp. 12f., 39.

54. Barber B. Conable to Moeen Qureshi and David Hopper, memorandum, Environment, April 13, 1989 [R-92-107] (Presidents' papers—Barber B. Conable—Haug subject files: Environment), WBGA.

55. *World Bank Annual Report 1991,* p. 12.

56. Barber B. Conable, address to Governors, September 30, 1986, in *The Conable Years,* p. 3.

57. Barber B. Conable, Poverty Task Force, FYI 86/133, December 17, 1986, Series 4534 (Administrative circulars and FYI), WBGA.

58. Barber B. Conable, address to the Board of Governors, Berlin, Germany, September 27, 1988, in *The Conable Years,* p. 68.

59. World Bank, *World Development Report 1990* (New York: Oxford University Press, 1990).

60. Barber B. Conable, address to the Safe Motherhood Conference, Nairobi, Kenya, February 10, 1987, in *The Conable Years,* p. 14.

61. *World Bank Annual Report 1991,* pp. 55f.

62. William S. Ryrie and Ernest Stern, memorandum to Bank and IFC operational staff, Cooperation between the World Bank and IFC, March 11, 1986, as communicated to Board, February 27, 1987, Sec M87-188 (Office of the Senior Vice President of Operations—Moeen Qureshi files—Subject files: IFC), WBGA.

63. Barber B. Conable to Executive Directors and Alternates, memorandum, February 3, 1988 (Office of the Senior Vice President of Operations—Moeen Qureshi files—Subject files: Private sector), WBGA.

64. William S. Ryrie to Barber B. Conable, memorandum, Private Sector Development, December 13, 1988 (Office of the Senior Vice President of Operations—Moeen Qureshi files—Subject files: Private sector), WBGA.

65. Gwin, pp. 52f.

66. Conable, interview, p. 11.

67. Gwin, p. 53; see also E. Patrick Coady, interview by William Becker and David Milobsky, April 19, 1993, Oral History Program, pp. 21ff.; Ryrie, interview, pp. 40ff.

68. Ibrahim F. I. Shihata to Barber B. Conable, memorandum, U.S.S.R. Membership, November 4, 1986, Series 49 (Presidents' papers—Barber B. Conable—Subject/Country files: USSR), WBGA.

69. U.S. proposal regarding a "special association of the Soviet Union with the World Bank and the IMF" made December 13, 1990, in a presidential press conference.

70. Barber B. Conable, address, Warsaw, Poland, February 22, 1990, in *The Conable Years,* p. 111.

71. Conable, interview, p. 7.

72. Barber B. Conable, address to the Board of Governors, Washington, D.C., September 26, 1989, in *The Conable Years,* p. 93.

73. Barber B. Conable, address to the Organization of African Unity, Abuja, Nigeria, June 4, 1991, in *The Conable Years,* p. 170.

74. Barber B. Conable, address to Governors, September 30, 1986, in *The Conable Years,* p. 10.

75. Barber B. Conable, address to the annual meeting of the Bretton Woods Committee, Washington, D.C., July 10, 1991, in *The Conable Years,* p. 175.

76. Conable, interview, p. 2.

Reflections

1. Articles of Agreement, Art. V, Section 5 (b).

2. Paul Lewis, "A 3-Way Race to Head the World Bank," *NYT,* February 13, 1995, p. D1; John M. Berry, "3 Top List to Head World Bank," *Washington Post,* February 15, 1995, p. F1.

3. George D. Woods, note, Desired Qualifications for President of the World Bank, n.d. G. D. Woods Papers (IBRD), Columbia University.

4. Ibid.

5. Articles of Agreement, Art. IV, Section 10.

Bibliographical Notes

The text itself and the chapter notes indicate the principal sources of information on the presidents of the World Bank and on their administrations. The following comments and suggestions are for readers who want to pursue the subjects further.

Only one of the seven presidents from 1946 to 1991 has written an autobiography or, so far as is known, kept a journal or diary in any sustained way. (Partial telephone logs, some of them mere notations, but others more extensive—occasionally a memorandum of conversation—may be found in the various archival collections mentioned here.) The one exception is Robert S. McNamara. His *In Retrospect: The Tragedy and Lessons of Vietnam* (New York: Random House, 1995) focuses on his role as secretary of defense during the Vietnam War. Yet it also discusses his earlier life, his education, and his "journey to Washington" and provides many clues to the person he was when he came to the Bank.

All seven presidents were national figures in the United States—in finance, law, or politics. Yet biographies have appeared of only four; this book has made extensive use of all of them:

Bird, Kai. *The Chairman: John J. McCloy, The Making of the American Establishment* (New York, Simon & Schuster, 1992).
Oliver, Robert. *George Woods and the World Bank* (Boulder, Colo.: Lynne Rienner, 1995).

Pusey, Merlo. *Eugene Meyer* (New York: Alfred A. Knopf, 1974).

Shapley, Deborah. *Promise and Power: The Life and Times of Robert McNamara* (Boston: Little, Brown & Co., 1995).

Trewhitt, Henry L. *McNamara* (New York: Harper and Row, 1971).

Unfortunately, only *George Woods* by Oliver deals with the details of Woods's presidency of the World Bank. All four, however, provide valuable information on and insights into the personal backgrounds—formative years, friendships, experiences, and the like—that the presidents brought to the World Bank Group. Those backgrounds shaped their initial views of the Bank and thus affected their administrations.

On the overall context of the Bank Group over the past forty-five years of the Bank, there is no shortage of books, journal articles, and daily press stories on people, issues, and events. Some are critical and some are laudatory. All are interesting for one reason or another, whether for what they say about the Bank Group and its CEO or for the light they throw on the writers themselves and what they represent.

A full listing of these publications might double the size of this book. Two, however, stand out as comprehensive overviews of the Bank Group. Both—one published twenty-three years ago and the other to be published around the turn of 1996–97, as the Bank passes its fiftieth anniversary—are the products of the Brookings Institution. Both are sympathetic, yet critical; comprehensive, yet detailed and analytical. They were instigated by the World Bank, which provided complete access to its archives, files, and staff but remained at arm's length from the writing. This book has made extensive use of both.

Edward Mason and Robert Asher wrote *The World Bank since Bretton Woods* (Washington, D.C.: Brookings Institution, 1973) on the occasion of the Bank's twentieth anniversary. John Lewis, Richard Webb, and Devesh Kapur are producing the fifty-year story, including the first quarter century but focusing on the second, and they have been good enough to share their draft manuscript, just as this one was made available to them. This is not to say that the views of the two books correspond, but only that each group of authors has had the benefit of seeing the other's draft. Together these two works will provide an indispensable overview of the Bank against which to consider its governance, policies, structure, and activities, as well as its presidents.

For the general reader especially interested in the early history of the World Bank, mention must be made of the story of the Bank's impact on people, described in James Morris (now Jan Morris), *The Road to Huddersfield: A Journey to Five Continents* (New York: Pantheon, 1963). This book was inspired by President Black, who was impressed by Morris's sensitive writing. Many efforts have subsequently been made to present the Bank's "human face." None has yet matched Morris's work.

For the more recent story of the Bank's activity, especially reflecting the Bank's enhanced focus on poverty, see the following:

Ayres, Robert L. *Banking on the Poor: The World Bank and World Poverty* (Cambridge, Mass.: MIT Press, 1983).
deVries, Barend A. *Remaking the World Bank* (Washington, D.C.: Seven Locks Press, 1987).
Please, Stanley. *The Hobbled Giant: Essays on the World Bank* (Boulder, Colo.: Westview Press, 1984).

An important source of information on the presidents' evolving views is, of course, their published speeches and articles. A selection of the most important of them has been published, such as:

Clausen, A. W. *The Development Challenge of the Eighties: A. W. Clausen at the World Bank. Major Policy Addresses, 1981–1986* (Washington, D.C.: World Bank, 1986).
Conable, Barber B. *The Conable Years at the World Bank: Major Policy Addresses of Barber A. Conable, 1986–91* (Washington, D.C.: World Bank, 1991).
McNamara, Robert S. *One Hundred Countries, Two Billion People: The Dimensions of Development* (New York: Praeger, 1973).

Many, if not most, of these speeches and articles had already been published individually by the Bank or in the *Proceedings* of the Bank Group's Annual Meetings.

The basic sources on the presidents are, of course, the documentary records of the World Bank and other archival collections to which the presidents may have left their papers. These include the files of the presidents' managerial councils and committees and the papers of their principal officers who participated in those councils and committees. Marie Gallup and David Milobsky have prepared a *Guide to the Archives of the World Bank (1946–1986)*, soon to be published by the Bank. The general policy on access is described in *The World Bank Policy on Disclosure of Information* (Washington, D.C.: World Bank, 1994).

Although the Bank is opening to the public an increasing amount of operational information, the material most relevant to the presidencies—not only what was said and decided, but also what was done—is not publicly available. Qualified outside researchers, however, may obtain access on request on an ad hoc basis.

Then there are the oral histories of key Bank staff, including some of the presidents. A valuable oral history program was initiated in 1961. It was used by Mason and Asher. Unfortunately, the program was not continued. It was sporadically revived and then petered out. When the Office of the World Bank Group Historian was created in January 1993, the reestablishment of an oral history program was an explicit part of its terms of reference. That program is under way and will go on as long as the office continues. Total interviews now available number about 130 transcripts of 88 individuals and should continue to grow. All may be found in the Bank's Archives.

Distinct from the Bank's Archives is the Executive Directors' Library Collection. It includes all the records of the boards of the Bank, IDA, the IFC and MIGA, the documents presented to them, and the proceedings of their meetings, both verbatim transcripts and formal decisions.

Other archival collections in the United States and elsewhere contain relevant records, notably:

Harry S. Truman Presidential Library, Independence, Missouri; for records on the first two presidencies and the start-up of the Bank
Library of Congress, Washington, D.C.; Eugene Meyer Papers
Amherst College, Amherst, Massachusetts; on John J. McCloy
Hargett Library at the University of Georgia, Athens, Georgia; on Eugene R. Black
Butler Library at Columbia University, New York, New York; on George D. Woods
The John F. Kennedy Library, Boston, Massachusetts; on Robert S. McNamara

So far as is known, neither A. W. Clausen nor Barber B. Conable has yet deposited relevant papers in any archive.

Index

323